95-42433

20-25
31-43
73-83
129-135
199-202

THE BUREAUCRATIC EXPERIENCE

THE
BUREAUCRATIC
EXPERIENCE

Ralph P. Hummel

ST. MARTIN'S PRESS
New York

Library of Congress Catalog Card Number: 76-28132
Manufactured in the United States of America.
0987
fedcba
For information, write: St. Martin's Press, Inc.,
175 Fifth Avenue, New York, N. Y. 10010

cover illustration by Masaaki Sato
                    executed by Patrick Vitacco

cloth ISBN: 0-312-10815-X
paper ISBN: 0-312-10850-8

Acknowledgments

Excerpts from TOWARD A RATIONAL SOCIETY: STUDENT PROTEST, SCIENCE, AND POLITICS by Jürgen Habermas. German text: Copyright © 1968 by Suhrkamp Verlag, Frankfurt am Main and English text: Copyright © 1970 by Beacon Press. Reprinted by permission of Beacon Press.

Excerpts from IDEOLOGY AND UTOPIA by Karl Mannheim. Reprinted by permission of Harcourt Brace Jovanovich, Inc., and by permission of Routledge & Kegan Paul.

Excerpts from SCIENCE AND HUMAN BEHAVIOR by B. F. Skinner. Reprinted with permission of Macmillan Publishing Co., Inc.

Chart entitled "Percentage Change in American Feelings of Political Distrust, Powerlessness, and Meaningless" from POLITICAL ALIENATION IN CONTEMPORARY AMERICA by Robert S. Gilmour and Robert B. Lamb reprinted by permission of St. Martin's Press.

"Klassen Told by a Senator that Mail Service Is a Joke" and excerpts from "Morale of Justices in New York Is Low." © 1973/1976 by The New York Times Company. Reprinted by permission.

Material in table on page 12 of THE ANGUISH OF CHANGE by Louis Harris. Copyright © 1973 by W. W. Norton & Company, Inc. Reprinted by permission.

To Pat Boughton

Preface

Everyone has trouble with bureaucracy. Citizens and politicians have trouble controlling the runaway bureaucratic machine. Managers have trouble managing it. Employes dislike working in it. Clients can't get the goods from it. Teachers have trouble getting an overall grip on it. Students are mystified by the complexity of it.

It would be useful to all of us — citizens, clients, politicians, administrators, functionaries, teachers, and students — to have a clear framework for organizing our thinking about bureaucracy and our dealings with it. The framework should be one that can be easily kept in our heads. It should not be esoteric. It should not be complex but essential. It should encompass the nature of bureaucracy, and it should have clear practical applications.

The framework proposed is this:

First, bureaucracy is an entirely new way of organizing social life. It succeeds society, just as society has succeeded community.

Second, bureaucracy, a world into which we are recruited,

differs from society, the world into which we are born, in five ways: (1) socially, (2) culturally, (3) psychologically, (4) power-politically, (5) linguistically. Bureaucracy is a new society and a new culture. Bureaucracy's functionaries represent a new personality type and speak a new language. Bureaucracy is a new way of exercising power.

Third, bureaucracy, because it differs from society in these five ways, poses special difficulties for people depending on where they stand. Grouped according to the type of problem they face, these people are (1) the citizen as taxpayer, voter, and nominal boss over bureaucracy, (2) the politician as immediate but still nominal boss, (3) the manager as the wielder of bureaucratic power, (4) the employe as the tool of bureaucratic power, (5) the client as recipient of bureaucracy's goods and victim of bureaucracy's power. Individuals in each of these groups must make different adaptations to bureaucracy if they are to succeed in dealing with it or working in it.

The assumption of the book is this: We will be better able to live and work *with*, *in*, or *against* bureaucracy IF we (1) view it as an entirely new world, (2) become aware of the practical impact of its differences from the world with which we are familiar, and (3) understand how that impact will vary for each of us depending on the form of our involvement with bureaucratic life.

Ralph P. Hummel
New York City

Acknowledgments

Perhaps as a reflection on our times, the greatest debt in the making of this book is owed to anonymous men and women in greater and lesser bureaucracies across the United States. Not even all the institutions can be listed here.

I remember with special warmth the men and women of the New York City Police Department, Fire Department, and Urban Corps. My first appreciation of the importance of bureaucracy and the rationalized professions, as against the polity, I owe to Robert Stierer, then city manager of Pontiac, Michigan, who led me to think during a short career as a reporter that the press should stop covering city council meetings and start covering administration instead. My most important contact with a thoroughly human career official was with an immigration officer in Windsor, Ontario, in whom I first detected the tension between social morality and bureaucratic duty. It is possible to forget a name, but not a kind act. The examples drawn on in the book stem from a variety of institutions ranging from departments of corrections to the U.S. State Department. Since I owe these institutions themselves nothing and since the employes to whom I owe everything must remain nameless, there is no point going into detail.

Institutions were responsible for the opportunity to engage in a number of activities which helped me when it came to writing this book. Among these was the chance to study behavioral genetics, do time in a think tank, teach semantic analysis as well as sociology, political science, and public administration, and establish an institutional basis of my own. Since institutions have now been proven not to be human, they deserve no thanks. I prefer to turn to the people who do.

Intellectual and professional debts are owed to

Dwight Waldo for lending support to the project at the very beginning;

Robert A. Isaak for his constant support and creative contributions;

Carl Nelson and Conrad Rutkowski for helping in my early ruminations on the psychology of bureaucracy;

Marc Holzer for his faith in me as a teacher of public administration;

Donna Lavins and Claudette Ford for giving me my first consulting opportunities in administration and internship training;

Hans Held for appreciating my early efforts in the form of a paper on technology and world politics; John Everett for instigating it;

Katherine Speicher for making available to me her work on operational codes and her friendship;

Max Mark and Louis Koenig for always being there to listen;

Edward Mazze for encouraging the discussions here of bureaucracy as applied to the private sector;

Roger Mazze for being as ever generous with his own work on everything from ghetto revolts to alcoholism;

Stephen Wasby for his early encouragement and dissemination of some trial papers;

Sandra Fish for finding in the phenomenology of bureaucracy something that could be applied to teaching speech and drama;

Paul Bernstein for desperately trying to straighten me out on the language chapter; Bruce Spender and Cliff Landers for lending computer expertise;

H. Mark Roelofs for being the center of my understanding of American politics;

Michael P. Smith for contributing the concept of "ritual politics" to my understanding of apolitics;

Douglas Fox, William Morrow, and Peter Woll for their careful reviews of the proposal and manuscript and their many helpful suggestions.

I think back with nothing but pleasure to the memory of Kalman Silvert, teacher and friend, who found value in the introductory essay but assured me that was not the way to do it.

In an increasingly dehumanized world, I have been kept alive by the talkative and supportive circle of an elective "family": Pat Boughton, Charles Hayes, and Harry Steinberg, as well as Roger Mazze and Rochelle Mazze and Barry Rossinoff. Finally, I want to thank especially Glenn Cowley and Carolyn Eggleston of St. Martin's Press.

R. P. H.

Contents

Introduction: Understanding Bureaucracy

This book is a practical guide to bureaucracy. It is practical because a group of twenty-five interns in the New York City Urban Corps challenged an academician to be practical.

THE CHALLENGE

The challenge came about three years ago in the form of an invitation. Would I, asked a voice at the other end of the telephone, come down to New York's City Hall and tell interns about to enter the city bureaucracy what to expect? No matter how down-to-earth an academician is in the classroom, there is only one reaction to such a request: stark, naked panic. After years of work in generalizations and abstractions, I was asked to give practical advice *that would be tested*. Not only was my own reputation at stake with the interns who would soon enough encounter the realities of bureaucracy, but the interns themselves would be tested by seasoned bureaucrats.

The credibility of the academic world and its relevance to society had been very much on my mind. I had just become director of a small consulting firm on urban educational and administrative problems. Half the reason for the existence of that firm was my own experience that academicians had created around themselves their own little world of unreality. The other half was founded on the remnant of an earlier faith that academicians still *did* have something to tell practitioners. Here was my first personal test.

What was bureaucracy all about? What could an individual expect the first day he or she walked into an office? What *should* he or she expect in order to survive?

What could I tell newcomers about modern bureaucracy?

THE KEY

A half century ago, sociologist Max Weber had recoiled from the bureaucratic future in personal horror. Like George Orwell and Aldous Huxley he saw a strange new world in which not the brave but the dehumanized would survive. What if, instead of parroting Weber's classic characterization of bureaucracy, we started taking seriously his condemnation of its inmates? After all, he did foresee a future populated by nonentities — "specialists without spirit, sensualists without heart; this nullity imagines that it has attained a level of civilization never before achieved."[1]

Planted like time bombs through his famous essay on bureaucracy, temporarily defused by the neutral language of his "constructive" insights, lay the fragments of Weber's vision of a terrifying reality.

Bureaucracy gives birth to a new species of inhuman beings. Man's social relations are being converted into control relations.[2] His norms and beliefs concerning human ends are torn from him and replaced with skills affirming the ascendancy of technical means, whether of administration or production.[3] Psychologically, the new personality type is that of the rationalistic expert, incapable of emotion and devoid of will.[4] Language, once the means for bringing people into communication, becomes the secretive tool of one-way commands.[5] Politics, especially democratic politics, fades away as the method of publicly determining society-wide goals based on human needs; it is replaced by administration.[6]

If this picture matched reality, I decided, the time had come to set off the time bombs. Newcomers to bureaucracy and oldtimers deserved to be told that they were not facing a question of minor adjustment but a challenge to alter all their orientations and behaviors. The severity of this challenge could be summarized in two ways:

1. The assertion that life in bureaucracy is radically different from life in society.
2. The description of just how that difference impinges on us socially, culturally, psychologically, linguistically, and politically.

One way of keeping these differences in mind is to visualize them in terms of misunderstandings and understandings of bureaucracy:

Misunderstandings	*Understandings*
Socially —	
Bureaucrats deal with people.	Bureaucrats deal with cases.
Culturally —	
Bureaucrats care about the same things we do: justice, freedom, violence, oppression, illness, death, victory, defeat, love, hate, salvation, and damnation.	Bureaucrats care about control and efficiency.
Psychologically —	
Bureaucrats are people like us.	Bureaucrats are a new personality type, headless and soulless.
Linguistically —	
Communication with bureaucrats is possible: we all speak the same language.	Bureaucrats find it in their interest to define how and when communication shall take place: they create their own secret languages.
Politically —	
Public bureaucracies are service institutions.	Public bureaucracies are control institutions.

In sum, the bureaucratic experience that awaits us differs from the social experience behind us in five ways: socially, culturally, psychologically, linguistically, and politically. Each of these five differences deserves exploration in depth. Toward this purpose the rest of this introduction, which is based on the lecture I delivered to those twenty-five interns three years ago, provides a survey; the following five central chapters provide the details.

BUREAUCRACY AS A STRANGE NEW WORLD

Anyone who has set out from his or her familiar daily life to tangle with bureaucracy knows that bureaucracy and society are worlds apart. The distance can seem as far as that from the earth to the moon. It is not impossible to get there and back, but to survive the journey means learning a new set of behaviors, attuned both to the home world and the new world.

The Bureaucratic Experience

This is true for the administrator who suddenly finds himself in charge and held responsible for an instrument of purported power and control that eternally squirms and wriggles to escape his grasp. It is true also for the newly hired worker in a bureaucracy who has to learn a new set of behaviors, norms, and speech patterns to get along in the bureaucracy and keep his job. And it is true for the outsider who wants to do business with a bureaucracy — whether get a tax refund, register a birth or death, secure a passport, license an enterprise, obtain police protection, or enter a child in school. Quite similar problems exist for the manager trying to control a corporation's sales force; the employe learning to talk, act, and think the way employes typically talk, act, and think at IBM, GM, or ITT; and the customer attempting to get Macy's credit system to correct a mistake the computer made.

If we have experienced bureaucracy in any of these roles, and none of us can long avoid such contact, we have to admit to ourselves that we have difficulty with bureaucracy — attuning to it, communicating our needs to it, and obtaining satisfactions from it. No matter how astute we are, these difficulties exist, and we may feel that if only we could explain the reasons for such tensions we might be able to do better for ourselves in future contacts.

Antisocial Encounters

The fundamental reasons for our difficulties were spelled out by Max Weber in warnings to which we seem not to have paid much attention. Perhaps to do so would be too painful a recognition of the vastness of the chasm between social life and bureaucratic existence. Bureaucracy in its modern form, Weber concluded, constitutes the creation of a new world of human interaction. A transformation of normal human life began specifically with the development of modern bureaucracy.

Normal human life is characterized by "social action." Weber wrote:

> We shall speak of "action" insofar as the acting individual attaches a subjective meaning to his behavior — be it overt or covert, omission or acquiescence. Action is "social" insofar as its subjective meaning takes account of the behavior of others and is thereby oriented in its course.[7]

But bureaucracy, Weber points out, is different. In normal human life people relate to one another primarily through the meaning each attaches to his or her actions — a meaning which the other tries to understand. The bureaucrat, on the other hand, is restricted to those actions that his work rules permit him and that fall within the scope of his jurisdiction. He, as bureaucrat, is not allowed to tune in to the subjective meanings and needs that a client of the bureaucracy is trying to convey; he must tune in only to those meanings and needs that have officially recognizable standing. For example, a welfare investigator is not officially permitted to take cognizance of the psychological stress that a mother on welfare experiences because welfare rules forbid her husband to live with her. Or a consumer advocate in a consumer protection agency cannot consider the intensity of poverty or the severity of psychic agony of a client who wishes to file a complaint but fails to produce the necessary sales receipt.

Bureaucratic action is not social action. Social action opens me up to the entire range of meanings and needs that relevant others try to convey, because only if I open myself up to as many of the meanings, connotations, and inner feelings that others attach to their actions will I be able to understand them, cooperate with them fully, fight them sufficiently — in other words, continue to exist with them in a shared social world. Such openness is forbidden in bureaucratic action, which follows its own rules to protect itself. It is a separate world and to break its rules is to threaten its boundaries. Against such threat, the bureaucratic world and those who have to exist within it defend themselves. It is in this sense that Weber wrote, "Bureaucracy is *the* means of transforming social action into rationally organized action."[8]

But "rationally organized action" can only mean, in this context, action that is logically coherent with the goals of the bureaucracy. These may in themselves be human and humane goals. It is just that other human and humane goals not encompassed by the system's purpose cannot be considered by those who carry out its functions — the functionaries. Such goals and needs standing logically outside the goals and needs of the bureaucratic system are, in the system's terms, "illogical" and therefore "irrational."

The extent to which the bureaucratic world is not the normal human world can also be understood psychologically. Weber himself pointed out in this regard that bureaucratization favors the development of "the [new] personality type of the professional expert."[9] Because Weber did not develop this theme further in psychological terms, we may have missed that he was speaking about the creation of a new type of human being. The bureaucrat has to be a truncated remnant of a human being. Bureaucrats are allowed to feel emotion, but only those emotions specified in the work orders. They are allowed to be responsible for their actions and in fact will be held responsible, but only if the action performed falls within their jurisdiction. The bureaucrat is not officially responsible and will not be held responsible for the action or nonaction of another bureaucrat in a different and independent part of the bureaucracy. The bureaucrat has a will, but it is an officially limited will: it cannot transcend his or her role. It is a will whose origins lie, not in personal conscience, but in machinery set in motion by a superior, the work rules, or the understanding of one's jurisdiction.

The psychological limits of a bureaucrat are already indicated when we speak of a *functionary* of a system. Ideally, from the point of view of their bureaucracy, bureaucrats are highly reliable cogs in the machine. They must be reliable because a bureaucracy is a complex organization of many individuals, all of whom are supposed to be so organized that the purpose of the bureaucracy will be carried out as precisely and efficiently as possible. No secretary of state wants to have to face subordinates making their own foreign policy. Welfare case workers who show personal sympathy to clients beyond what is officially permitted may pay out extra money. This could lead other clients to perceive the bureaucracy as unfair and taxpayers to see it as wasteful. But to the extent that bureaucrats are cogs in a machine, they cease being free agents — the human beings of social action who freely orient themselves to other human beings and engage in social projects with them. Bureaucrats lose their own power and become instruments of power. It is in this sense that Weber wrote, ". . . bureaucracy was and is a power instrument of the first order for one who controls the bureaucratic apparatus."[10] The use of the term "apparatus" cannot be accidental.

Bureaucratic Psychology

But what type of individual best fits psychologically into this subordinate role? Sigmund Freud defined a normal human being as one whose ego is in control of a superego and an id. The ego was considered by Freud the controlling center of the individual's psyche, the core by which he organized his responses to the external challenges and problems that originated in the social and physical environment. The superego was a set of social norms learned by the individual and internalized early in childhood until he perceived them as a part of his self. The id was the set of biological drives and urges built into every human being by genetic inheritance. In the human being as a relatively free agent in society, the superego might painfully insist on observance of its set of norms. However, these norms seemed to the controlling ego to come from within. They were obeyed because to not obey them meant to lose part of one's self. This also meant that some parts of the superego might have to be sacrificed if their continued operation threatened the overall existence of the self. Such decisions, however, were all perceived by the individual as being internal to himself. He was, in the words of the poem, the Master of his Soul.[11]

In contrast, bureaucrats are officially asked to take their guiding norms from a reservoir of norms designed by the bureaucratic system and its makers. When these come into conflict with personal norms, settled in the superego, these personal norms and part of the superego must be sacrificed. The normal human being faced with such daily sacrifices would face a daily loss of self. Yet when people become bureaucrats, they are asked to accept such daily losses. To the extent that they do, their self gradually ceases to exist. The inner superego yields to an external superego reposed in work rules, superiors, bureaucratic peers, and the system at large. Disobedience is ultimately punished by dismissal.

Freud's normal human being, then, has a psyche composed of a triad of superego, ego, and id — with the ego at the apex. In contrast, bureaucrats lack a superego and possess only a very truncated ego. Adaptations that control individual survival, pain, or gratification are ultimately made somewhere in the system outside and above the self. In this sense psychologist B. F. Skinner is right that in the modern world it is now clear that the individual is a being "beyond freedom and dignity"[12] — that is, *without* either quality.

The Paradox of Needs

The paradox of bureaucracy is already inherent in the new type of action and the new type of personality it requires. Each person involved with bureaucracy — administrator, employe, client — experiences this paradox in his or her own way. Each stands in a different location in relation to the bureaucracy and therefore has his or her own perspective.[13]

The client approaches the bureaucracy with a full repertoire of human needs. These are often interrelated, but the bureaucracy is designed to satisfy only one or a few of them. In American society, where demonstrated ability and willingness to work define an individual's dignity and self-esteem, a "welfare mother" with eight children will find some of her material needs satisfied by the welfare bureaucracy, but she is also likely to have her self-esteem needs challenged. Part of that challenge may be attributed to inadequate design of the bureaucracy's goals: no one has yet figured out a way to combine material help with help for a bruised ego in a cultural situation in which to accept material help means to lose self-respect. So far the nature of bureaucracy cannot be held responsible. But the other part of the challenge is likely to derive from the nature of bureaucracy itself — the fact that it requires the client's submission to rationally organized action and the abandonment of his or her attempts at problem solving using the full repertoire of social action.

The story of Mrs. Pamela Ashcroft, a divorced mother of three children, and her attempt to obtain enough heating fuel provides a typical example:

> The poverty agency in Augusta [Maine], the Southern Kennebac Valley Community Action Program, gave her 10 gallons on Dec. 27, a friend bought 5 gallons on Jan. 2 and she herself bought 50 gallons last Monday.
>   This most recent delivery, which cost $20.05, was financed with the $219-a-month Mrs. Ashcroft receives from Aid to Dependent Children, a federally supported program that is her only means of support. She expects the fuel to run out in two weeks. The sudden cold that marks this event is especially hard on her 2-year-old daughter, Mrs. Ashcroft said. The girl has had a hacking cough for six weeks.[14]

The employe at the Aid to Dependent Children agency to whom Mrs. Ashcroft might go with her concern for her daughter's health is not, however, permitted to engage in full social action with her to work out her problem. Determination of aid to dependent children is based on quantifiable measures and is not susceptible to adjustment because of ill health, the worry of a mother, or even the threat of continued ill health and the eventual death of a child. Such concerns belong to what are largely the unquantifiable values of everyday social life, not to the quantified measures that guarantee bureaucratic efficiency and administrative control.

While Mrs. Ashcroft, as a client, is likely to think that the rationally organized bureaucracy is cold, rigid, and inhuman, the employe of the bureaucracy with whom she has dealt is likely to feel his or her own special agony.

The only way the employe can help Mrs. Ashcroft over and beyond the allotted aid is personally. Not only are the resources for such action limited, but such a personal response requires a deliberate, if only temporary, emigration from the bureaucratic world and its rationalistically organized action.* Whatever empathy or sympathy he or she may feel urges the employe to engage in social action — that is, to become attuned as fully as possible to the meanings attached to the client's pleadings and to the needs behind them, to engage in mutually responsive action with the client, and to come to terms with both their needs in a social relationship.

Stepping from the world of bureaucratic logic can be a wrenching experience when the bureaucrat is suddenly confronted with the fullness of social action after periods of bureaucratic isolation. But not

---

*"Rationalistic" in terms of the goals and conditions of the bureaucratic system, *not* in terms of the situation involving the employe and the client as human beings engaged in social action.

to step out of the world of bureaucracy can be a denial of perfectly natural human impulses.

The Bureaucratic War

Weber recognized the difference between bureaucracy and society as a culture gap, that is, a gap in the pattern of norms that guide behavior in each environment.

Two Cultures

Bureaucrats are expected to fulfill their tasks "without anger or predisposition"[15] — or, as Weber says elsewhere:

> "*sine ira ac studio*," without hatred or passion, and hence without affection or enthusiasm. The dominant norms are concepts of straight-forward duty without regard to personal considerations. Everyone is subject to formal equality of treatment; that is, everyone in the same empirical situation. This is the spirit in which the ideal official conducts his office.[16]

But personal needs, often intimate ones, are frequently the reason the client approaches the bureaucracy. To the registrar of births and the county clerk, the addition of a new member to my family is just "another birth," the addition of a simple mark in their books of accounts; to me the birth of my son is an event full of affection, enthusiasm, joy, emotion, passion, and import. He is *my* son. He has my eyes. My feelings about him make me laugh and cry. He is my redemption, my future, my burden, the transcending testimony of love, my wife's and mine. To the Social Security official, a man's death is just another form filled out; to his wife that death is the death of her beloved or hated husband and all he meant and all the things they ever did together. To the welfare case worker, you and I are "cases" or we are not "cases." If we are not "cases," the "case" worker is not allowed on eventual pain of losing his job to recognize us or our troubles. Even if we are "cases," our troubles are troubles only if they fall within the bureaucracy's predefined "cases" of trouble.

As Weber summarized them, the norms of bureaucratic life are "precision . . . stability . . . stringency of discipline . . . reliability . . . calculability of results . . . formal rationality . . . formalistic imper-sonality . . . formal equality of treatment."[17] In contrast, the traditional values of normal social life that serve as guiding and binding norms are, in the words of Jürgen Habermas, "justice and freedom, violence and oppression, happiness and gratification, poverty, illness and death, . . . victory and defeat, love and hate, salvation and dam-nation."[18]

Where the norms of bureaucratic detachment are carried out, the client is bound to feel himself treated with a certain coldness and without a sense of caring. In dealing with private bureaucracy he may respond with irritation and shift buying habits in the market system. *The New York Times*, for example, has chiseled into the marble of its lobby, and doubtless in the minds of its reporters, the motto ". . . to give the news impartially, without fear or favor, regardless of any party, sect or interest involved . . ."[19] — an echo of Weber's words *"sine ira ac studio."* The result of this formal requirement of balance and fairness is at times the elimination of the emotional substance of everyday life, which is neither balanced nor fair. Readers of an unbureaucratized bent may turn to *The Daily News*, in which consideration of the passionate norms of everyday life abounds.

The Revolt Against Control

But there are more serious reactions against the often mindless cold-heartedness of bureaucracy in public service. One is the attempted return by the over-organized to more traditional social life; the other, the search for charisma, a power of which Weber said, "In a revolutionary and sovereign manner, charismatic domination transforms all values and breaks all traditional and rational norms."[20]

Bureaucracy and its minions* tend to derogate the traditional administration of goods and services. Nevertheless, such administration still exists today, usually in the form of patriarchal, or personal, power. The inability of bureaucrats and professionals to maintain their even-handed tone when dealing with remnants of personal power may in itself be evidence of their subconscious recognition that such power constitutes a threat to formal rationalism and is, therefore, "the enemy."

Thus *The New York Times* reported on Mayor Richard J. Daley's primary victory, on his way toward a sixth term as mayor of Chicago and head of the Daley machine, in this manner:

> Mr. [Edward V.] Hanrahan [one of Daley's opponents in the primary], who once was a Daley protege but fell out of favor, said:
> "The people of Chicago are going to get the kind of government they apparently want and deserve — inefficient, wasteful and immensely corrupt."
>   . . .
> Mr. Daley told a wildly cheering throng of loyalists, "I shall embrace charity, love, mercy and walk humbly with my God."[21]

---

*The disdainful word is here used to represent "professionals" who unconsciously pursue their self-interest in collaborating with bureaucracies while maintaining an image of disinterested nonpartisanship.

Perhaps, however, Daley's recurrent victories lie exactly in the emotional motivations that bureaucrats, professionals, and reformers imply and decry. As one black leader said about his relations with the mayor, "The mayor doesn't give us everything we want, but he knows what we have to have — and that he gets for us."[22] It would be difficult to find a similar statement made by blacks in reference to the welfare bureaucracies.

A war between cultures need not be fought in the open. When the enemy is overwhelming, as the forces of bureaucracy are, the other side may withdraw into guerrilla warfare. Even a fantasy war may serve. A best-selling book of our time is *The Godfather*, which describes the patriarchalism of organized crime in America and perhaps glorifies it.* The concern of the book, and of the film, with the values of social life is perhaps most concisely expressed in Michael Corleone's response to the suggestion that the attempt to kill his father, Don Corleone, was "business, not personal":

> Tom, don't let anybody kid you. It's all personal, every bit of business. Every piece of shit every man has to eat every day of his life is personal. They call it business. OK. But it's personal as hell. You know where I learned that from? The Don. My old man. The Godfather. If a bolt of lightning hit a friend of his the old man would take it personal. He took my going into the Marines personal. That's what makes him great. The Great Don. He takes everything personal. Like God. He knows every feather that falls from the tail of a sparrow or however the hell it goes.[23]

When millions turn to books and films like this for escape, an organized modern society may experience their temporary departure into fantasy as a safety valve, functioning to briefly expel frustrated individuals only to ingest them again in a "safe" state.

At points, however, the frustration of emotions and other natural human characteristics, as demanded by bureaucratization, may have, and has had, more serious consequences.

At the end of his *Protestant Ethic*, having characterized the rationalized social structure of the modern world as an "iron cage," Weber raises the possibility that frustration of inmates' emotions and their search for human meanings may find in charismatic leaders a carrier that will return them to power. "No one knows who will live in this cage in the future, or whether at the end of this tremendous development entirely new prophets will arise."[24]

Nowhere does Weber anticipate with what violence the possibility he raised would come true. He had begun writing the *Protestant Ethic* in

---

*If by "glorify" we mean making the Mafia look better than many a faceless bureaucracy, which should not be too difficult a job considering that the first involves human feelings and the second does not.

1913. Exactly twenty years later, as bureaucracy, legality, and rationalism failed under the impact of irresolvable economic problems and a crisis of faith in modern legal-rationalism, a charismatic leader took over Germany. In a sense the outcome of the world war that followed can be understood as a victory of modern industrial production and bureaucracy over traditional organization, charismatically led.[25]

This is not the place to predict a war between the bureaucratized, and therefore rationalized, parts of the world and the world of premodern social life. Such a war is conceivable only as a civil war. It would rest on the expectation of people in the social world that the bureaucratic world is, or should be, a meaningful and controllable zone of everyday life. Or it would rest on the forceful intrusion of bureaucracy into all activities of social life so that people would be forced to deal with bureaucracy on its dehumanizing terms.

Current indicators do not show a clear direction of development. The self-creation within the Catholic church of a group of intensely religious believers calling themselves "charismatics" might indicate that the sacerdotal bureaucracy (hierocracy) of the church has failed to meaningfully convey the sacred "goods" through its administrative body. But the opening up of church ritual, the abandonment of the "secret" Latin language, and the turning of the priest to the congregation, might also be signs of the hierocracy's adaptation to salvationist demands. Weber warns in this connection that behind the need for salvation "stands always the taking up of a position toward something which in the real world is sensed to be specifically 'meaningless' . . ."[26]

Similarly, the recently recorded drop in public confidence in all major professions and institutions, ranging from 7 to 28 percentage points,[27] indicates that where professions and bureaucracies have most protected themselves they have failed their clients, but it does not yet indicate client action.

Some bureaucrats themselves explicitly or implicitly revolt, guerrilla fashion, against the matter-of-fact administration of human beings as things and the truncation of their own personalities. An employe of the Office for Economic Opportunity involved in processing grants to other poverty agencies complains:

> You wish there was a better system. A lot of money is held up and the grantees . . . want to know why they can't get it. Sometimes they call and get the run-around on the phone. I never do that. I tell the truth. If they don't have any money left, they don't have it. No, I'm not disturbed any more. If I was just starting on this job, I probably would. But the older I get, I realize it's a farce. You just get used to it. It's a job. I get my paycheck — that's it. It's all political anyway.
>
> A lot of time the grantee comes down to our audit department for aid. They're not treated as human beings. Sometimes they have to wait,

wait, wait — for no reason. The grantee doesn't know it's for no reason. He thinks he's getting somewhere and he really isn't.[28]

From this example, it is difficult to tell whether the prohibition against full social interaction is bureaucratically commanded or is in itself a response to the truncation of social action and human personality that tends to develop within large-scale organizations. It is clear, however, that whatever the reason, including the possibility of mismanagement, individual employes try to fill the gap between official restrictions and the potential fullness of a self-managing personality engaged in social action. This rebellion may not necessarily be in the direction of humanizing bureaucracy on the behalf of clients, but it is aimed at making life more bearable for the employes by asserting ego against the system:

> Oh, we love it when the bosses go to those long meetings, those important conferences. (Laughs.) We just leave in a group and go for a show. We don't care. When we get back, they roll their eyes. They know they better not say anything, 'cause they've done nothing when we've been gone anyhow. We do the work that we have to.[29]

For the administrator, the employe's attempt to fill the vacuum between bureaucratic existence and full social life has its own inevitable consequences. From his perspective, he experiences a loss of control over his organization. But every action on his part to reassert control from the top down means a widening of the gap between bureaucracy and society at the bottom. Weber may indeed be right when he notes that "bureaucracy was and is a power instrument of the first order for one who controls the bureaucratic apparatus."[30] But the degree of power and control is dependent on the degree to which human relations within the bureaucracy can be made to resemble an "apparatus" — a machine. For the individual employe the consequence of that fact is equally clear. In Weber's own words, "Of all those powers that lessen the importance of individual action, the most irresistible is *rational discipline.*"[31]

Five Foundations of Conflict
The fate of the employe-functionary is unenviable from the viewpoint of personal psychological integrity and other standards of social life. The gap between bureaucracy and the rest of society is horrendous. The gap exists on five grounds that grow out of the very nature of modern bureaucracy itself.

Power-politically, it is exactly the degree to which a bureaucracy is a control instrument from the top down that it is welded into a powerful machine against which the individual, standing in the less-organized patterns of social life is always relatively powerless. In fact, he may be forced to submit to control by a competing bureaucracy to exercise some power over the bureaucracy whose power he resists. Thus consumer organizations can become as dictatorial as the enterprises and public bureaucracies they are set up to fight.

Culturally, the need for internal control over the bureaucracy, as defined by the terms of modern science and technology, forces the imposition of new norms for behavior that are, in fact, the norms of mechanics as a subdivision of physics. The more relationships between human beings can be welded into an apparatus, the more control can be exercised from above. To the extent that functionaries can be taught and inwardly motivated by such mechanical standards as "efficiency," "calculability of results," and "impersonality," the less need there is for direct use of pains and pleasures as punishments and rewards. The inward acceptance of machine norms becomes a precondition for the well-oiled bureaucracy, even as it becomes the major cause for rejection of the norms of social life with which outsiders approach the bureaucracy.

Psychologically, a new psychology of dependency spreads throughout the bureaucracy, for only individuals so inclined can easily accept the mechanical norms and are likely to survive the rigors of accepting orders unquestioningly even when these go against personal values. In Weber's words:

> The honor of the official is the ability to carry out an order on the responsibility of the commanding official conscientiously and exactly in such a way as if it accorded with his own conviction, [even] when the higher authority insists, despite his protests, on an order that appears wrong to him. Without such ethical discipline in the highest sense and self-denial the entire apparatus would disintegrate.[32]

Such self-denial means, as previously shown, the submission of an amputated or fragmented ego to an externalized superego in return for the immediate satisfaction of id needs and avoidance of id pains.

The result is that the clients of a bureaucracy encounter in the official not merely an individual whose obedience belongs internally to an authority in the hierarchy and whose thinking is different from the norms guiding social life, but an individual whose *being* is different from themselves. The bureaucrat, to the extent he or she has become bureaucratic, is psychologically a being different from people in social life.

Socially, interaction between bureaucrat and human being becomes a frontier. If they want to survive politically, bureaucrats are not allowed to take account of the needs and intentions of clients in their fully complex humanity; only "cases" and "categories" that fill voids on forms can be recognized officially. Culturally, bureaucrats are constantly surprised at clients' recalcitrance to behaving in ways that can be fitted into bureaucratic norms. To the extent that bureaucratic norms have become second nature to them, bureaucrats are unable to understand the behaviors of clients since these rest on different norms. And psychologically, bureaucrats will perceive any attempt by clients to develop a human relationship with them not only as officially "out of order" but as a challenge to their own dependency-oriented identity. To bureaucrats, humanizing efforts by clients always constitute aggression. In fact, they are aggressions against their bureaucratic identity. For these reasons, bureaucrats gladly embrace the injunction against full personal interaction with clients. Such interaction threatens their identity, challenges their norms, and endangers their power position.

Full social interaction at the frontier between bureaucracy and society, therefore, is rejected for two reasons. First, the goals and work rules of bureaucracy define the limits of interaction. Second, functionaries find it in their political, normative, and psychological self-interest not to expand these limits set to interaction.

Linguistically, the separation between bureaucracy and society is given its final form. A language, by limiting what can be said, defines what we can talk about. An agent of the Internal Revenue Service can talk to me about "exemptions," "exclusions," and "penalties," but if I try to put in my two cents' worth about what these terms mean to me, he becomes inflexible and refers to the definitions in the internal revenue code. With the predefinition of the language he can use and its meaning, the reality with which he can deal is also predefined. All languages, indeed, define reality. But bureaucratic language defines reality from the top down. Language of that kind becomes a one-way instrument of power for those who assume the right to set down the definitions. Such languages are nothing new, but have been developed "wherever power interests of the given structure of domination *toward the outside* are at stake."[33] Weber noted, for example, that "the Treasury officials of the Persian Shah have made a secret science of their budgetary art and even use a secret script."[34] A typical example today is the classified ad on the following page. What deserves further investigation, in a time of the proliferation of secretive administrative arts and computer languages, is the ultimate effect on human beings when communication is transmuted into *in*formation — the shaping of thought and language exclusively from the outside.

When seen from the viewpoint of client, citizen, and politician, the bureaucracy's "integrity" becomes "secrecy." Language itself is merely the form that protects the two types of knowledge bureaucrats seek to monopolize for their own self-protection: professional knowledge (to Weber, *Fachwissen*, or expert knowledge of a substantive

```
┌─────────────────────────────────┐
│                                 │
│       IBM DUAL 370/168          │
│      INSTALLATION NEEDS         │
│         2 SUPERVISORS           │
│      2 CONSOLE OPERATORS        │
│                                 │
│          OS/MVT/ASP             │
│          EXPERIENCE             │
│          PREFERRED              │
│                                 │
│           3 day week            │
│        excellent benefits       │
│                                 │
│       Write: X7031 TIMES        │
│                                 │
└─────────────────────────────────┘
```

field)[35] and bureaucratic knowledge (*Dienstwissen*, or administrative knowledge of the forms of applying substance).[36] Specialized language constitutes the outer frontier of what Weber called "the most important means of power of officialdom — the transformation of bureaucratic knowledge into *secret knowledge.*" This, he wrote, constitutes, in the last analysis, "merely a means to safeguard the administration against supervision."[37]

The lessons that might be drawn from the analysis of bureaucracy as a separate culture with its own norms, behaviors, psychology, language, and political structure, cannot even be outlined in an introductory essay such as this. In general, however, each of the persons most concerned with tackling the problems bureaucracy presents — manager, functionary, and client — might begin to recognize that the challenge is not one of making minor adjustments, such as "humanizing" management, "psyching out" the job in order to keep it, or "getting access" to get the goods.

Managers who "humanize" or "personalize" some of their relationships with their hierarchy (they obviously cannot personalize *all* relationships given the size of most bureaucracies) are not simply stepping on the toes of some people who will be jealous of such relationships from which they are excluded. They are, in fact, subverting the basic structure of modern organization: they are opening up to question the taken-for-granted values system that provides most functionaries with guidelines for success, attacking the identity of functionaries as organizationally defined and thus frightening the excluded to their very core, and factually and legally engaging in "corruption" in the true sense of the word by propagating emotional relationships that threaten death to rationalistically legitimated ones.

For functionaries the problem is not merely one of making a minimal adaptation to the bureaucracy. In most cases they must allow themselves to be brainwashed into new norms, change their personality structure from self-orientation to dependency, make the bureaucratic language their own, submit and uphold the hierarchic power structure, and cut themselves off from personal empathy and relationships with clients. To the extent they do not, the probability of failure rises.

Clients are in the most difficult position. Without the initial institutional support given to recruits into bureaucracy, clients must learn a new language, tune in to new norms, bow properly to immense institutional power, understand and flatter the bureaucratic personality, and try to become a "case." Paradoxically, especially in welfare bureaucracies, only to the extent that clients surrender their humanity are they given the bare promise of material support by which to uphold that humanity.

Each of these problem areas deserves separate investigation.

NOTES

1. Max Weber, *The Protestant Ethic and the Spirit of Capitalism*, trans. Talcott Parsons (New York: Scribner's, 1958), p. 182.

2. Max Weber, *Economy and Society: An Outline of Interpretive Sociology*, 3 vols., eds. Guenther Roth and Claus Wittich, trans. Ephraim Fischoff *et al.* (New York: Bedminster Press, 1968). All of the points made here are in the essay entitled "Bureaucracy," pp. 956 – 1005. On the transformation of social relations, Weber writes, p. 987: "Bureaucracy is *the* way of translating social action into rationally organized action."

3. Ibid., p. 975: "Bureaucracy develops the more perfectly, the more it is 'dehumanized,' the more completely it succeeds in eliminating from official business love, hatred, and all personal, irrational, and emotional elements which escape calculation."

4. Ibid., p. 998: Bureaucratization favors development of "the [new] personality type of the professional expert." P. 968: Bureaucracy develops "the official's readiness to subordinate himself to his superior without any will of his own."

5. Ibid., p. 992. This is my expansion on Weber's comment regarding bureaucracy's interest in secrecy, extending even to the use of a "secret script." See chapt. 4.

6. Ibid., pp. 987 and 991. See also p. 1403.

7. Ibid., p. 22.

8. Ibid., p. 987.

9. Ibid., p. 998.

10. Ibid., p. 987.

11. Based on Sigmund Freud, *The Ego and the Id*, in James Strachey, ed., *The Standard Edition of the Complete Psychological Works of Sigmund Freud* (London: Hogarth Press, 1955). This psychology is also weakened in industrial and business technology; see R.P. Hummel, "The City in the Year 2000," *urbia*, 1 (Spring/Summer 1974), 12.

12. B.F. Skinner, *Beyond Freedom and Dignity* (New York: Bantam, 1972).

13. The theory of how social place affects what we get to see of reality belongs to

the sociology of knowledge. See especially Karl Mannheim, *Ideology and Utopia*, various editions, and Peter Berger and Thomas Luckmann, *The Social Construction of Reality* (Garden City, N.Y.: Doubleday, 1967).

14. "A Maine Man's Determined Effort to Keep his Home Warm," *The New York Times*, January 12, 1975, p. 43.

15. Max Weber, *Staatssoziologie — Soziologie der rationalen Staatsanstalt und der modernen politischen Parteien und Parlamente*, 2nd ed., ed. Johannes Winckelmann (Berlin: Duncker & Humblot, 1966), p. 45.

16. Max Weber, *Economy and Society*, p. 225. Here "*sine ira ac studio*" is rendered differently. The German terms Weber used in *Staatssoziologie* are "*ohne Zorn und Eingenommenheit.*"

17. Ibid., pp. 956 – 958; cf. pp. 224 – 225. Similar norms hold for bureaucracy in private enterprise. See ibid., "The Conditions of Maximum Formal Rationality of Capital Accounting," pp. 161 – 164.

18. Jürgen Habermas, *Toward a Rational Society* (Boston: Beacon Press, 1971), p. 96. This summary of norms has been taken from Habermas merely because of its brevity and cogency. Weber makes the same points in his discussion of administration in traditional (nonmodern) societies (Weber, *Economy and Society*, pp. 226 – 241), where he notes that the distribution of goods and services under traditional authority turns about personal dignity (*Eigenwürde*), p. 227; personal loyalty, p. 227; ethical common sense, . . . equity, . . . utilitarian expediency, . . . not formal principles, p. 227; wisdom, p. 227; favoritism, p. 228; fealty, p. 230; sacred traditions, p. 231; age differences, p. 231; personal rights, pp. 232 – 233; ritual, p. 234; blood relations, p. 234; and so on. Specifically absent under traditional rule are "(a) a clearly defined sphere of competence subject to impersonal rules, (b) a rationally established hierarchy, (c) a regular system of appointment on the basis of free contract and orderly promotion, (d) technical training as regular requirement, (e) [frequently] fixed salaries, in the type case paid in money," p. 229.

19. From the wall of *The New York Times* lobby, 229 West 43rd Street, New York City. The words are those of Adolph S. Ochs, the founder of the modern *Times*. For details see Edwin Emery and Henry Ladd Smith, *The Press and America* (Englewood Cliffs. N.I.: Prentice-Hall, 1954).

20. Weber, *Economy and Society*, p. 1115.

21. *The New York Times*, February 27, 1975, p. 23.

22. Quoted by Andrew M. Greeley, "A Scrapyard for the Daley Organization?" *Bulletin of the Atomic Scientists*, February 1973, p. 11.

23. Mario Puzo, *The Godfather* (Greenwich, Conn.: Fawcett, 1969), p. 146.

24. Weber, *The Protestant Ethic*, p. 182. Weber also holds open the possibility of charismatic irruptions into other kinds of rationalized cultures in his *Gesammelte Aufsätze zur Religionssoziologie (Collected Essays in the Sociology of Religion)* 3 vols. (Tübingen: J.C.B. Mohr, 1920 – 21).

25. On the emotional base of charisma ascription, see my "Freud's Totem Theory as Complement to Max Weber's Theory of Charisma," *Psychological Reports*, 35 (1974), 683 – 686.

26. Weber, *Gesammelte Aufsätze*, I, p. 253.

27. Louis Harris, *The Anguish of Change* (New York: W.W. Norton, 1973), p. 12.

28. "Diane Wilson" in Studs Terkel, *Working* (New York: Pantheon, 1974), p. 348.

29. Ibid., p. 351.

30. Weber, *Economy and Society*, p. 987.

31. Weber, *From Max Weber: Essays in Sociology*, trans. and eds., H.H. Gerth and C. Wright Mills (New York: Oxford University Press, 1958), p. 253. The slightly different translation of this passage in *Economy and Society*, pp. 1148 – 1149, is not apropos here. The peculiar form modern Western rationality takes, as well as its content, are described by Weber in his *Protestant Ethic*.

32. Weber, *Staatssoziologie*, p. 45.

33. Weber, *Economy and Society*, p. 992. Italics are Weber's.

34. Ibid., p. 992.

35. Weber, *Staatssoziologie*, p. 77.

36. Ibid.

37. Ibid. See also *Economy and Society*, p. 1418, where the passage is rendered similarly. *Staatssoziologie*, of course, constitutes Johannes Winckelmann's incomparable effort to compile and edit all Weber's fundamental insights on politics and administration into a synthesis. Weber had planned such a synthesis and even written an outline that would have appended the work to *Economy and Society*, but was prevented by death from completing the work. Citations from *Staatssoziologie* will therefore appear familiar to the Weberian, since they often repeat other sources, although the synthesis has not been translated.

1

Bureaucracy as the New Society

Bureaucracy is the means of transforming social action into rationally organized action.

— *Max Weber*[1]

What does it mean in a practical sense when we warn a newcomer to bureaucracy in Max Weber's words that "bureaucracy is *the* means of transforming social action into rationally organized action"? Even without knowing what is meant by "social action" and "rationally organized action," it is clear that Weber is warning us about a *difference* between the two.*

HOW PEOPLE ACT

The Citizen versus Bureaucracy

The man in the street experiences that difference every day. It has to do with the coldness and impersonality with which he is typically treated by the street-level functionaries of a bureaucracy. Before he walked

*As throughout the book, each difference between society and bureaucracy is here first treated experientially. Analysis of the difference in social relations begins in the second section of the chapter.

into the doors of, say, the New York State Motor Vehicles Department, our man in the street was a proud car owner, a man of substance because he could own a car, a man of some degree of self-esteem because he just steered that car through difficult traffic — in other words a human being with class, status, and unique personality. Once inside the door, he is told to stand in line, fill out forms just so, accept the rejection of the way he filled out his forms, told to stand in the same line again to wait another hour or so, required to answer the questions of the man or woman behind the desk, directed to another line, and so on.

> They made me feel like a kid, like I didn't have a brain in my head. The whole thing didn't make sense. First one line, then another. Then they sent me back to my insurance agent for my F-1 form I didn't know I was supposed to have. I told them I just took off the day to get my license plates and couldn't take off another. Couldn't they just give me my plates and I would mail in my form? No! The rules say . . . blah, blah . . . another day shot.
>
> — *Man interviewed outside a Motor Vehicles Department office*[2]

"They made me feel like a kid . . ." The client here commits his first and almost universal error in misunderstanding bureaucracy. Actually, he is turned into less than a child in the eyes of the bureaucrat. He is turned into a "case." The bureaucrat has no time and no permission to become involved in the personal problems of clients. From his point of view the more he can depersonalize the client into a thing devoid of unique features the more easily and smoothly he will be able to handle the cases before him.

Here is where the client commits a second mistake of misunderstanding. In the world from which the client has just come, the world outside the bureaucracy's door, there are many areas of life in which it is absolutely necessary to take into account the unique personality of the person with whom you are dealing. Friendship and salesmanship are two of these areas. When you come for help to a friend, he or she helps you in a personal and intimate way exactly because you are unique — because you are you, a friend. If you are trying to sell door-to-door, whether it is Fuller brushes or life insurance, you had better take into account the unique state of mind of the individual you are selling to. It may make a difference to know that a housewife's husband has just put her on a strict budget or that the person you are trying to sell life insurance to has just that day lost a relative.

Yet when the Fuller Brush man and the salesman from Prudential walk into the Motor Vehicles Department, they see themselves treated in exactly the opposite way that they would treat their clients, their customers. The normal assumption, the second misunderstanding engaged in, runs along the following lines:

Those goddamn bureaucrats behind the counter got it soft. They got Civil Service, can't get fired. I knock myself out with every customer; they can just kiss me off. They should have my job for a while, they'd try harder.

— *The same man interviewed outside the Motor Vehicles Department*[3]

The misunderstanding is typical. What the client here fails to understand is that the pressures on the bureaucrat behind the counter are such that the very same behaviors that a client finds objectionable guarantee the bureaucrat "success" within the rules of his or her bureaucracy — not just this bureaucracy, any organization running on the modern bureaucratic model. In Weber's words, "Bureaucracy develops the more perfectly, the more it is 'dehumanized.'"[4]

This kind of statement seems to fly in the face of all common sense. Is not a public-service bureaucracy, especially, set up to provide public service? The answer has to be yes. By definition it is set up to provide service. But it is also set up to be a bureaucracy!

The Bureaucrat and the Client

There are many ways of giving public service. The Salvation Army gives public service. Parishioners in your local church collect money to give to the poor at Christmas. Society women hold a charity ball. You give to a poorly dressed man holding out his hand on a street corner. Whether any of these ways of giving are bureaucratic remains to be examined. The last two examples are likely to be unbureaucratic.

Service Without a Smile

Bureaucracy is a particular strategy, chosen from among others, through which public service can be given. Weber indicated the chief characteristic of bureaucracy as a specific organizational strategy for giving service: it is characterized by "rationally organized action," not by "social action." In fact, it transforms social action into rationally organized action.

In brief, the way bureaucrats relate to clients is analagous to the way people in one country relate to people from an entirely different country. Bureaucrats can't help the way they act — if they want to remain employed members of bureaucracy. There is something innate in bureaucracy that turns bureaucrats into people who provide service coldly, impersonally, without a frown or a smile.

The newcomer to a bureaucracy, intending to keep the job, and the client approaching a bureaucracy, wanting to get service and still remain sane, had better understand the difference in the codes of behavior built into society and bureaucracy; that is, the conflict of "social action" versus "rationally organized action."

The alternative, even for the experienced bureaucrat, can be eternal puzzlement. A social worker for Catholic charities talks about her attempts to get humane, personal attention from welfare case workers for her clients:

> In dealing with clients we would eventually have to take certain clients down to welfare, Social Security, the board of education and they would see a case worker.
>
> Still, no one is interested in what your problem is. The case worker screens you like you have applied for a Banker's Trust loan.
>
> Eventually you get pretty tired of all the bullshit questions and ask, Are you so inhuman that you can't deal with the client as a person? Then, being the dedicated case workers that they are, they'll give you some crap about the manual not allowing for that.
>
> If you still continue along this line of questioning the case worker — or, as they call it, harassment of the case worker — they will read you the rules and regulations of the welfare department.
>
> All of this keeps you in line and keeps them uninvolved. . . .
>
> Bureaucracy, as you say, is *the* means of transforming social action into rationally organized action. Which is what any well-organized agency will do, in that they cut through the bull and get to *their* main objectives, not *yours*.[5]

Ultimately, functionaries who cannot accept the restrictions of bureaucratic service leave, or are forced to leave, the bureaucracy. A former social worker tells of the frustrations that led to her being fired:

> For two and a half years, I was a social worker for a private child caring agency which cared for dependent and neglected children. Since these children were all from New York City, our agency was funded by the City of New York and thus we were bound by the rules of the Bureau of Child Welfare of the city's Social Service Department.
>
> My job was to provide casework services to the children and their families. The goal was to come up with some long-range plans for the child — hopefully to reunite him with his family or to place him in a long-range foster home. I had a regular caseload and visited the families every two weeks.
>
> I had a difficult time adjusting to some of the rules set up by both New York City and the agency that employed me. We always had to become somewhat detached from our clients. It was not my job to get involved in determining how much welfare money my clients received. Almost all of them were receiving public assistance and it was easy to see that it wasn't enough.
>
> I recall using my own money to buy Christmas gifts so that the parents would give them to the children when they spent the holidays with them. I occasionally brought food with me to my clients because it was easy to see that their public assistance allotment wasn't enough.
>
> I never told this to my employer.

Our agency had a rule that the parents could come and visit the children every other Sunday. I remember feeling frustrated over this, as I felt that it was hardly enough contact. I remember asking how this decision was arrived at and being told by my supervisor that he didn't know: it had always been that way.

I always felt that the bureaucratic process placed a great gap between the social worker and the client. This created much frustration because I guess I felt some human feelings toward these people and couldn't give them what I wanted to. There were too many regulations and forms that got in the way of what I considered to be a good relationship based on needs and feelings.

Thus, I didn't last long.

— *Elaine G., currently personnel director*
for a detention shelter for juveniles[6]

Despite puzzlement, resentment, and an overpowering sense of frustration, both the Catholic charities social worker and the child-care agency social worker put their finger on essential characteristics of bureaucracy. Their only problem is that they perceive these essentials as pathology.* In their own words, these essentials are:

1. Bureaucracies "get to *their* main objectives, not *yours*."
2. "Regulations and forms" get in the way of "a good [social] relationship based on needs and feelings."

Why is this so? Why should this be so?

What Price Efficiency?
Bureaucracy is an efficient means for handling large numbers of people. "Efficient" in its own terms. It would be impossible to handle large numbers of people in their full depth and complexity. Bureaucracy is a tool for ferreting out what is "relevant" to the task for which the bureaucracy was established. As a result, only those facts in the complex lives of individuals that are relevant to that task need be communicated between the individual and the bureaucracy.

To achieve this simplification, the modern bureaucrat has invented the "case." At the intake level of the bureaucracy, individual personalities are converted into cases. Only if a person can qualify as a case, is he or she allowed treatment by the bureaucracy. More

---

*The citizen of the social world typically has this difficulty of being unable to believe that the dehumanizing characteristics of bureaucracy are the result of design rather than the result of a systems breakdown. This is exactly equivalent to the story of an old Italian immigrant to the United States who remembers: "When I first came to New York, off the boat, I thought the people were crazy. They couldn't even speak Italian." This observation neglected the fact that Americans were all crazy the same way: they all spoke English.

accurately, a bureaucracy is never set up to treat or deal with persons: it "processes" only "cases."

Once this is understood, the uncanny fact is explained that within a bureaucracy you will never find clients in the form of human beings. They can have existence for the bureaucracy only as truncated paper ghosts of their former selves — as cases.

Since this simple fact of bureaucratic life is seldom communicated to prospective clients in any explanatory way, and since clients therefore continue to assume they are addressing the bureaucracy for help as they define it in all their complex individuality, the intake section of a bureaucracy usually resembles a theater of war. In fact it *is* a theater of war. The war is one between two cultures. It is conducted by two totally different personality types, according to two totally different rules of war. The opposing armies cannot even shout threats or imprecations at one another very well: their languages are too different.

When Patricia Hearst, granddaughter of the late newspaper tycoon William Randolph Hearst, was arrested after some time as a fugitive, she was badgered by a clerk with the repeated and remorseless demand that she must give her occupation for the purpose of filling out a jail form. Finally her patience cracked and she cried out, "Urban guerrilla!" It was a response to categorization that was to haunt her in later legal battles. Her self-categorization not only satisfied a clerk, it served to satisfy a whole army of prosecutors, who took the exasperated remark as a confession. Patty Hearst could now be treated under a label, "urban guerrilla," that could be fitted into the overall category of "self-confessed criminal."

The Functionary and the Manager

The dehumanization of the functionary-client relationship is hard to understand, especially in public-service agencies. After all, such agencies were set up to serve clients, or so clients keep saying. The classic remonstrance from a client with taxpayer consciousness is and always has been: "You're *my* employe. My taxes pay your salary. Now let's get some service around here!"

Bureaucracy as Organization
Yet this attitude ignores the nature of bureaucracy. After all, why do we have bureaucracy? If we stop thinking of it for a moment in its negative, dehumanizing role and compare bureaucracy to previous forms of organizing administration, we are left with one answer only. Bureaucracy, as a form of organization, is the most powerful instrument yet developed for getting people to work together on monu-

mentally large common tasks. Modern bureaucracy harnesses more power than any, and possibly all, of the great projects of antiquity. As a form of organization, it makes possible the control of literally millions of people. And all these millions can be directed to one big project — bigger than building the pyramids, larger than the Roman Empire.

We live, as Weber pointed out, in an age of "universal bureaucratization."[7] "In a modern state," he wrote, essaying the impact of World War I on the process of bureaucratization, "the actual ruler is necessarily and unavoidably the bureaucracy . . . "[8] Similarly, in a more recent work, Henry Jacoby explores, as the book's title indicates, "The Bureaucratization of the World."[9]

What underlies this triumph of bureaucracy is its ability to amass and direct power. It does so better than any competing organization. And it does so whether in the private sector, as in the organization of modern business or industry, or in the public or political sectors, as in public service or the organization of political parties. The world over, those countries that have resisted "modernization" — that is, the introduction of bureaucratic organization and its norms — have been pushed aside and into the backwaters of history by modern, bureaucratized countries. In this sense the organization of China's Communist party is as much a triumph of bureaucracy as *the* form of modern organization as was the conquest of countries and continents by Western European nations in the nineteenth century.[10] Similarly, the state apparatus of one of the largest political organizations, the Soviet Union, has become one of the most successful control mechanisms in the world for exactly the reason that Weber predicted when socialism was first introduced in Russia, "Increasing 'socialization' today unavoidably means increasing bureaucratization."[11]

Bureaucracy as Control

What does the victory of bureaucracy as a control instrument of unparalleled power mean to people in everyday life? Listen to the complaint of a functionary in the personnel department of the Cleveland, Ohio, Board of Education:

> For a long time, I felt my role within the bureaucracy was to deal with human needs. In recent years, accountability has become so important, however, that I now must spend more and more time completing forms and compiling records. In many instances this work is duplicated by others and there is less time devoted to rendering service.
>
> My program director is caught up in this control situation and is constantly seeking new control methods and reactivating dormant rules. We had the sign-in and the sign-out procedure, the daily log, weekly, bi-weekly, monthly and yearly reports; now, we have a management information retrieval system.

When similar information about all workers in the program is placed in the system, management can then analyze this data and attempt to control the daily work schedule and work distribution. Before all this paperwork there was more productivity. It seems that accountability and productivity are not compatible.

— *Richard W., curriculum specialist*[12]

Here a functionary has put his finger on two countervailing pressures of bureaucracy that express themselves in the meaning of "rationally organized action."

Rational Action
In bureaucracy action is rational on two grounds: first, if an action is a logical means to a clearly defined end; second, if and only if action is performed in such a manner that its means-ends logic is visible. Action within bureaucracy must not only be action; it must also be subject to control. If it is not subject to control, it is not action. Or, rather, it may be action, but bureaucracy itself cannot take official notice of it.

This double aspect of action as defined in the modern era stems from our concept of science and pervades all the kinds of technology that institutionalize action. Science recommends this definition; technology, including modern bureaucracy as the technology of management, enforces it.

A social scientist, like sociologist Talcott Parsons, will include the double demand for both logic and visibility in a definition:

Action is rational in so far as it pursues ends possible within the conditions of the situation, and by the means which, among those available to the actor, are intrinsically best adapted to the end *for reasons understandable and verifiable by positive empirical science.*[13]

And a bureaucracy will enforce the double aspect by insisting both that work be done in a manner suitable to an overall purpose and that it be done in a visible manner so it can be checked and controlled from above.

Functionaries have a hard time accepting the double aspect. "Why," they typically ask, "do I have to spend hours filling out reports, when anybody can see that I've got my work done." The demand for visibility is especially irritating to civil service workers whose work is already highly visible to them. A battalion chief in the New York City Fire Department complains:

When the fire's out, the fire's out. Anybody can see that. We've done our job. There's a lot of satisfaction in that.

I don't even mind going over what happened at a big fire with the captains involved. I think it's necessary to debrief. You learn from that. Other people can see things that happened that you missed.

But then there are the reports. And the second guessing from upstairs. And the insisting on regs [regulations]: does your watch guy have his shirt buttoned, are shoes shined, are buttons on?

If I've got a good team that turns out a topnotch performance at a fire, I'm going to hassle them about a missing button?[14]

Yet bureaucracy is a control instrument and a control instrument without compare. Control is the source of power for this type of organization, and it is natural that those charged with control will emphasize the visible portions of what their subordinates do. As a result, instituting standard operating procedures and basing assessment of performance on observed compliance with these is a natural and normal solution to the problem of control experienced by an organization that grows larger and larger.

The results of such emphasis on the visible are also inevitable. Eventually control comes to mean largely checking that procedures are followed — instead of looking at output.[15] In other words, for the sake of visible procedures that can be easily supervised by control personnel (management), the first condition of modern rational action — that action be logically connected to some end or purpose — is finally abandoned. Formality conquers substance.

A classical example of this last point is the way teachers are forced to organize their teaching in most public schools. In an essay on alienation and bureaucracy, Michael P. Smith puts his finger on exactly that point at which the demand for controllable, visible work, with no other reason for being than its visibility, actually destroys work that is purposeful:

> In many urban school systems excessive bureaucratization also has resulted in the routinization of teaching practices, which, in turn, has added to the deindividualization of the learning process. Even those teachers and principals who are person-oriented rather than task-oriented can be constrained by the weight of procedural strictures and paper work emanating from the central headquarters staff. In the St. Louis public school system, for example, teachers at the elementary level are required to organize their entire work week according to a printed form. Such behavior leaves little room for spontaneity or that leap of imagination we call creativity.[16]

This example actually contains two truths about the nature of bureaucratic action:

1. In bureaucracy, action can be recognized and rewarded even though it has become totally detached from people, as in the contrast between person-oriented and task-oriented school personnel.
2. In bureaucracy, action can be recognized and required even though it has become totally detached from an object — the teaching process from what is being learned, for example.

Bureaucratic Action

This leads us to a summary statement about bureaucratic action. Social action is normally initiated by a human being who has certain intentions or purposes. The action is intended to convey such goals or purposes and is addressed to a social partner whose understanding of the action is a key part of the purpose. Social action, then, consists of a human initiator, the action itself, and a human recipient, or co-actor.

Bureaucratic action is reduced to the action itself. It does not have a human originator in the sense of expressing the private will or intentions of a human being; it originates — and this is a key characteristic of bureaucracy as a system — in an office whether or not a specific human being fills the role of office-holder. (In automated bureaucracies, the action may originate in a computer.) Next there is the operation or function itself. What makes it an operation or function, however, is not primarily related to the logical end point which was the original purpose of the action. What makes it an operation or function is determined by whether or not the action meets the values and standards of higher offices charged with control.

Bureaucratic action, therefore, is motion amputated from origin and purpose. It is, however, never uncontrolled motion. I first understood this difference between action and motion when a disgruntled client told me about a bureaucracy with which he was having difficulty, "They went through a lot of motions, but I didn't get any action."

The novice bureaucrat especially must keep this difference between social action and bureaucratic action in mind if he or she is not to be eternally puzzled by a fundamental absurdity of bureaucracy: if there is ever a conflict between actually rendering a service to clients and thereby endangering internal control within the organization, control must be put first. That is the bureaucratic imperative for self-preservation.* The alternative is that the bureaucracy dies, as nearly happened recently to New York State's Urban Development Corporation, which the former governor said was intended to render service even at the risk of bankruptcy.†

Bureaucratic Structure

All of the often-complained-about structural characteristics of bureaucracy — like the division of labor, which gives no single function-

---

*For a detailed discussion of control as the bureaucratic imperative in public service, see chapter 2. But it should be obvious even at this point that, without its much vaunted claim to be the most powerful instrument of control in the history of the world, bureaucratic organization loses its raison d'être.

†The rise and fall of this almost unique bureaucracy, which abdicated the prime imperative for maintaining control as the means for self-preservation, is traced at the end of chapter 2.

ary enough power to do anything alone but allows him or her to specialize, or the requirement that the functionary treat clients not personally but as cases — are derived from the imperative of control.

The division of labor, for example, has two purposes. On the one hand, it makes a functionary capable of developing highly specialized skills. The advantage of this may be that the bureaucracy can bring to bear on a specific problem an individual who has the ideal capacities to resolve that problem. It makes possible the development of the expert. On the other hand, exactly because of that specialization, it is often impossible for one expert to solve an overall problem without the cooperation of other experts. But for this purpose of mobilizing cooperation we need the manager.

We now have arrived at a most important insight into the whys and wherefores of the structural arrangements of bureaucracy. People's work is divided, not only to make them expert and more efficient, but to make them dependent on managerial control.

If you want to survive as a bureaucrat, you will never forget that the prime relationship you engage in is that between you and your manager, not that between you and your client. And that functionary-manager relationship is a control relationship. The successful manager never forgets this.

In many public-service bureaucracies the choice between service and control is being made every day. A policeman on the beat may truly want to render a service to a citizen.[17] In fact, contrary to popular misconception, the kind of behavior of which police are most proud and which they recall with great self-respect are instances of personal service they have rendered to citizens. An anonymous patrolman in a Midwestern city provides an example:

> The things you really do for people, you never get credit for.
> I remember picking up this kid out of the gutter three times. High on dope. The fourth time, I start taking him in. His mother comes running up to me and says the kid is going into the army in a couple of days. The medical corps. He'll straighten out. He'll never be on the stuff again. I'm supposed to give him another chance. Three times before!
> I must've been out of my skull. I let the kid go. Kid goes in the medical corps, gets his training. Now he's in medical school, becoming a doctor. Once in a while he still keeps writing me letters saying how I saved his life.
> Imagine me putting that into my day report![18]

Here is a clearcut case of an officer of a public-service institution rendering an individual citizen a human service. No matter how laudable the patrolman's humanity might be, however, his act also represents a clearcut breakdown of bureaucratic control. It is a threat against the very existence of the police department as a modern organization which is at least potentially under the control of legitimate political authority.[19]

Against this deterioration of control, the manager who intends to keep his job as sergeant, lieutenant, or captain of police will defend himself by such techniques as introducing the use of "shoo-flies" (internal police spies), tightening up on the number of times a patrolman has to report in by radio, and demanding more written reports on how and on what time was spent.

All these assertions of control, of course, take time away from service. But it is a choice a manager cannot help but make.

WHAT THE EXPERTS SAY

What people experience, experts should explain. In the preceding, we have seen that social relations — how humans encounter humans — differ radically between bureaucracy and society. How has this difference been explained by the experts?

Max Weber

The classical, and still leading, expert on bureaucracy is Max Weber. Weber also gives us a definition of social action outside bureaucracy that underlies much of current sociology.

Social Action
In *Economy and Society*, the theoretical groundwork for his sociology, Weber offers this definition of action and social action:

> We shall speak of "action" insofar as the acting individual attaches a subjective meaning to his behavior — be it overt or covert, omission or acquiescence. Action is "social" insofar as its subjective meaning takes account of the behavior of others and is thereby oriented in its course.[20]

What does he mean, and how is what he means relevant for any attempt to distinguish between social action in bureaucracy and in society?

If we take Weber personally, his meaning becomes clear. I am engaged in action when I do something and attach some sort of meaning to what I do. For example, I may be swinging an ax and hacking away at a piece of wood. This behavior, in itself just a physical exercise, becomes action when I attach to my swinging and hacking the intention of ending up with some kindling for the fire.

So far Weber's point about action is merely definitional. He is simply saying to us: This is how I shall define "action" in a purely arbitrary way. But, of course, he has a hidden purpose, and this becomes apparent when we look at the definition of *social* action.

Social action is action not simply of the sort to which *I*, as the actor, attach my personal meaning. It is action in which I take into account the meaning that *others* may attach to it.

For example, if I am in the woods by myself and want some kindling, I may swing and hack at anything that comes along. If there is another person with me, however, I do not want him to misunderstand my wild swinging and hacking as an attack on him. I therefore chop in a very organized way at one piece of wood at a time, hoping he will recognize in my care and direction the meaning I attach to my action: "Hey, Joe, I'm chopping at this piece of wood, you see? Not at you!" When I so design my actions that I take into account how others might react, I have begun to transform action, with its purely personal meaning, into social action, which is intended to have meaning for myself and at least one other person.

From this, Weber progresses to the term "social relationship." "The term 'social relationship' will be used to denote the behavior of a plurality of actors insofar as, in its meaningful content, the action of each takes account of that of others and is oriented in these terms."[21] Now we have at least two actors, you and I for example, and each of us acts in such a way that the other can understand the meaning of the action. I, for example, am now writing these words with the intention of having you understand them. And, you, to the degree that you want to engage in a reader-author (social) relationship with me, read with the intention of understanding me. To the extent that we each direct our actions toward the other, we are engaged in a social relationship.

Now let us ask ourselves to what extent bureaucrats are allowed to engage in either social action or social relationships with their clients. To answer the question, we can simply ask ourselves:

1. To what extent do bureaucrats intend to have their actions understood by clients?
2. To what extent do bureaucrats intend to engage in social relationships with clients — relationships in which all action rests on mutual understanding?

In ordinary human life, we treat people as people. We try to understand them and give them a chance to understand us. But what of the bureaucrats' position? Do they wait — *can* they wait — until they are engaged in a relationship of mutual understanding with their clients? The fact is that the machinery of bureaucracy must grind on long before that. If you are handing out license plates, forty more clients are waiting behind the one with whom you are dealing. Even if this particular client has a special problem for which he needs extraordinary understanding on your part, your work rules do not allow you to go into his problem as an individual: he must remain a case. Nor, if you are a clerk at a branch of the New York State Motor Vehicles Department, with a quota of clients to handle and the clients themselves clamoring for faster service, do you have the time to make sure your action is understood by each client. Because of the pressures of being a bureaucrat, you will often engage in simple, one-directional action — "Here are the forms, fill them out" — and never advance even to the level of social action in which you at least look to see if you are understood. These are the facts of bureaucratic life. And this is exactly what Weber was talking about when he said, "Bureaucracy is *the* means of transforming social action into rationally organized action." What Weber meant to tell all of us working in and living with bureaucracy is that the pressures we feel from being unable to deal with clients as human beings are not occasional. They are not symptomatic of something gone wrong in bureaucracy. They are built into bureaucracy. They are essential to bureaucracy if the great claims of modern organization to greater efficiency and the ability to manipulate large masses of people are to be achieved. Bureaucracy *is* the rational organization of action.

That leaves us with one more of Weber's terms to understand. What is rationally organized action?

Rationally Organized Action
Weber clarifies the character of rationally organized action in another essay, "Some Categories of a Sociology of Understanding," in which he distinguishes between social action, defined as "action based on mutual understanding," and "institutionally commanded action."[22] The first type of action is most developed in that socio-historic stage of social development traditionally called "community." It is also called "communal action" (*Gemeinschaftshandeln*). "We shall speak of communal action," writes Weber, "wherever human action is related in terms of its subjective meaning to the behavior of other human beings."[23]

"Institutionally commanded action" (*Anstaltshandeln*)[24] gradually replaces communal action as community becomes "society" — that is, as human relationships become "socialized." In this new form the actions human beings engage in are designed by others. Individuals are expected to obey society's rules even if they did not have a chance to contribute to their design. Eventually there is the possibility that they can expect to be *forced* to obey.

In the first kind of action two individuals are considered to be of the same mind, sharing an understanding of each other, because they have contributed to that understanding. In the second type of action two individuals are of the same mind because they are *forced* into it.[25] This is the kind of action found in society. Society imposes general rules for proper social behavior, but personal discretion is allowed, providing plenty of room for actions based on mutual understanding. As society becomes more bureaucratic, however, rationally organized action finally collapses that room: in its never-ending search for control over its functionaries, bureaucracy must destroy discretion.

Rationally organized action is thus associated with the step that follows community and society in the formation of human life. These stages and their associated types of action can be portrayed as follows:

community = action based on mutual understanding
society = social action: general rules; discretion for exercise of understanding within the rules
bureaucracy = rationally organized action: design of all action from above; shrinkage of discretion

The insight that bureaucracy is a new type of social relationship, first outlined by Weber, is subsequently developed in three directions. Talcott Parsons and the functionalists accept rationally organized action as a necessary condition of the large-scale organizations into which human beings have fitted themselves for survival in the twentieth century.[26] Jürgen Habermas, a successor of both Weber and Karl Marx, criticizes the decline of true social relationships of a personal kind and penetrates the farthest of any academician into the consequences of the new form of human relationships in spheres such as education, technology, and politics.[27] But the third direction in which Weber's insight was developed contributes musti intimately to the understanding of our personal experience with bureaucracy. This direction is pursued in the phenomenological sociology of Alfred Schutz.

Alfred Schutz

Phenomenology in this context refers to nothing more than a technique for reducing our experience of life in bureaucracy to its basics. Phenomenology is an analytical method that brackets out from our experience all that is accidental and unessential. After such an analysis is applied to bureaucracy, we are left with what fundamentally makes up the bureaucratic experience — those characteristics without which life in bureaucracy would not be life in bureaucracy.

We-Relationships
Where Weber distinguished between "social action" as normal everyday social life and "rationally organized action" as bureaucratic life, Alfred Schutz analyzes this distinction down to the basic elements of each life form by differentiating between the "pure we-relationship" and the "they-relationship."

In the pure we-relationship I create my social life with others who have intentions similar to mine. In the they-relationship the social world has been preconstructed for me and my contemporaries, and the problem becomes to get to know them in terms of the significance and role already assigned them by the system. It is easy to see that the we-relationship describes the situation between close friends, whereas the they-relationship describes that between bureaucrat and client, with the bureaucrat being forced to think of the client in terms predefined by the bureaucracy.

The same distinction can be observed between creative or revo-lutionary political action and institutionalized political action.[28] In creative politics, at least two individuals must go through the effort of determining what each of them wants or intends. If their goals or intentions are similar, they then can work out a shared social act that will bring them together, laboring toward those goals. Once this act has worked for them in achieving their shared goals, they may want to repeat it under the assumption: We have done it once, we can do it again. But at that point, institutionalization of politics begins. The second time around, the problem of achieving a want or intention does not have to be apprehended anew. All the participants have to do is identify the want or intention. If it fits into the category of a want or intention previously accomplished by a political action, all they need to say is: It fits under Political Routine No. 1001B; let's do Political Routine No. 1001B. Typical routines of action replace original and creative action. Bureaucracies and specifically their organiza-tional structures are such routines frozen into permanently repeated patterns; that is, they are institutions.

In normal social life we are forced to a large extent to accept the ever-changing, unfolding, blossoming, and eventually decaying con-crete reality of the human beings we encounter in all their uniqueness. To the extent that we do not, we isolate ourselves from them; that is, they perceive us as cold, insensitive, inhuman, and they isolate us. We lose the we-relationship — a most painful experience when the "other" in the we-relationship is a mother, a father, a beloved, a dear friend.

Routines of social action do, of course, serve us even in intimate social action, for example, using language ritual to reassure friendly others that I still include them in the we-relationship: "Hi there, fella!" "Good morning, Mother!" and so on. And so do everyday stereotypes of others: mothers are expected to act like Mothers, fathers like Fathers, friends like Friends. What makes social life especially human is the fact that *my* father interacts with *me* in the complexity of his uniqueness as the only father of the stereotype Fathers that I recognize as mine. What makes social life appear human is a kind of intimacy I gain from interacting in depth with my consociates — the members of the little world whose center I am and which I enlarge by including you in the we-relationship. In fact, the more I make an effort to understand you in your complexity and the closer to you I feel, the more meaningful and satisfying life in the social world appears to me.

They-Relationships

In contrast, they-relationships tend toward just the opposite pole. Routines, stereotyping, recipes for action coded in work rules — and the even-handed application of these to *all* comers — dominate they-relationships of which the relationship between bureaucrat and client is easily recognized as the extreme example. Not that human relationships of a personal sort are never used, but they represent a deviation from the essential characteristics of bureaucratic life. The bureaucrat who becomes deeply involved in the life of a client is regarded as either undependable or corrupt.

When we think of bureaucracy in the value-free sense, neither condemning nor approbating, we think of the organization of human labor into methodically applying overall institutional goals and functions. The essential characteristics of such a human apparatus can be defined in terms of the inner logic such an apparatus must come to possess if it is to carry out its predetermined purposes. These terms will be spelled out in the next section, but for now it already appears evident that bureaucracy is the ideal type of the Schutzian they-relationship world of contemporaries, located at the polar opposite end of the we-relationships of consociates. In the world of contemporaries, Schutz writes, "we never encounter real living people at all."[29] It is not the face-to-face we-relationship in which "the partners look into each other and are mutually sensitive to each other's response."[30]

Schutz's concept of the they-relationship corresponds to Weber's concept of action that is not social. If we recall the example of the clerk in the license-plate office, pressed by office rules and the number of clients, Schutz's concept helps us understand more closely the situation the clerk is in:

> I cannot assume, for instance, that my partner in a They-relationship will necessarily grasp the particular significance I am attaching to my words, or the broader context of what I am saying, unless I explicitly clue him in.[31]

For me, as a hardpressed clerk, there just isn't enough time to penetrate through the cloak of anonymity that having to treat people as cases has thrown over them. "As a result, I do not know, during the process of choosing my words, whether I am being understood or not . . ."[32]

Few bureaucracies have standards for the functionary's behavior that measure the client's understanding of what the functionary has done or said. Schutz points out, "In indirect social experience there is only one way to 'question a partner as to what he means,' and that is to use a dictionary — . . ."[33] This again argues the one-directionality of communication in a bureaucracy. Functionaries are allowed to utter any statement they like from within a repertory assigned them by the organization. They need not see to it that this organizationally approved statement is understood. On the other hand, clients have to bend over backwards to learn the bureaucratic language. Otherwise they suffer the denial of service. Clients who do not understand the language used by the Internal Revenue Service are not only likely to make mistakes on their tax returns, but they also lack essential information for cutting down their tax bills. It is, of course, in the interest of both the lawyers who write the tax laws and the bureaucrats who administer them to keep most of such information to themselves. As long as such information and the language that encodes it remain essentially secret, both professionals and bureaucrats will keep their jobs.*

Two Separate Worlds
According to Schutz, the worlds of we-relations and they-relations remain distinct. As a client dealing with a bureaucrat, our ideal type of they-relationship, I am not allowed to know him intimately ". . . unless, of course, I decide to go to see him or to call him up; but in this case I have left the They-relationship behind and have initiated a face-to-face situation."[34] As Schutz indicates, travel between the two worlds literally involves a special effort on the part of the client to gain personal access to the functionary. Of course an infinite number of devices — ranging from failure to hand out a telephone number to claims of bureaucratic secrecy, purportedly intended to protect the client's anonymity — protect the bureaucracy and its functionaries from becoming accessible to what Weber called social action and what Schutz calls the we-relationship:

> In the We-relationship I assume that your environment is identical with my own in all its variations. If I have any doubt about it, I can check on my assumption simply by pointing and asking you if that is what you mean. Such an identification is out of the question in the They-relationship.[35]

Ultimately in the world of contemporaries (the world I have here used to include the world of bureaucracy) "we never encounter real

---

*See chapter 4 for a discussion of bureaucracy as a country with its own language.

living people at all. In that world, whether we are participants or observers, we are only dealing with ideal types. Our whole experience is in the mode of 'They.'"[36] In other words, we are dealing only with cases. But cases are artificial constructs that bureaucracy requires real people to become before they can be considered for service. The motorist must have an insurance form, a driver's license, and an application form, and must be free of driving tickets before qualifying for a license plate; that is, before flesh-and-blood uniqueness can become a generalized case that the bureaucracy is predesigned to handle. In Schutz's words:

> Observation of the social behavior of another involves the very real danger that the observer will naively substitute his own ideal types [case characteristics] for those in the minds of his subject. The danger becomes acute when the observer, instead of being directly attentive to the person observed, thinks of the latter as a "case history" of such and such an abstractly defined type of conduct. Here not only may the observer be using the wrong ideal type to understand his subject's behavior, but he may never discover his error because he never confronts his subject as a real person.[37]

The results for the functionary-client relationship can be disastrous. A mother and her children applying for welfare may suffer and die because the mother is one child short of becoming a "case." A patient is denied treatment at a hospital, not on medical grounds, but on grounds of being an insurance card short of qualifying financially for admission.

Bureaucracy Penetrates Society
But these are extreme cases. More widespread, and affecting us all, is the ever-present pressure of a multitude of bureaucracies demanding that we think and act at all times like cases. Certainly it cannot escape any of us that, to the extent that we guide our personal behavior according to bureaucratic standards, we qualify for the endless variety of services or goods that bureaucracies provide. To the extent that services such as those provided by police, licensing and taxing bureaus, and banking and credit facilities have become necessities, all the pressures for conformity in social life channel the individual in a bureaucratic direction. In other words, bureaucracy penetrates society. Society is transformed into bureaucracy, even outside the formal institutional confines of the modern organization.

Further, the attitudes that Schutz describes turn functionaries themselves into cases. That is, functionaries see themselves as called into action only when specific conditions prevail that constitute a "case" of having officially to act. Functionaries thus lose in their own self-images, the power and creativity of ordinary, but free human beings. Both their emotions and actions, to say nothing of their wills, are bound by the structure to which they have surrendered their souls for the sake of a salary and institutional identity.

It is exactly this boundedness, of course, that turns bureaucracy into the powerful machine that it is. As long as functionaries accept the roles and instructions assigned to them, the machine can grow to immense proportions, and people at the top can control masses at the bottom through the tools of control and service that the functionaries in the middle have become.

But this means a final conversion of the human being into the bureaucrat. The functionary is also considered a case by his superiors. His foreman or direct supervisor means it when he says, "Nothing personal in this, Joe, but you just don't measure up. You're fired." Just what is it that Joe doesn't measure up to? Not the ability to work out his fate through direct social action with his supervisor. In fact, any attempt to engage in such action, to explain one's motivations or intentions, will be seen as an excuse. Or more accurately, from the perspective of the system of case work which the organization represents, such action is not even "right" or "wrong": it is "functional" or "dysfunctional" in terms of the goals of the organization, and an "excuse" is nothing more than a response that doesn't work.

In conclusion, Schutz can show us, through his exposition of they-relationships, that in bureaucracy social life has ended. And he shows us the reasons why. If we first define what social life consists of — what Weber called social action and Schutz the we-relationship — then it becomes possible to measure the distance away from these standards of social life that human beings are forced to go. The distance, it becomes clear, is that between opposite poles. At the one pole, human beings interact freely and spend time and effort trying to fathom each other's meanings and intentions. At the other, the functionary acts in one direction, deprived of the time and right to understand the individual needs of the other, to engage in the we-relationship, or to construct a world on the basis of mutual understanding and mutual effort.

Peter Berger

The complaint that bureaucrats are robots, not human beings, is commonly voiced by disappointed clients. It is just as commonly dismissed as a kind of folk wisdom. Yet, Max Weber and Alfred Schutz, as leading sociologists and founders of important schools of thought, confirm that there is a central element of truth in this popular perception. Similar supporting evidence comes from sociologist Peter L. Berger, who following Schutz is the current head of the phenomenological school in American sociology.

Acutely aware of the transformation of social action into bureaucratic action, Berger and his co-workers argue that "technological production brings with it *anonymous social relations*"[38] in industry as well as in bureaucracy:

> Actually, it is not concrete individuals but abstract categories that interact in the bureaucratic process. The bureaucrat is not concerned with the individual in the flesh before him but with his "file." Thus bureaucracy is an autonomous world of "papers in motion," or at least it is so in principle.[39]

Constructing Society

This understanding of the difference between society and bureaucracy has its roots in earlier work Berger did with Thomas Luckmann, also a student of Schutz's.[40] This work was a description of how society is created to begin with. It runs as follows:

Human beings create society. They begin this process by each expressing his or her needs or wants or designs for society, interacting face-to-face with others, and engaging with others in the construction of the social world. This first step of expressing one's intentions is called *externalization*. The process of constructing the social world, beginning with simple social relationships and ending with institutions, is called *objectification*, and the products — the formations of social reality that I encounter outside myself — are called *objectivations*. These objectivations, when they are encountered as parts of a reality "out there," are then in turn taken by individuals as guidelines for future conduct. That is, human beings internalize the patterns of their social reality and behave according to the standards explicit or implicit in them. This last part of the dialectic of constructing and living within the social world is called *internalization*.* In the words of the authors, "*Society is a human product. Society is an objective reality. Man is a social product.*"[41]

All three phases of society construction are here considered as perfectly normal and legitimate. Human beings have a natural need to externalize, to express their designs *for* the world and impress these designs *onto* the world. Human beings also need external objects, whether human or inanimate, connected into patterns: it will not do to have to recreate the New York City subway system all over again every

---

*In this triad of externalization, objectivation, and internalization, Berger and Luckmann combine the sociological insights of Weber, Marx, and Durkheim into an attempted synthesis.

time I get up in the morning and want to go to work. And human beings have a natural tendency to learn the patterns in the objective world, that is, to internalize them.

The problem relevant to the understanding of bureaucracy is that there is an immense gap between the creative activities of social life involved in externalization and the passive activities that are forced on individuals by their need to accept existing social structures as guidelines and background for everyday behavior.

Berger argues that the initial face-to-face situation is the matrix of all forms of social relations. The face-to-face relationship is for him the foundation of social life. It is in this situation that "the most important experience of others takes place."[42]

> In the face-to-face situation the other is appresented to me in a vivid present shared by us both. I know him in the same vivid present I am appresented to him. . . . I see him smile, then react to my frown by stopping the smile, then smile again as I smile, and so on. Every expression of mine is oriented toward him, and vice versa, and this continuous reciprocity of expressive acts is simultaneously available to both of us. . . .
>
> In the face-to-face situation, the other is fully real . . . [He] becomes real to me in the fullest sense of the word only when I meet him face to face.[43]

Here Berger, in describing the essential interaction in society in much the same words that Weber and Schutz used, already presents us with a situation that we hardly ever find in bureaucracy. It is exactly the fullness of the face-to-face relationship that is absent there — and it is commanded to be absent!

Bureaucratizing Society

But Berger does more than describe the creative phase of society in contrast to its objectivated phase, which we may begin to associate with bureaucracy as an objectivation. He shows how and why bureaucracy is a natural product of society.* This in turn helps us understand why the inhuman characteristics of bureaucracy exist, not as mere accident and mistakes, but as logical extensions of a perfectly natural human tendency.

Berger ultimately treats bureaucracy as a kind of objectivation and, in the extreme case, as an example of *reification*, a process in which human beings so lose consciousness of their potential and their past as creators that they treat their social institutions as if they had a life of their own above and beyond human control.

---

*The fact that objectivations, although a logical product of human needs, turn against humanity can be understood in terms of contrary needs — for order and for creativity.

Objectification in this context is a process in which human subjective consciousness produces certain products. These then embody it and are available in the world we share with others. Reification is a step beyond objectification. While objectification is absolutely necessary for society and for human survival, reification is a process in which the link between the producer and the product is broken. The world humans have produced now appears to them as an *alien* reality. Reification is a phenomenon of unconsciousness. The experience of reification is a dwindling of consciousness to the point where humans forget they have made their world. Eventually, consciousness fades to such a point that "the real relationship between man and his world is reversed in consciousness. Man, the producer of a world, is apprehended as its product, and human activity as an epiphenomenon of non-human processes."[44]

Thus students become the "products" of universities, workers become the "tools" of management, and individuals holding roles within an institution become subsystems performing functions within a system — "functionaries."[45]

The fact that this is a distorted picture of the place of human beings within their social reality has been repeatedly demonstrated in the recent past and present. When students at American universities left their classes to engage in protest demonstrations in the late 1960s, the universities suddenly discovered that students were not simply products, but constituted one pole of a teaching-learning relationship without whom teaching could not proceed. Thus teachers and administrators were suddenly confronted with the termination of their own institutional identity. They could no longer be teachers or administrators as long as the students stayed away. Calling in the police to arrest some students so that others might be intimidated to return to class must be understood in these terms: teachers and administrators, long the profiteers of having the university understood by students as a reification, sought to save their existence by any means possible.

Similarly, the underlying nature of business and industry as a social relationship is exposed whenever workers strike. So is the fragility of public-service institutions in instances where public servants engage in "job actions" and call in sick *en masse*.

Such instances point out not only that society and bureaucracy, as examples of externalization and reification, are polar opposites, but also that the claim of bureaucracies to be something other than social relationships is intrinsic to them. In other words, as long as bureaucracies can lower consciousness, leading clients to perceive them as reifications without which life would be unthinkable, if not "unnatural," that is as long as they will survive. But to achieve this deception of clients, bureaucracies must continuously deny them opportunities for engaging in full social relationships, in we-relationships, or in the mutual construction of new solutions to individual problems through externalization. For such experiences are actually exercises in power on the part of those who in modern organizations are supposed to have the least power — clients and street-level functionaries. They thus threaten the concentration of power at all levels of the ever-ascending hierarchy.

Bergerian analysis shows that the supercession of fundamental human relationships by dehumanized relationships is a condition for bureaucracy's very existence. All attempts to "humanize" relationships between a bureaucracy and society must therefore be considered as suicidal or window-dressing when they come from within bureaucracy itself, and as declarations of war when they originate in society.

Talcott Parsons

One way to understand the difference between action in bureaucracy and action in society is to compare the "social" view of action taken by Weber, Schutz, and Berger with the "systemic" view of action taken by Talcott Parsons.

Action Defined by the System

Parsons's view is both interesting and relevant to the study of bureaucracy because he is a founder, within sociology, of systems analysis and functionalism — two views of the world especially palatable to those who design, run, and analyze modern organizations. Here is part of Parsons's definition of action:

"Action" is a process in the actor-situation system . . .[46]

Already at this point Parsons parts company with the ordinary human being's experience of action as well as with the definition of anyone who puts such experience at the center of any explanation of human behavior. As far as ordinary human beings are concerned, you or I might think action is something you do. Not so, says Parsons; action is from the very beginning part of a "system."

Now, Parsons has every right to label as "action" anything he wants to call action. In the same way, the first man to call a dog a dog, instead of a c-a-t,* had the right to label as he saw fit. I, of course, being an ordinary human being, would call that act of first labeling an "action." Parsons, of course, can't ever get around to calling a dog a dog for the first time because action exists only where there is a system, which I take to mean, where we already have a taxonomy that separates dogs from c-a-t-s.

*I spell out this word in deference to my dog, Max.

What all this apparent charivari means is that I am concerned with the origins of actions, in fact with individual and original and creative acts, and Parsons must be held responsible for endorsing as action only those behaviors that are already part of systems. I would conclude from this that, since my definition gives me freedom to engage in action even when nobody is around, I am likely to be at my best in *creating* systems. On the other hand, Parsons will not let us *do* anything unless it makes sense in terms of somebody's system. In other words, you and I are not going to have a lot of fun.

Seriously, though, it is easy to see, even with this short beginning excerpt, that Parsons's view of the world will be welcomed very happily by people who are in a system, especially by those who run it. Anytime you want to engage in action proper to that system, you have to get permission.[47] And just in case you think I exaggerate, take a look at Parsons's definition of an act:

> But acts do not occur singly and discretely, they are organized in [guess what?] systems.[48]

Contrast that with, for example, Alfred Schutz's definition of action: "The term 'action' as used in this paper shall designate human conduct devised by the actor in advance, that is, conduct based upon a pre-conceived project."[49]

Or, as a commentator on Schutz, Maurice Natanson, said a bit more elegantly: "Dr. Schutz defines 'action' as human conduct self-consciously projected by the actor."[50]

With such definitions you and I are back in business again. We can engage in action no matter whether there is a system or what it thinks of us. Eventually, of course, we may want to elaborate a bit on what we think action is. For example, we may want to be understood in our action by others. But for at least the initial understanding, we do not as yet need a system. We can just experiment until the other person understands that when we consciously flash a smile we do not intend to attack. This, of course, is a risky business, and setting up a system of understanding that will settle once and for all the action routine "My smiling means I'm friendly" will eventually come in handy. But for a beginning it makes all the difference in the world in the way we treat one another whether we are allowed original and creative action or whether our actions are valid only within a system.

Admittedly, there may be the handicap that "in commonsense thinking we have merely a *chance* to understand the Other's action sufficiently for our purpose at hand," as Schutz himself confesses.[51] But the difference between those of us who come from society and those whose acting and thinking are integrated into bureaucracy is that we would just as soon take that chance.[52] They want to be sure all the time.

Intentionally or not, Parsons has constructed a theory of action that better reflects action in bureaucracies than in society. In bureaucracy, of course, there is only one meaning for any official action — one that is predetermined, written, encoded, and handed down to you, and you had better know what it is if you want to keep your job.

All of which should also help us understand why even the way people act seems strange to us when we emigrate from society into bureaucracy.

It seems that at least two things can be learned from the experts who write about bureaucracy and society:

1. They can explain why some of the strange differences between bureaucracy and society exist, in this case as regards social action.
2. Some of the experts themselves are more at home in society than in bureaucracy — Weber, Schutz, Berger — and their ways of defining social action reflect this. Others, beginning with Parsons, take views of social action and social relationships more suitable as apologies for bureaucracy.

BUREAUCRACY AS SOCIETY

Bureaucracy replaces society. This claim may seem farfetched — but only at first. Examine the place of bureaucracy *in* society. At first, bureaucracy is only a tool. It is intended to be the extension of my hand as taxpaying citizen. Through that extension I reach out to other citizens who become the clients of bureaucracy.

Bureaucracy, The Divider

Bureaucracy, initially, is a bridge between citizens as taxpayers and citizens as clients. It links those who have something to give with those who expect to receive — taxpayer with welfare recipient — as distinct individuals. But bureaucracy also links me as taxpayer to myself as car driver in need of a license and license plate, as the victim of crime in need of police protection, as a member of a nation needing protection from other nations. The New York State Motor Vehicles Department, the Los Angeles Police Department, and the Defense Department in Washington — all are links between me in one role (taxpayer, productive worker, voter) and me in my other roles (driver, crime victim, target for international attack).

When we think about the size of the huge machinery needed, so we are told, to link one part of our selves to major other parts, a sense of a vast absurdity breaks through into our consciousness: the machinery intended to *link* me with my fellow citizens is also the machinery that separates me *from* them. The bridge has become a chasm.

Separating People

In the realm of welfare, bureaucracy exists not only to channel welfare funds from me to people whom taxpayers like me have decided are worthy of getting our help. The welfare bureaucracy in its size and complexity puts a vast physical distance between me and the welfare client. The welfare bureaucracy makes certain that I, as taxpayer, will never be confronted face to face with a welfare recipient.

Compare this with the normal social relationship involved if you, as a friend, come to me for help when your house burns down, when your children are ill, or when you run out of food. I meet you face to face. If I have any empathy at all I will feel for you in your trouble. I tell myself: there, but for the grace of God, go I. You tell me of your children's pain, of your fear over lack of shelter, of how it feels to be hungry. We tune in to each other and our needs, we talk of basic human feelings.

As taxpayer I have none of that experience. I do not see the person to whom I give. There is no opportunity for experiencing a sense of satisfaction at helping alleviate another human being's suffering. And there is never any demand to involve my emotions — except perhaps the anger I feel when I am invited down to the tax office for a review of my returns. The welfare bureaucracy has destroyed all of the ingredients of the traditional social relationship involved in giving between friend and friend, or between human being and human being.

The recipient moves from immediacy into anonymity. He or she is never an individual to me, but merely a stereotype within the mass. Where there was warmth and human appeal, there is now coldness and impersonality. Where there was a face-to-face meeting, there is a third person intervening, not as a person, but in the shape of a robot. That robot presents the recipient with a sheaf of forms to fill out, not with a face to talk to. It treats the recipient not as a human being, but as a case. And it never has any contact at all with me as giver — except indirectly if I threaten to withhold my taxes or when politicians, on behalf of their constituents, write new rules on how welfare should be bureaucratically given.

Bureaucracy separates the giver from the taker, the giver from the bureaucrat, and the bureaucrat from the client. All three relationships cease to be personal, emotional, and social and begin to be impersonal, "rational," and machine-like. Here is the meaning of Max Weber's original insight that "bureaucracy is *the* means of transforming social action into rationally organized action."

Splitting the Self

Bureaucracy effects a further separation, that of myself from myself. Many Americans recently experienced an amazing phenomenon when they were displaced from a role as wage earner to a role as member of the corps of unemployed: they suddenly shifted from self-respect to self-hatred. Many of us have difficulty accepting unemployment benefits, relief, and free health services. To take such goods and services after long providing taxes to supply them seems to reduce us in our self-esteem to less-than-human beings. Yet I, as an employed person, contributed through my labor to funds that are set aside for people not employed. Why then, when I become unemployed, should I be unwilling to receive from the funds which I helped create?

The Protestant work ethic, under which a person is considered human only if he or she works, is one source of difficulty. But bureaucracy is another. It gets *between* me and my different roles.

When I stand in line to receive my license plates, I forget, as I am treated as just another "case" to be shouted at by overworked functionaries, that I am also the citizen and voter responsible not only for setting up that bureaucracy, but for the small budget with which it has to work. I may burst out in frustration with a typical comment: "I'm a taxpayer, let's get some service around here." But I have so little experience — very likely none at all — with relating to a bureaucracy from my position as taxpayer that I have very little sense that how I am treated as client depends on how I acted toward setting up that bureaucracy as taxpayer. The distance separating citizen and politician from eventual manager and bureaucratic functionary is too great.

Left alone I might sense that I am responsible when an ax-head I poorly attached to the handle flies off and hits me on the head. The separation between my roles as tool-maker and tool-user is infinitesimally small. It is small enough for my self to be able to oversee both roles. Yet when the tool is bureaucracy — and it is supposed to be our tool — the tool itself breaks us up into widely separated roles. It also induces an amnesia of responsibility when we shift from the role of citizen to the role of client. And, through its vast institutional presence, it breaks us up further into disparate selves. These selves no longer recognize each other. And a major function of bureaucracy is to see to it that they don't. The alternative to that is too threatening for the survival of bureaucracy itself.

Individuals who cease to dumbly play the single role of client when they stand in front of a post office window do so because they have, for a moment, reunited that role with some other role — such as citizen, taxpayer, politician, or worker — that provides them not only with a sense of independence, but with the power to integrate their various roles into a coherent self. Always when such, usually shortlived, connections are made by individuals, they feel a surge of power, of consciousness, and they escalate their demands. Such demands, unless controlled by the bureaucracy, represent threats to its functioning processes and therewith to the security of the bureaucrats whose livelihoods depend on the roles provided for them by existing processes.

Bureaucracy, then, separates human beings in two ways: (1) it separates individuals from other individuals with whom it was supposed to provide a link; (2) it separates individuals from themselves. This involves two forms of separation — separation between roles, and the detachment of roles from an integrating self.

People as Cases

Socially, bureaucracy exists wherever people treat one another in the abstract as cases rather than concretely as human beings. If we think of all possible social relations as classified into three categories — intimacy, friendship, and anonymity — social relations in bureaucracy are characteristically typified by anonymity. Neither the client nor the functionary knows the other as a person. The three realms of social contact can further be visualized as three concentric circles, each farther removed from the central self than the next:

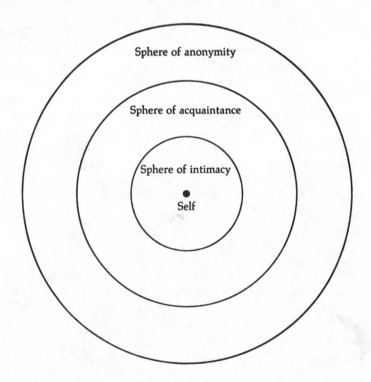

Knowing and Loving

The ultimate irony of the case approach to social relations is here revealed: we spend most of our working and even living hours with those on the periphery of our knowledge, those whom we know least. This is a reversal of communal or social life in which we know best those with whom we come into contact the most — members of our family, for example.*

This reversal has an important separating impact on the traditional human tendency to integrate cognition and affection — knowing and loving. With few apparent exceptions, human beings have in the past displayed a tendency to attach feelings of love to things and persons close to them in the sphere of intimacy.[53] In society, I love my wife, child, and even the family dog, but seldom the mail carrier. The first are familiar objects of my daily intimate life; it would be difficult not to have feelings about them. The mail carrier will tend to serve me no matter how I feel about him or her.

A transitional example of the bureaucratic reversal of the relationship between knowing and loving is the man who "loves his work" but is indifferent to his wife. What does it mean to say "I love my work" in this context? It means something very human: I have attached positive affect to the operations of my official life with which I occupy most of my waking hours. But if I work in a "good" bureaucracy, the paradox is that while I am allowed to attach affect to my actions as long as these are in line with official values, I am not allowed to attach affect to the persons toward whom these actions are directed. I am allowed to be happy in my functioning, as it is officially defined, but I am not allowed to be happy with one superior over another or one client over another. My social relations with fellow workers, superiors, or clients are supposed to be marked by an absence of affect.

Thus life in a bureaucracy has the effect of separating me from my ability to love people and of forcing me into the habit of associating affect only with processes — things I do. And, because I, in my unconsciousness, associate the things I do with myself rather than with the system of which I am merely a function, I become fundamentally narcissistic in my social relations. I take joy not in the *product* — having helped a person receive the services my office is charged with providing — but in the *process* — providing functions officially associated with that service.

---

*The beginnings of growing closeness of the anonymous are, of course, already present in society, as a transitional form of social organization between community and bureaucracy. For example, a businessman may sense himself very close to others with whom he does business, though there can be, of course, no talk of them rivaling the intimacy he shares with his family.

If we then return to the question, with whom do bureaucrats have their most intimate relationships, we must list these in the following order:

1. Their most intimate relationships are not with people, but with the things they do.
2. Their closest relationships with people are with their fellow workers, superiors, or clients in as much as these make handy objects toward which "doing things" can be directed.
3. Their most distant relationships are with those people who do not constitute objects of their official capacity to serve — for example, their spouses.

Loving the Job

The judge who says, "I love my work," does not mean he loves the lawyers, fellow judges, or accused with whom he deals. He loves the power of the process of dispensing justice. Having come this far, he may, in his confusion of consciousness, which separates him in general from contact with all humanity except that categorized into cases, allow the affect attached to his operations to spill over onto his cases.

It is in this sense that police officers and criminals develop love-hate relationships. Without the handy criminal, the police officer cannot exercise the satisfying official powers of duty. In fact, without criminals, officers would have no official existence at all because their jobs would be abolished.*

In this sense, because of the impact of their presence on official function, the people one knows least — those with whom one has only official contact — become indirectly the objects to whom one attaches affect.

An End to Intimacy

For the thoroughly bureaucratized, the intimate family becomes, for reasons they seldom understand, an arena of powerlessness. Here the bureaucrat does not experience the same fullness of power and purpose that he experiences at work where the full machinery of bureaucracy is behind him. Not only does the thoroughly bureaucratized individual have difficulty attaching positive affect to any person whom he does not officially "serve" — that is, in the service of whom he cannot flex his official muscles — but he is likely to attach negative affect to an individual, such as his wife, who insists on

---

*This could be empirically tested by research, well worth doing, on policemen dismissed from their positions when taxpayers find the fight against criminals less important than avoidance of higher taxes for police salaries. Examples abound.

intimacy. Intimacy is the best way to break stereotypes. But official life is cases, a series of relationships with only stereotypes. There is nothing in the bureaucratic experience that prepares the functionary to live at home the kind of nonbureaucratized life demanded by the traditional intimate family.

In the end, as bureaucratic orientation becomes more and more the standard for all life, bureaucracy destroys the family for exactly the same reasons that society destroyed the communal kinship system. Society's free-floating family, able to move wherever the early modern economy provided income, replaced extended kinship systems, such as clan, caste, or tribe. In kinship systems affect *had* to be attached to a great number of relatives, regardless of their behavior, as a matter of communal duty. In the family affect was restricted centrally to spouse and children, and only selectively to outlying uncles and aunts.

Bureaucracy carries this process of the lifting of affect a step further. The entire training of human beings subjected to bureaucratic life is (1) not to attach affect directly to any person, (2) to attach affect only to their own functions, successfully performed according to systems standards, and (3) to attach affect only to the exercise of power.

As a result, when the bureaucratic type engages in what used to be known as personal relations between the sexes, his behavior is characterized by (1) an absence of love, (2) a great deal of emphasis on, and attachment of affect to, technical performance in sexual inter-course, and (3) the narrowing of the range of affect to feelings of power — i.e., the replacement of love by sexual aggression.

I leave it to others to answer whether this effectively describes the new types of relationships touted as replacements for the family — open marriage, serial monogamy, and the gamut of purely sexual combinations and recombinations. My purpose here has been to give only an example of the socially expectable effects bureaucracy has on relations between human beings as human beings.

SUMMARY

The social separation of the actor from his actions as well as from other human beings creates a new orientation. Human beings become accustomed to engage in functions — actions neither on behalf of themselves nor of someone else. Rather they act on behalf of an abstract system, the purposes and logic of which they do not fully understand because of the nature of functions themselves.

Since a function is an action detached from original intentions, and even from the object or person toward which it is intended, it is impossible for a single functionary to trace its origins or its ultimate ends. Bureaucrats must therefore trust in an action's functionality to the system at large; they are no longer competent to judge the success or failure of their actions, their functionality or dysfunctionality. The lack of mastery in the psychological sense, which is discussed in a later chapter, is already implicit in the "freeing" of action from the actors, that is, in their official detachment from it. Ultimately, "the system" decides whether its inhabitants act functionally, i.e., whether their actions are linked to an overall origin and purpose of the entire bureaucratic machinery.

Analysis of the changed nature of social action in bureaucracy, then, reveals that the most common complaints and perceptions by bureaucrats themselves are not at all inaccurate. These include complaints about (1) one's inability to tell whether one is performing a useful or meaningful action; (2) the unwillingness and inability of supervisors to make final judgments and take final responsibility; (3) an awareness that it does not much matter whether I personally perform my functions because, even if I am absent, an anonymous someone will; (4) an inability to become personally attached to one's official work product because such attachment is punished; and (5) the resulting attachment to and relative overvaluation of activities not officially required or sanctioned.

Especially striking is bureaucrats' unusual emphasis on developing "personal" relations with other functionaries. Such relationships become an outlet for the frustration of the very human tendency to attach affect to one's work. Personal relationships become marked by an insistence on personal responsibility in friends, an emphasis on behavior that is ethical within the informal confines of the work group, and an exaggeration of what, in society, would have been minor breaches of personal conduct into major issues worthy of intraoffice feud and interoffice war.

Humor becomes an essential tool to bridge the gap between what, from the social point of view, is meaningless or absurd and what, from the system's point of view, is necessary official action. Used in banter among functionaries, viewing themselves in their private capacities, humor serves as an apologia for the fact that they retain a personal sense of both social ethics and responsibility, a sense against which the work group privately judges the necessity of having to commit senseless and detached bureaucratic functions. Humor here bridges the gap between bureaucracy and society. It enables the functionary to stand with one foot in both worlds, to display a consciousness of human social obligations when confronted privately by the social conscience of his or her co-workers taking a break from duty.

Apart from an initial and persistent illusion of immense power over subordinate functionaries or clients, bureaucrats are overwhelmed by an abstract "freedom." This "freedom" marks the loss of the individual's self-perception as a truly social being who is locked into personal responsibility for his or her actions and for the impact of these actions on other human beings.

NOTES

1. Max Weber, *Economy and Society: An Outline of Interpretive Sociology*, 3 vols., eds. Guenther Roth and Claus Wittich, trans. E. Fischoff *et al.* (New York: Bedminster Press, 1968), p. 987.
2. Interview conducted by the author. All such interviews in this chapter were conducted in the period 1974 – 1976, except where noted.
3. Ibid.
4. Weber, *Economy and Society*, p. 975.
5. A social worker in New York City, anonymity requested. Interview conducted by the author.
6. Written report to the author, May 1974.
7. Weber, *Economy and Society*, p. 1401.
8. Ibid., p. 1393.
9. Henry Jacoby, *The Bureaucratization of the World* (Berkeley: University of California Press, 1973). Originally published in German in 1969. My thanks to Dwight Waldo for calling this work to my attention.
10. Contrast the victory of modernization in China today against Weber's own description of the antimodern cultural barriers of traditional China at the turn of the century. See Max Weber, *Gesammelte Aufsätze zur Religionssoziologie*, 3 vols. (Tübingen: J.C.B. Mohr, 1920 – 21), vol. I, pp. 308 – 309 ff.
11. I have taken the translation of this passage directly from Max Weber, *Gesammelte Politische Schriften*, 2nd ed., ed. Johannes Winckelmann (Tübingen: J.C.B. Mohr, 1958), p. 310. In the English translation, in *Economy and Society* cited above, the translators use the term "public ownership" instead of Weber's "'socialization'." While his use of the term "'socialization'" undoubtedly signified "public ownership," the translators took an unjustified liberty. Weber meant socialization, with direct reference to Russia and socialism. His use of quotation marks always indicates that he means to use a term ironically or not in the sense in which it is routinely used. Here the use is ironic. Weber meant to indicate that what was taking place in Russia in terms of "'socialization'" was not socialist in Marx's sense, but was a case of conversion to state capitalism. See also *Gesammelte Politische Schriften*, p. 505.
12. Written report to the author, June 1975.
13. Here the regular print includes the demand for logic; the italicized part, the demand for visibility. Talcott Parsons, *The Structure of Social Action* (New York: McGraw-Hill, 1937), p. 58.
14. Personal conversation with author.
15. Official rules become so structurally embedded in everyday regulation of performance that the functionary spends more time looking over his shoulder at the rules than looking forward at the product.
16. Michael P. Smith, "Alienation and Bureaucracy: The Role of Participatory Administration," *Public Administration Review* (November/December 1971), p. 660. For further research into the bureaucratization of the teacher, begin with the older but still valid analysis by Willard Waller of what teaching does to teachers in *The Sociology of Teaching* (New York: Wiley, 1932), pp. 375 – 409.
17. For the motivations of police, see my "Teaching Human Beings: A Socio-

Psychological Role Model of Relationships with the New Student," paper presented at the 1976 annual meeting of the New York State Political Science Association, Albany, N.Y., March 26 – 27.

18. Personal interview with the author, August 1975.

19. For numerous reasons the cop on the beat exercises immense discretion, and the costs of supervision to limit that discretion are usually considered too high. On patrolmen's discretion, see James Q. Wilson, *Varieties of Police Behavior: The Management of Law and Order in Eight Communities* (Cambridge, Mass.: Harvard University Press, 1968), especially chapter 2.

20. Weber, *Economy and Society*, p. 4.

21. Ibid., p. 26.

22. Max Weber, "Ueber einige Kategorien der verstehenden Soziologie," in *Gesammelte Aufsätze zur Wissenschaftslehre*, ed., Johannes Winckelmann (Tübingen: J.C.B. Mohr, 1968), p. 471. The fact that Weber here defines social action in the same way he defines social relationship in *Economy and Society*, and thereby vitiates the distinction between the two, should not be held against him. Great men are allowed to be inconsistent, and besides it is difficult to engage in social action without waiting to hear a signal from a partner and thus engaging in a social relationship.

23. Ibid., p. 441 especially; also pp. 452 – 464.

24. Ibid., p. 467.

25. Ibid., pp. 465 – 466.

26. The tone for this acceptance was set in Parsons's own classic, *The Social System* (New York: Macmillan, 1951).

27. Perhaps the fundamental essay in which Habermas develops these implications is "Technology and Science as Ideology," in Jürgen Habermas, *Toward a Rational Society: Student Protest, Science and Politics* (Boston: Beacon Press, 1970).

28. This distinction is further developed in Robert A. Isaak and Ralph P. Hummel, *Politics for Human Beings* (North Scituate, Mass.: Duxbury Press, 1975), especially chapters 2, 3, and 12.

29. Alfred Schutz, *The Phenomenology of the Social World* (Evanston, Ill.: Northwestern University Press, 1967), p. 205.

30. Ibid., p. 202.

31. Ibid., p. 204.

32. Ibid.

33. Ibid.

34. Ibid.

35. Ibid.

36. Ibid.

37. Ibid.

38. Peter Berger, Brigitte Berger, and Hansfried Kellner, *The Homeless Mind: Modernization and Consciousness* (New York: Random House, Vintage Books, 1974), p. 31. Emphasis in the original.

39. Ibid., p. 47.

40. Peter L. Berger and Thomas Luckmann, *The Social Construction of Reality: A Treatise in the Sociology of Knowledge* (Garden City, N.Y.: Doubleday, Anchor, 1967).

41. Ibid., p. 61.

42. Ibid., p. 28.

43. Ibid., p. 29.

44. Ibid., p. 89.

45. This is exactly how modern organizational psychology treats human beings in bureaucracies. For a striking example, see the work of Edgar H. Schein, reported in chapter 3. For a classic example of the distortion of a university away from its origins as a teacher-student relationship see *Crisis at Columbia: The Cox Commission Report* (New York: Random House, 1968). For a classic example of emphasis on administrative structure and processes as representing a primary reality into which workers are fitted as epiphenomena and interchangeable pieces, see the top-down process of position classification advocated by the U.S. Civil Service Commission in *Basic Training Course in Position Classification* (Washington, D.C.: U.S. Government Printing Office, 1965),

especially Part I, "Fundamentals and the Federal Plan," pp. 1 – 19. and Part II, "The Classification Process," pp. 1 – 20. These parts are reprinted in Gilbert B. Siegel, ed., *Human Resource Management in Public Organizations: A Systems Approach* (Los Angeles: University Publishers, 1974), pp. 90 – 123. An attempt to right the balance between systems needs and individual capacities, if not human needs, is represented by Jay F. Atwood, "Position Synthesis: A Behavioral Approach to Position Classification," originally printed in *Public Personnel Review*, 32 (April 1971), 77 – 81; reprinted in Siegel, *Human Resource Management*, pp. 180 – 184.

46. Talcott Parsons, *The Social System* (Glencoe, Ill.: Free Press, 1964; orig., 1951), p. 4. There is no point in giving in to a theoretical opponent's demand that we absorb all his terminology all at once. The full first sentence of Parsons's definition runs: "'Action' is a process in the actor-situation system which has motivational significance to the individual actor, or, in the case of a collectivity, its component individuals."

47. This is literally true if you want to act in organizations. Action in modern organization is organized into roles. The prescribed action bundled into a role is so powerful that, experts on the role concept agree, the role usually changes or dominates the needs and dispositions of the individual conceived as personality. See Frank Sherwood, "The Role Concept in Administration," *Public Personnel Review*, 25 (January 1964), 41 – 44, and Victor A. Thompson, *Modern Organization* (New York: Knopf, 1961).

48. Ibid., p. 7.

49. Alfred Schutz, "Common-Sense and Scientific Interpretation of Human Action," in *Collected Papers*, vol. 2 (The Hague: Martinus Nijhoff, 1967), p. 19.

50. Ibid., p. xxxiv.

51. Ibid., p. 24.

52. Our everyday assumption that other people may have at least a little difficulty understanding all we intend to convey in all our actions is simply, says Schutz, "a principle of constructing course-of-action types in common-sense experience." (Ibid., p. 25.) It is good to wait and see.

53. An apparent exception might be the affective closeness we experience even in society to such figures far away in physical or social distance as presidents and prophets. Freud, however, explains such apparent closeness in terms of our projection of part of our intimate self onto the object in question. See Freud's *Totem and Taboo*.

2

Bureaucracy as the New Culture

Since bureaucracy has a "rational" character, with rules, means-ends calculus, and matter-of-factness predominating, its rise and expansion has everywhere had "revolutionary" results . . . as had the advance of rationalism in general.

— *Max Weber*[1]

The *cultural* conflict between bureaucracy and society is between systems needs and human needs. In society, culture is the pattern of norms and behaviors that have proved adaptive in keeping society and its members alive in the past. These patterns are frozen into standards to keep society and its members alive in the present and future. In bureaucracy, whose creators prided themselves on the independence of this form of organization from the actual people who fill its offices, the purpose of culture is to keep the bureaucracy alive whatever that does to the human beings who are the bureaucrats.

The conflict can be summarized by comparing the norms of bureaucratic life with the norms of social life:

Important in Bureaucracy[2]	Important in Society[3]
precision	justice
stability	freedom
discipline	violence

Important in Bureaucracy	Important in Society
reliability	oppression
calculability of	happiness
results	gratification
formal rationality	poverty
formalistic imper-	illness
sonality	death
formal equality of	victory and defeat
treatment	love and hate
	salvation and damnation

WHAT PEOPLE BELIEVE

People experience the conflict between these norms or values most acutely at three points — (1) when bureaucracies are born, (2) when bureaucracies die, and (3) when living bureaucracies collide with living societies. Often people caught at these points of collision accurately perceive the wrenching at their values involved.

When Bureaucracy Is Born

Judges
"I love the work, but I hate the job," laments a New York state supreme court justice caught in a recent change-over from a judicial system run by judges to a system run by court administrators. What we see is a conflict between personal gratification and the changing value-concerns of bureaucracy — efficiency, formal rationality, discipline, and calculability of results. These concerns become apparent in the following article in *The New York Times*:

> There was a time when conversation in the judges' lunchroom atop the State Supreme Court Building in Manhattan centered on fine legal points — the handling of a motion, say, or the implications of a decision.
> Now, discouraged by cuts in their budgets, distracted by charges of corruption in the courts, and vexed by an administrative struggle that they contend threatens their independence and dignity, judges are exchanging notes on the lack of morale.
> "I love the work," one judge commented recently over lunch, "but I hate the job."
> After frequent informal discussions of the problem, the 120 State Supreme Court justices in New York City were invited to join a committee last week to "act as one voice in a time of crisis."
> . . .

The committee's acting president, Justice Edward J. Greenfield, said that the justices' first worry was how they would be able to function without their confidential aides, who were scheduled to lose their jobs today for budgetary reasons. The aides type decisions, answer phones, and perform other clerical functions for the justices.

More generally, Justice Greenfield said his colleagues were concerned about their reputations and credibility, which they maintained have been damaged by the charges being made by Maurice H. Nadjari, the special state prosecutor investigating corruption in the criminal-justice system.

But the issue that has preoccupied the judges, according to Justice Greenfield, is how to fight domination by the state's Office of Court Administration under the direction of Justice Richard J. Bartlett.

"We want the right to give the orders," said Justice Moses M. Weinstein, deputy administrative judge in charge of Queens, who is also a member of the committee. "Who knows the courts better than a judge right on the scene?"

At issue is who should oversee the nonjudicial matters of State Supreme Court: the Office of Court Administration or deputy borough administrators under the direction of Justice David Ross.

Up until last November Justice Ross and his deputies were responsible for the management of nonjudicial personnel: court officers, secretaries, stenographers, and so on. In November this authority was signed over to Justice Bartlett's office. The justices' fight is to regain this responsibility. They view the matter as crucial to maintaining the judiciary's independence.

Justice Bartlett, a Glens Falls judge who was appointed state administrator in January 1974 by Chief Judge Charles D. Breitel of the State Court of Appeals in a move to spur statewide improvements in the judicial system, said he viewed the matter in terms of efficiency.

"There are many advantages," said Justice Bartlett, commenting on centrally managed personnel. "Nonjudicial needs could be viewed from a citywide perspective, the city court system could be viewed as a single budgetary entity and costs could be handled on a uniform basis."

The justices contend that they are not opposed to centralization as such but rather are concerned about taking directions from a central administrator who is not a judge. Peter Preiser, Justice Bartlett's deputy administrator in charge of the city's courts, is not a judge. The judges maintain that Mr. Preiser's appointment is a first step to taking judicial power away from the judiciary.[4]

In terms of the conflict between bureaucracy and society, the crucial sections of this report are those that expose the changing situation of the judges as a clearcut example of bureaucratization.

Until November 1975 administration over nonjudicial personnel had been in the hands of one of the New York City justices — Justice

David Ross. This meant that management of nonjudicial personnel, ranging from court officers to stenographers and secretaries, was, in contradiction to bureaucratic principles,[5] in the hands of a judicial officer, not of a manager. The rationalization for this is, "Who knows the courts better than a judge right on the scene?" It is the same complaint that people in practical work always make against those charged with the administrative coordination and control of that work.* What they are asserting is a principle — their right to personal mastery over a piece of work. The judge's statement, "I love the work," is directly related to that sense of mastery.

But what are the bureaucratic values being asserted against that sense of personal gratification? And are they in some sense valid?

"There are many advantages" to centrally managed personnel, says the judge who became the new central state administrator under bureaucratization. Specifically he mentions:

1. Nonjudicial needs could be viewed from a citywide perspective.
2. The city court system could be viewed as a single budgetary entity.
3. Costs could be handled on a uniform basis.

And ultimately all these advantages are justified in terms of "efficiency." Here, then, we have reached a typical society-bureaucracy conflict — personal *gratification*, based on mastery over judicial work, versus *efficiency*, as seen from a central managerial perspective.

Where social values are being succeeded by bureaucratic values, bureaucracy is being born. That bureaucracy is just now penetrating the New York State Supreme Court indicates the lack of modern organization in the court's administrative system. This points up the widespread fallacy that large organizations are necessarily modern organizations. A simple way to test whether an organization is modern or premodern — whether it has the coordinated power of bureaucracy

---

*See the distinction between "visible" and "invisible" work made in chapter 1. This is also the distinction between *work*, perceived by the worker as actions that are suitable means to achieve a given end or task, and *labor*, defined by accountants as units of measurable activity whether task-related or not. Managers, of course, tend to equate efficiency with visible work. Efficiency to them refers to the degree of integration between *visible* segments of work seen as elements in a means-ends chain. In contrast, workers ultimately relate all work done — whether visible or invisible to higher authority — to energy expenditure and psychologically to personal or professional judgment about the relevance of a work action to a work goal.

When managers speak of efficiency, they therefore mean work done in such a way as to become visible to them and to enhance their control. When workers speak of efficiency, they refer to the appropriateness of an action to work being done.

Failure to understand managerial appeals to efficiency as attempts to assert control leads to confusion over what the basic values of bureaucracy really are, as, for example, in James D. Thompson, *Organizations in Action* (New York: McGraw-Hill, 1967), pp. 5 – 6.

or is a fragmented shadow of what it could be — is to match its major activities with the values of bureaucracy and society as listed at the beginning of this chapter.

Firefighters

I recently had the challenge and opportunity to orient fifty battalion chiefs in the New York City Fire Department to a new management system — management by objectives (MBO).[6] Because management by objectives places emphasis on translating work activities into measurable objectives, its introduction into the fire department constituted, without doubt, the imposition of modern managerial norms — that is, bureaucratic ones.

Conversations with firemen I had taught earlier at John Jay College of Criminal Justice, and with each group of battalion chiefs, indicated that this department, admittedly one of the most effective in the city, was still being run on the basis of traditional, social norms. One example may suffice. Battalion chiefs were given a choice between two descriptions of systems of authority and asked to pick the one that most closely described their own command experience.

The first description delineated a system of authority involving leaders and followers. Orders from above were couched in terms of command and obedience from below was described as based on trust. Motivation for work on the part of followers was described in terms of inner motivation based on a sense of duty to peers and commanders and a sense of vocation, or calling.

The second description delineated a system involving managers and employes. The giving of orders from above was labeled by the term management in contrast to command. Obedience from below was described as based on clearly defined rewards and promotional opportunities. Motivation was described as based on legal commitment to observe a contract specifying duties, hours, and pay. Employes were said to work on the basis of having sold their labor for a specific time in return for which they would be reimbursed. In other words, motivation was described as based on external incentives, not internal obligations.

In each group of ten battalion chiefs, only one or two felt the fire department operated primarily on the basis of the manager-employe system. All the battalion chiefs involved agreed that authority was shifting more and more from the leader-follower to the manager-employe model. There was at least tentative evidence here that the fire department of the City of New York, with a history of effective fire fighting for more than 200 years, had only recently (within the last six to ten years) entered the bureaucratic era. And there was evidence of not only considerable hostility, but also of considerable pain at the change-over. Again and again during the introduction of the new management system the question was raised: "Why us? The city admits we're the most effective department. Why us?" Or, in a theme repeated over and over by old-timers in command and expressed most poignantly by one commander: "My men used to go into fires to save lives because they knew it was right. They risked their lives, and they died for the city. No more. When morale goes, what can I put in its place? I can't order the guy to get himself killed. He'll either want to take that risk because he feels he has to, or he won't. More and more, he won't."[7]

"Victory and defeat, love and hate, salvation and damnation" have been, as Habermas said, the categories of human life and work for millenia. To break the emotions involved is both the power and the agony of modernization. Perhaps at some future date the cost in human terms may be deemed too high. For the present, all we can do is begin to understand the cultural difference between the two opposing worlds, bureaucracy and society.

When Bureaucracy Dies

A Postmaster General
"I don't give a damn what politicians say," said the postmaster general to the senator. The time was 1973, and the Post Office Department of the United States had just died and been reincarnated as the Postal Service. What provoked the outburst? What does it mean in our discussion? The following article in *The New York Times* sets the context:

> Postmaster General E.T. Klassen was told at a Senate hearing today that, despite a major reorganization, the mail delivery service has deteriorated to the point where it was a national joke.
> "Postal Service jokes have become a national pastime," said Senator Alan Cranston, Democrat of California, in asserting that the reorganization of the Post Office Department into the United States Postal Service had failed to speed service or to slow down rate increases.
> Mr. Klassen, meanwhile, apologized to the Senate Post Office Committee for remarks that he made to a reporter before the opening of the hearings yesterday when he said, "I don't give a damn what politicians say."
> "I want to apologize for it," he said today. "It was not my intent now, nor has it been my intent, to show disrespect for Congress."[8]

A full analysis of the apparent conflict between the postal service chief — a bureaucrat — and the United States Senate — a political institution within society — is not possible. For this we would need data on the comparative performance of the Post Office Department, with its highly political characteristics, as against the Postal Service, with its vaunted modern organizational characteristics. But our aim is not to cast judgment. Our task is to make clear what values are involved in the conflict.

One reason that the Post Office Department yielded to the government-chartered but management-run agency of the Postal Service was that delivery of the mails had declined to levels where at one point it was slower than in the days of the pony express. The Postal Service, less politically dependent, promised to be more efficient. Efficiency is an internal characteristic of bureaucracy. Cost and service are external expectations society has of bureaucracy. A common misunderstanding of bureaucracy on the part of outsiders is that the chain of efficiencies inside a bureaucracy will necessarily relate to social inputs (costs) or social outputs (services). In this sense it is entirely possible to explain the postmaster general's outrage at senators. As the chief bureaucrat of his service, he knows of specific efficiencies he has instituted through modern management techniques. He is also aware of the constraints put on him in instituting these efficiencies by a cost-conscious Congress and by policies that require the agency to handle mail of a type that doesn't pay (third-class mail, for example). The degree to which he can modernize his agency, then, is limited by political considerations imposed by society.

On the other hand, citizens and politicians — the amateurs of social life in contrast to the experts of bureaucracy — have little interest in how the process of mail delivery is organized as long as the mails are delivered and stamps are cheap. This concern is expressed in Senator Cranston's complaint that the new postal service had failed to speed service or to slow down rate increases.

Whether or not the bureaucratic value of internal efficiency can ever catch up in this case with societal demand for cheaper and faster service — that is, low input and higher output — cannot be determined here. What can be observed is this: when an institution, like the original Post Office Department, declines to such an extent that the service it was intended to perform is no longer performed, society judges such institutions not according to their internal standards, but according to its own external standards. Is the mail delivered? Are stamp prices within reach?

The death of an organization always brings out the basic conflict between bureaucracy and society. Bureaucracy is concerned with means, society with ends. Here lies the essential difference in the cultural norms associated with each. It is essentially a conflict between control and service. Service, as its name implies, is the outer imperative for which public-service bureaucracy is established. Control is the inner imperative of any bureaucracy, public or private. The tendency of any bureaucracy is to substitute inner control for outward service.

This brings about one of the most outrageous examples of the paradoxical experiences private citizens have had with bureaucracy: toward the end, the Post Office Department was one of the most complex bureaucracies around — but it could not deliver the mail.

On the other hand, a bureaucracy will come in conflict with society's demand for accountability on the spending of financial resources when the bureaucracy provides services but shows a lack of inner control.

A Governor
Managers who do not adhere to bureaucracy's basic control imperative, aimed at keeping bureaucracy alive, are severely called to task. Sometimes, so are their bosses — the politicians. The death and resurrection of New York State's Urban Development Corporation (UDC) is an example.

The UDC was created in 1968, charged with building low-income housing and engaging in urban renewal. It defaulted in February 1975, having collapsed financially in an environment of shrinking fiscal resources. It finally required a $258-million loan and a direct state appropriation of $200 million in the spring of 1975 to resurrect the agency, which had been intended to be self-financing.

The chief financial officer of the corporation, which financed its operations by selling securities, had warned its director, Edward J. Logue, in 1971 that UDC might be spending money faster than it had a chance of raising it. To this warning the director responded in a letter in December of 1971:

> I do not believe there is any evidence to support your conclusion, and I do not propose to go looking for any. We are going to build as much as we can. The need is here now. When, having managed our affairs, we have gone as far as we can go, and we can't borrow any more, that is another day.[9]

A key characteristic attacked by various sources, including the report of the commission that investigated the collapse, was the lack of control exercised by the governor as chief state administrator over the agency and the degree to which legislative control was made impossible by the way the governor insulated the agency from legislative oversight. The Moreland Commission in charge of the investigation concluded, "The relationship between UDC and the executive chamber was one of cooperation and partnership, rather than one of control."[10]

Asked to testify about the collapse, former Governor Nelson A. Rockefeller clearly asserted the primacy of service over control in the operations of the agency:

We were not running a bank, not running a corporation for profit. We were trying to build housing for people who need it.

Sure there was some risk, but I was always willing to err on the side of achieving social objectives.[11]

Given an agency head who admittedly shared the governor's concern for service, those concerned with control were clearly shunted aside:

Mr. Rockefeller brushed off testimony by previous witnesses cited to him by Mr. [Sheldon H.] Elsen [counsel to the Moreland Commission]. Of budgetary officials who complained that they could not get his ear, he said their job was to carry out his orders, not dictate policy.[12]

Here the normative conflict between the survival needs of a bureaucracy and its mission of public service is clearly spelled out. As a representative of the political will of the people of New York, Rockefeller was, of course, on defensible grounds: a politician's prime legitimate task is to provide public service, in this case the achievement of "social objectives." But as chief administrator of the state's bureaucracy, a responsibility he clearly accepted when he told complaining budgetary officials to carry out orders, Rockefeller was nevertheless called to task.

Unlike politicians and the rich, typical managers cannot so easily escape responsibility — and they know it. They therefore recognize and respect the fundamental imperative of the bureaucratic enterprise, which is to keep its activities, no matter how purely and socially motivated, within such bounds that the bureaucracy will survive them. From that survival orientation they derive their cost consciousness. And from that cost consciousness they derive their need for tight control over their subordinates and for ever-continuing drives for efficiency.* Efficiency is a measure of managerial control internal to a bureaucracy — that is, to what extent managers are able to join one link to another in the long chain of administrative means that converts public expenditures into public services. The more control they exercise over this process, the more easily they can bring their organization's action into accord with the demands for accountability

---

Efficiency is here distinguished from *effectiveness*. *Efficiency* denotes the process internal to bureaucracy of logically connecting means to means with the least cost. *Effectiveness* denotes joining the internal processes of bureaucracy (means) to external products or services (ends). A bureaucracy can be highly efficient in all or part of its processes, and yet there can be a breakdown at the boundary it shares with society; the result is that, while there is efficiency, there is little or no effectiveness. For evidence of confusion on these concepts and an attempt to reach consensus on efficiency, effectiveness, productivity, etc., see Charles R. Wise and Eugene B. McGregor, Jr., "Government Productivity and Program Evaluation Issues," *Public Productivity Review*, 1 (March 1976), 5 – 19.

made by legislators and executives in the political institutions above them. Efficiency in this sense means the managers have their organization well in hand. As the case of UDC proved, not only are having an organization in hand and delivering public service not the same thing, they may on occasion be antithetical goals. Managers who allow the service goal to impair the control goal risk both their jobs and their organization's capacity to survive into the future.

All of the norms of bureaucracy listed at the beginning of this chapter favor inner stability and the survival of the bureaucracy, whereas the norms of society are external expectations that become pressures capable of eventually draining the capacity of the bureaucracy to survive. Power once expended is no longer power. Service once expended is no longer power. It is in the interest of every bureaucrat to hoard such power.

Collision Between Bureaucratic and Social Life

The conflict between the culture of bureaucracy and the culture of society arises not only in times of crisis. It pervades everyday life. Human needs collide with systems needs, and the individual suffers.

A Corrections Officer

Consider the story of a California corrections officer who was forced to make a choice between his survival in the job and the survival of his mother:

> I was at work. My mother called me and expressed a desire to be taken to the hospital. (My mother is 73 years old and lives alone.)
>
> At this time I made application to the personnel office for time off. Why did I do that? It was as though I had asked for his right arm. He immediately responded in the negative, giving no consideration to the seriousness of the problem.
>
> All he was interested in was: by letting me go, it would cause a shortage of personnel.
>
> His inability to react to me in a humanistic manner turned me off completely. It was all I could do not to react violently.[13]

Here one functionary of a bureaucratic system makes a decision that puts the needs of the system before those of another functionary. The possible death of a functionary's mother was not a concern with which the bureaucracy could be ultimately concerned. In addition, we can be almost certain that the personnel manager was protected from censure, should the woman die, by a system of personnel rules that took absolutely no account of an employee's external family obligations.

We are assuming here that the manager did not act arbitrarily. We are assuming that he acted according to the work rules. But if the objection is raised that such work rules, which did not cover the case of illness in a functionary's family, were insufficient and should be amended in a "good" bureaucracy, we have to protest.

Ultimately, conflicts between individual human needs* and systems needs are unavoidable no matter how many adjustments are made. The argument being made here is that managers must always make their decisions within the constraints of the situation — given rules and suddenly arising demands for deviation. When such conflict arises, the tendency built into the system is to put the system first. This means internal security and survival needs — expressed in demands for efficiency, reliability, and so on — predominate. For no bureaucracy will decree its own death to assure the fulfillment of its functionaries' needs when these contradict its own needs.

In summary, people high or low experience the confrontation of bureaucracy and society in terms of incompatible values and beliefs. Bureaucracy was instituted to allow people to achieve social goals and to achieve them better, more quickly, more cheaply, and most of all on a larger scale. Yet the managers of such a modern organization may be forced to make a decision to have their bureaucracy survive rather than provide services. The governor of a state, aware of this proclivity toward protecting self-interest, may make a conscious decision to set up a bureaucracy in a way that will put service first, even at the risk of

---

*The term "human needs" used throughout my argument refers to a concept of essential characteristics that make human beings human in all times regardless of civilizations or cultures. In a modified sense, I distinguish human needs in a social context from systems needs. Through the process of socialization, human needs in society are modified into needs adaptive to society as a whole just as social values are modified to meet human imperatives. When systems theorists, like James D. Thompson, for example, speak in a laudatory manner of the advantages of "open systems," they are speaking, without realizing it, of society. Society is an open system toward its environment in that it must adapt to environmental challenges to survive. It is also an open system toward its inner biological components — the human beings that comprise it — shaping them and being shaped by them. Society, when it is successful, is the mediating tool between humans and their natural environment. The human needs it shapes are nevertheless affirmed by it; otherwise society fails as an adaptive device.

No such saving grace can be ascribed to bureaucracy. Because of its immense power, and often immense size, it can conquer or at least hold in abeyance the power of its environment — as happened with industrial pollution — until the environmental reality strikes back with an iron hand. Bureaucracy, therefore, may temporarily look like an adaptive device expressing human needs only to be exposed long-term as the best possible device to negate human needs, whether these are conceived as essential and fundamentally unchangeable or as socially modified needs. The reason for this is that bureaucracy has so much power that, as an instrument, it can afford to lack the corrective processes built into society. We thus have no assurance that what bureaucracy makes any one of us do at any time has any relationship whatsoever to human needs — individual and essential or social.

All this by way of explicating the extreme polarization of human needs versus systems needs developed in the above.

having the organization die. Functionaries on the line — firefighters and their battalion chiefs, for example — struggle between the work they see has to be done, such as a fire that has to be put out, and the pressure for control from above, which demands not simple but measurable performance. How to put a measure on a firefighter's willingness to risk his life for another human being? Like the firefighters, judges in New York City, and very likely elsewhere, struggle between the personal gratification work can give and the need to subordinate that gratification to accountability, efficiency, cost consciousness, and productivity — all related to a largely unseen system and beyond to unseen taxpayers and citizens.

Between all these poles stand the managers as guardians of the new culture of bureaucracy. But they are guardians who are themselves imprisoned. How can that imprisonment be explained, not only for the managers but for all the rest of us?

WHAT THE EXPERTS SAY

The Imperatives of Capitalism and Bureaucracy

Capitalism and bureaucracy are human activities. To understand capitalism and bureaucracy as activities means to go behind their structures and find out why people engage in these activities.

What makes either capitalism or bureaucracy "tick" as modern economic and administrative structures is the motivation of the people who must live in these structures. If we can understand these motivations, we should be able to derive a whole series of imperatives of behavior without which the individual cannot survive in capitalism or bureaucracy. For what is a motivation for action to the actor becomes, once converted into action, the condition for further action on the part of anyone wanting to join that structure of action. One person's beliefs and norms become another person's imperatives.

It is in this sense that I speak here of "built-in," or "innate," tendencies of bureaucracy as a form of administration, whether in the public or the private sector. It is necessary to distinguish exactly *what* is built in for each case because the administration of business and the administration of public-service institutions do differ; but for both, real understanding requires the search for central norms and motivations deriving from them.

Capitalism
As Max Weber said of capitalism:

> The capitalistic economy of the present day is an immense cosmos into which the individual is born, and which presents itself to him, at least as an individual, as an unalterable order of things in which he must live. It

forces the individual, insofar as he is involved in the system of market relationship, to conform to capitalistic rules of action. The manufacturer who in the long run acts counter to these norms, will just as inevitably be eliminated from the economic scene as the worker who cannot or will not adapt himself to them will be thrown into the streets without a job.[14]

This should be a lesson of practical value to the manager of the private business or public institution, as well as to the entering employe who must make certain personal and moral decisions.

To the extent that the norm of a modified and secularized Protestant ethic — the idea that work alone brings human dignity and that endless accumulation of capital is evidence of that dignity — still provides the motivation behind all industrial or business enterprise, the owner or manager of such an enterprise who allows anything else to come before profit and capital accumulation is committing economic suicide. This is especially obvious in small- to medium-sized enterprises. The owner or manager of these can be certain of one thing: his competitors are not likely to forget what business "is all about." They will squeeze costs if he does not; they will undersell him in the still relatively open market if he does not. And all his pleadings that he was driven out of business because he paid his workers a decent wage, or because he felt the public deserved his goods at a low price and high quality, will not help him one iota in bankruptcy court. Large corporations can, on occasion, permit themselves the luxury of introducing "human relations" approaches to the management of workers, or even sell some goods at below cost (often to drive a smaller firm out of business) simply because their largeness allows them a measure of cushioned security that a smaller competitor does not possess.

But a manager, even of a large enterprise, who forgets over the long run that he is *fundamentally not* in the business of providing social clubs, coffee breaks, and baseball teams for his employes will soon discover that powerful remnants of capital-accumulating norms still dominate even the modern corporation.*

The worker who allows himself to be hornswoggled by mana-

---

*This is not at all to deny the shift from robber-baron capitalism, with its dominant risk-taking mentality that risked all for a gamble at expansion, to the more security-conscious mentality of the modern corporation. This shift has been explored in depth by John Kenneth Galbraith in his *The New Industrial State* (Boston: Houghton, Mifflin, 1956). But the immediate fact remains that the underlying norm, that capital accumulation is the best cushion for continued security, is not touched by his analysis. The fact remains that Lockheed Aircraft Corporation and New York City, both recently bailed out by the federal government, nevertheless, for many breathtaking moments, actually did face the fate of bankruptcy and default. In both cases this resulted from administrative failure to keep costs down and to accumulate cushions against unforeseen environmental exigencies.

gerial distractions, such as sports, credit, or cheap increments in status in the form of medals or awards, similarly misunderstands the categorical imperative of the institution for which he works — whether public or private.*

The fact that all else — including structure, personnel policies, budgeting, and attitudes toward clients — follows from a central motivating norm, which becomes the categorical imperative of modern public bureaucracy, may not be as obvious as in the case of private business. But isn't it a fact that, even when we critically give a public bureaucracy the once-over from the outside, we expect certain specifically "modern" performances on its part? Isn't it true that the "good" citizen will not "stand for" maldistribution of public services to those who "do not deserve it"? And that the "good" politician will be ever watchful of any tendency in bureaucracy to be "wasteful" and "inefficient"? There is indeed something which makes modern bureaucracy "modern" in popular political judgment, and the honest, sober, responsible citizen — as he is wont to see himself, especially during America's repeated paroxysms of "reform" — demands that this "something" be implemented, especially when he thinks about how his tax money is spent.

Bureaucracy

Just as capital enterprises in general have as their categorical imperative the endless accumulation of capital and the cost-squeezing and market-controlling *rationality* that derives from this, modern bureaucracy, as a public or private administrative tool, is considered modern only as long as its managers and employes work in the interest of two underlying imperatives — efficiency and control. But these themselves are simply reflections of the prime categorical imperative of any modern bureaucracy in modern society — to keep costs down. Any citizen outside the bureaucracy thinks himself capable, at least in

---

*Proof that modern private organizations are still consciously run on the basis of a categorical imperative of capitalistic business was found in a recent survey of thirty-three selected industrial companies as reported in John P. Campbell, Marvin D. Dunnette, Edward E. Lawler III, Karl E. Weick, Jr., *Managerial Behavior, Performance, and Effectiveness* (New York: McGraw-Hill, 1970). "Most authors feel little need to comment upon the fruits of effective management in order to define it," the authors write. "In contrast, respondents to our survey of current practices . . . placed heavy emphasis on the products of effective management. Stated most directly, our respondents see effective managing as yielding *results*! But what are results? Depending upon the firm, results include maximizing profits, maintaining organizational efficiency, promoting high employee morale, and producing (selecting, training, developing) effective subordinates who will be capable of taking on added responsibilities and of maintaining the firm in the years ahead." (pp. 8 – 9)

All three of these concerns — profit as an end, efficiency and morale as means, and maintenance of the organization over the long run — are easily recognized as elements of the capitalist imperative.

modern democratic society, to be ultimate judge of whether or not his public-service institutions are performing according to that norm. Admittedly public bureaucracy encounters some difficulties not encountered in cost-cutting efforts by private enterprise: it is not officially allowed to husband profits and engage in endless capital accumulation. It is not supposed to be a profit-making enterprise at all; the client is supposed to be served as cheaply as possible from his viewpoint, too. (This is understandable when we consider that the citizen, as taxpayer, usually meets himself within the halls of some bureaucracy or other in his other incarnation of citizen as client — to get a dog license, to put children into public school, to serve in the army.) But despite this double amputation of the potential mechanisms for acquiring resources for its operations, the modern bureaucracy is nevertheless supposed to, and expected to, operate on a cost-cutting basis, even in the public institutional sector. Managers, of course, engage in desperate measures to gain a cushion against the stingy taxpayer and the waste-hunting politician who makes his career out of that adjective — strange practices such as ballooning last year's budget expenditures to increase next year's appropriations are a typical example — but in the end theirs is not an extractive resource-accumulation system, but a distributive one.

Thus for managers and employes of the public bureaucracy, the imperative of cost cutting is an even more inexorable one, and the entire structure of modern bureaucracy, with its much-vaunted characteristics of efficiency and control from the top down, is derived from that concern. Woe to the manager or employe who thinks he can ignore that imperative and its structural commandments. Clients may need help, but first the bureaucracy must survive. Workers may deserve to be treated as human beings, but if managers weaken their hold on the imperative, they are exposed as having lost "control." They will be replaced by managers not quite so "humanistic," and so on.

Actually such difficulties seldom beset the top managers who, especially in the United States, are recruited from the top echelons of business. From their business experience they understand quite well that accumulation is both the categorical imperative of business and the key norm in the public ideology. Even as they enter the non-accumulative public institution, they act as if all the structurings and behaviors that served business so well in achieving its imperative still hold true. To a surprising extent, of course, these structurings — control from above, hierarchy, specialization, etc. — and norms — calculability, efficiency, etc. — translated into behavior do hold true in public bureaucracy. And so the impression that business practices can be transferred by the business leader turned public administrator is easily sustained.*

In any case, there seems to be plenty of evidence that the peculiar structures, behaviors, language, and even psychological orientations and identity of the bureaucrat derive from a few fundamental imperatives that sit at the bottom of modern administration, whether public or private. It would be worthwhile to ask what these imperatives are if we are to understand the nature of not only the "cultural norms" of the world of bureaucracy, which are the concerns of this chapter, but the strange demands made on us by bureaucracy as these are exposed in other chapters of this book.

Max Weber: The Imperative of Capitalism

Those of us interested in understanding the conflict between bureaucratic and human values can learn something from the fact that bureaucratic norms surround us everywhere — not only in public service but in the bureaucratic components of private enterprise.

All businessmen at all times have always wanted to make money. But there is only one way to succeed as a businessman today. And that is to recognize that modern capitalism is a specific way of making money superior to previous forms of doing business. The proof of the pudding lies in the fact that an entrepreneur not using modern business practices simply cannot compete against one who does. There seems to be a central set of rules — a modern capitalist imperative — which, if followed, puts the modern businessman at an advantage over his more traditional predecessor.

Profits Through Growth

The owners of my favorite donut shop down the street understand this imperative of modern business perfectly. If the donut shop is to stay in business and overcome slow days when income is low, the more money is accumulated the greater its margin of security. Money can

---

*The business leader turned public servant actually may have an advantage: he or she will look around for something to accumulate and will usually find it in the form of "debts," "promises," "deals," and so on that can be made with political supervisors and budgeters. In much the same way the business leader turned politician finds that the "capital" of politics is votes. Similarly, the typical American social scientist, indoctrinated often quite unconsciously into the prevailing business ethic and its language, will make the transition from the economic to the scholarly, and supposedly value-free, analytical realm and continue to speak in the terms of the former: the "coinage" of politics is votes; the "coinage" of economics is money (of course); the "coinage" of society is "social transactions," and so on. I am thinking here of Talcott Parsons.

then be directed into two channels: it can be put away as a cushion against bad times, and it can be reinvested into another donut machine to increase sales and further profits. Growth and security are intimately related.

But to know how much of a cushion is needed or how much profit can be reinvested, operating costs (rent, labor, materials, depreciation of machines) must be calculated. In addition, the owners have to determine how many donuts must be sold to break even. How many customers have to go in and out of the shop each hour, on the average, to let them reach their break-even point?

The owners of the shop, in other words, are highly modern businessmen. They understand that profits are not just to be spent, but are a guarantee for the stability and growth of the shop. And they understand that sound use of investment and reinvestment can be achieved only through calculating everything — not only material, machines, and sales personnel but also customers and consumption.

They have understood the imperative of modern capitalism: capital stability and growth through sound reinvestment achieved by the calculation of everything. This imperative can be analytically divided into two parts, the goal and the means. The goal is growth of capital. The means is calculation — or, in terms with which we are already familiar from our discussion of bureaucracy, rationalization. In other words, bureaucratization of business practices becomes the means through which capital growth as the imperative of modern capitalism is achieved. The private bureaucracy of the accounting office is the first pillar supporting capital enterprise.

This is an important point for understanding the imperative of public as well as private bureaucracy. The imperative of bureaucracy, from the first, has always been control. It was through the bureaucratization of his accounting methods, personnel selection and use, and market calculations that the first modern capitalist became truly modern and therefore superior to his less calculating predecessors.

Max Weber contributed mightily to this understanding of both modern capitalism, with bureaucracy as its control instrument, and modern public bureaucracy as the control instrument of the political system. Bureaucracy in both cases is the outgrowth, according to Weber's investigations, of a unique Western belief that everything in the world could be calculated and thereby be brought under human control. This attempt to bring the world under the command of calculating reason — rationalization — becomes not only an inner tool for capitalism but an outward condition. Again and again Weber, in his explorations of capitalism, reminds us of the rationalistic control component of the overall bureaucratic imperative, for example, in this definition of the manufacturing type of modern capitalism as "orientation to the profit possibilities in continuous production of goods in enterprises with *capital accounting.*"[15]

So much for the internal norms of capital enterprise. To the extent that accounting spells control, they are entirely within the range of the list of bureaucratic norms drawn up at the beginning of this chapter.

Environmental Stability

But elsewhere Weber's extensive researches[16] also establish that modern capitalism can exist only in an environment in which general rationalized norms, including bureaucratic ones, also become the external conditions of existence.

In drawing up his summary of the conditions under which modern capitalism can develop, Weber includes these three points:

1. Complete calculability of the technical conditions of the production process, that is, a mechanically rational technology.
2. Complete calculability of the functioning of public administration and the legal order and a reliable purely formal guarantee of all contracts by the political authority.
3. The most complete separation possible of the enterprise and its conditions of success and failure from the household or private budgetary unit and its property interests.[17]

These points summarize the dependence of the capitalist imperative — profit-making through capital reinvestment — on the concurrent of modern technology, modern bureaucracy, and modern economics.

For the manager, functionary, or client still expecting any support for purely human values from this rationalized world built on the calculability of everything, including people, there is indeed little hope. Nevertheless, managers make recurrent attempts at "humanizing" administration. Functionaries continue to expect and demand treatment as persons rather than as quantifiable things. Clients and customers continue to await from public service and private enterprise the satisfaction of human needs.

The fact that such needs may not be intrinsically compatible with the overall imperative of modernity, including the imperatives of capitalism and bureaucracy, is simply not one we can easily face. Nevertheless, let us advance to a closer examination of the bureaucratic imperative.

Max Weber: The Imperative of Bureaucracy

The imperative of bureaucracy is control. This is true, for historical reasons, whether bureaucracy is master or tool.

Control Through Rationalism

In capital enterprises, the first office to be bureaucratized was the accounting office. Rationalistic methods of accounting, embedded in regularized procedures and office structures, which are themselves susceptible to rational oversight, allow entrepreneurs to "account for" any and all operations of their enterprises and how each affects the other. The final measure of such accounting is "the bottom line" — the profit-loss statement. The bureaucratization of accounting is the starting point for bringing financing, raw-material supply, machine and labor operations, and sales into a tight relationship with profit outcome. By demanding the rationalization of the labor process — that is, its description and organization in quantifiable terms — the accounting office could adjust the labor process as a means to maximize profit as an end. The logical and effective linking of means and ends in this way constitutes the very definition of the concept of modern rationality. Bureaucracy becomes the practical carrier of the rationalization process inherent in Western civilization.

But what makes this emphasis on rationalistic control the imperative of bureaucracy when applied to public service? The answer seems to be that modern bureaucracy was specifically conceived as a control instrument to be applied to public service from the very beginning. In this sense it has always been more master than tool.

One of Weber's contributions is that he calls attention to the need that capitalism, as an economic enterprise, has for the bureaucratization of the social and legal world. In this context, the outstanding value that bureaucracy offers to capitalism is that it makes the behavior of labor, fellow capitalists, and consumers predictable. Especially in law, bureaucracy freezes into relative permanence behaviors that are in the interest of capitalist entrepreneurs to have permanent. The previous types of capitalists, with their innate tendency to play for high risks and take their money and run, come to an end when not only the methods of production but the stabilization of the external environment make reinvestment of capital for ever greater growth a good risk. On the behalf of this growing class of entrepreneurs, state bureaucracies set norms of contract among entrepreneurs and marshaled the power to enforce them. They also regulated the ways in which workers could and could not sell their labor and began regulating markets to protect entrepreneurs from foreign and domestic fluctuations.

The central value that public bureaucracy offers private enterprise is stability against the tendency, found in previous types of administration, to allow flux through the arbitrary and unpredictable application and enforcement of policy. Such previous policy was, of course, the policy of kings, nobles, and landholders. Thus from the very beginning, bureaucracy served the purpose of limiting and regulating the exercise of political power by providing conditions of stability favorable to the exercise of economic power.*

The means through which bureaucracy ensured this relative permanence in contractual, labor, and market conditions was through its structure. Instead of being left to the good will of individuals, policies became embedded in offices or, more accurately, became the operating procedures of permanent offices which, if followed, guaranteed the income, status, and institutional identity of its temporary occupants.† By making the structure of administration inflexible, bureaucracy made an ever-changing world permanent. To accuse later bureaucracies of inflexibility is therefore to display an ignorance of the origin and nature of bureaucracy as an administrative concept.

Today there is every evidence that economic enterprises of the capital-reinvesting kind can satisfy their need for ever-expanding markets only if conditions of social flux prevail. For every new condition and problem created by such a state of flux, industry and business can then provide a new product. At the same time, this kind of enterprise still needs the maintenance of relative stability to guarantee that they will be paid for their products. It is therefore necessary to regulate the money supply, enforce people's willingness to pay their debts, make both labor and the suppliers of raw and machined goods necessary for production stick to their contracts, and so on.

While these needs for social change and social stability may be contradictory, many of the demands and criticisms of contemporary bureaucracy rest on such contradictory needs. Modern bureaucracy may in this sense be outmoded and in need of replacement by a postmodern administration. But, if anything, such a possibility makes more clear than ever that what is often considered a pathological development of bureaucracy — its tendency toward permanence, inflexibility, and rigidity — was from the beginning the very value for which bureaucracy was treasured as a form of administration. In this sense, if our needs now have changed, it is not modern bureaucracy that has failed us, but we who have failed to rethink what form of administration can best serve our turbulent postmodern needs.[18]

This is one way of getting at the central imperative of bureaucracy. The other way is to review once again that when Max Weber first analyzed the central characteristics of modern bureaucracy, he also isolated its central values by a comparison. But his comparison

---

*The ultimate replacement of politics by administration was in this sense a tendency already built into bureaucracy from its inception. See also chapter 5.

†On identity as the ultimate reward for bureaucrats, see chapter 3.

was with the dominant system of administration that preceded it. Weber's famous six characteristics of bureaucracy, as we shall see shortly, mean little and reveal none of their values biases if they are read out of context — that is, out of the comparison with the preceding forms of patriarchal and patrimonial rule.

An overall view of Weber's six points shows that his theme was to contrast a new form of administration, moving toward permanence of control, against the occasional, haphazard, and often unpredictable form of arbitration associated with feudal kings and ancient empires. Each of the six points describes conditions that will prevail if a permanent and predictable administration of control is achieved. Bureaucracy itself is the institutionalization of that form of administration. In other words, the builders of early modern bureaucracy recognized that if they could make the people, processes, and structures within bureaucracy stable, the impact on society would be stable. For this reason, Weber's six points not only describe structures and procedures, but often explicitly point to a psychology of bureaucracy that is aimed at stabilizing the behavior of its staff.

One look at the sequence of the six points indicates that the points are probably arranged in an arbitrary manner; Weber does not seem to have paused to arrange them in a deductive fashion, with the most important first and the latter deduced from them. The six points are, however, not meaninglessly arranged if we think of each as related to an overall concern for control and, to emphasize this very purpose, contrasted against older, less control-oriented forms of administration. To bring out this emphasis on control through comparison more strongly, I have below taken the central ideas of each paragraph, explained them in terms of the control aim, and related them to comparisons against older forms of administration that stem mainly from Weber himself. The full text is available in a number of reprinted versions,[19] and to reprint it once more would be to give those interested just another thoughtless presentation of the kind that has not been understood in the past.

Characteristics of Modern Bureaucracy
1. Bureaucracy is characterized by "fixed official jurisdictional areas."[20] *Jurisdiction* literally means to speak the law. Jurisdictional areas become areas of the exercise of law which in themselves are clearly defined, systematically differentiated within a system of legal-rational legitimacy, and assigned to specific offices. They are the beginning of a rationalistic *division of labor* which is structurally carried out throughout bureaucracy.

In its own internal structure, bureaucracy is initially a rational model of patterns of behavior which it is designed to impose on the outside world. Once the world itself has become ordered, bureaucracy is intended to reflect that order in its internal structure.

In contrast, the precursors of modern bureaucracy are patriarchal and patrimonial systems. Premodern organizations that survive today include the family, especially the extended family of some ethnic groups, political machines, and the Mafia. In such premodern organizations, the law is what the father-ruler says it is, within the confines of tradition.[21] Areas of responsibility may be delegated, but not systematically, and they are subject to the arbitrary will of the father as sovereign. The vague and overlapping boundaries of jurisdiction reflect the lack of clear social organization. This is frustrating, especially to the rising classes of modern entrepreneurs, merchants, and industrialists who require stable laws and administration regarding labor, raw materials, markets, and contracts binding one another.

1.a. Bureaucracy is characterized by "official duties."[22] Duty is defined by law and by superiors in their capacity of office-holders. A favorite saying of functionaries is: "I just did my duty; nothing personal." The psychologically compelling source of duty is an external one.* Functionaries are obedient to rationally traceable, external command.

In contrast, work in premodern organization is done out of a sense of personal obligation. The source of the sense of obligation is conscience; that is, it is *internal*. † A favorite saying of subordinates is, "I owed it to him; I couldn't live with myself if I didn't pay off my debt to him." Subordinates act as if they obeyed an inner voice. In premodern organization, the reasons why someone obeyed cannot be traced rationally by comparing actions to a list of prescribed duties; they become a matter for depth psychology.

1.b. In modern bureaucracy, authority is "distributed in a *stable* way."[23] Here Weber elaborates on Point 1: the emphasis on stability favors predictability and control. To the bureaucrats it means they can expect to see different types of orders always come from different places: the payroll department orders you to submit timecards, personnel rules on your fitness for the job, line supervisors give task commands. In a different sense, the bureaucrat learns to associate distinct forms of behavior with occupancy of distinct offices. Authority is clearly structured into permanent offices.

A further subpoint is that "authority . . . is strictly *delimited* by *rules* concerning coercive means."[24] Rules, in other words, are in existence and are published before administrative behavior takes

---

*Specifically, as we will see in chapter 3, the source is an externalized superego.
†What Freud would call an internalized superego.

place. The range of sanctions is strictly limited and assigned to specific offices.

In contrast, under premodern rule, authority is centralized in the paternal ruler and either not clearly distributed, if delegated, or not distributed at all. A contemporary example is the unstable fate of a White House staffer whose authority not only may overlap with others, but who has no permanence since the president may relieve him at any time; nor are his functions usually clearly delineated or clearly understood by others. Contrast this with authority distribution in any of the permanent cabinet departments.

In contrast to the delimitation of authority by rules, consider the family as a leftover of premodern organization. Here rules may not exist until a child engages in behavior not approved by the parent. Rules are often *ex post facto*. Notably, the purpose of administration in the family is not primarily control but growth. The range of coercion is infinite to provide for a vast range of possible behaviors and family needs: the Roman head of household could kill the child; the mother today can torture the child psychologically to develop control mechanisms of guilt and shame even as the child grows through individuation to material independence. Any member of the family can apply psychological torture to any other member; there is no official office of torturer, though there tends to be a chief executioner. In traditional families, it is the father.

Similarly, in the political machine, rules regarding reward and punishment for graft collection are never published. They change with the recipient, though an ethic related to it is understood.

1.c. Bureaucracy is characterized by "continuous fulfillment of . . . duties."[25] Such an arrangement favors the client's expectation that the administration of rules and behaviors in a functional area is permanent.

In contrast, premodern organization offers no such reliability, fulfillment of duties being dependent on the whim of part-time administrators whose interests in administration and assigned authority are ever changing. Such lack of continuity makes it impossible to develop expectations of finding the same market conditions, the same enforcement of contracts, the same administration of freedom of commerce, or a labor supply from one day to the next. This in turn makes impossible the rational calculation of means and ends for entrepreneurs or, for that matter, the rational planning of state tax levies to continue to support the administration without interruption of pay.

Secondly, permanent assignment and fulfillment of duties gives rise to "corresponding rights."[26] Rights are habituated expectations on the part of people that they will be rewarded in exactly the same way for an exact repetition in their performance of assigned duties. Without clear definition of duties and guarantees of the continuous application of sanctions and rewards to ensure their fulfillment, there can be no development of rights for either the functionary or the citizen.

In contrast, in patrimonial and patriarchal systems, exactly because they lack administrative structures to continually exercise duties, there are no "rights," only privileges bestowed by the ruler and left to the holders to assert as best they can.

Third, those employed to carry out duties must "qualify under general rules."[27] Again this provision enhances both the orderliness of administrative structure and the orderliness of administrative behavior in the environment. Functionaries picked according to their qualifications by standard rules can be expected to behave in an orderly and standardized fashion. Further, such standards can now be task related rather than remaining ruler related.

In summary, in bureaucracy: (1) there are qualifications related to the task; (2) these qualifications are established in regulations; and (3) they are universally applied.

In contrast, in premodern organization: (1) there may not be task-related qualifications, loyalty to the ruler taking precedence; (2) there are no official regulations, only ad hoc rules stemming from the ruler's temporary will; and (3) the ruler's will varies from case to case. No way to run a railroad.

2. Bureaucracy is governed by the "principle of office hierarchy . . . levels of graded authority . . . a firmly ordered system of super- and subordination."[28] Again orderliness favoring control is fostered. Whereas jurisdictional areas provide a vertical division of labor, hierarchy provides a horizontal division between levels of administration concerned with matters of different scope and importance. It is also the control mechanism that holds the vertical division of labor together. This latter point is of great importance to the psychology underlying bureaucratic control: the division of labor weakens the possibility of anyone acting successfully on his own, especially in situations where the division has been carried out to such an extent that one functionary's action completes only a fraction of an authorized administrative act. At this point the individual functionary becomes dependent on guidance from the next higher office as to when and how to perform his or her action in such a way as to integrate with the actions of other functionaries. It is this dependence, based on the division of labor, and the management of that dependence by ever higher offices in the hierarchy that constitutes the immense power of modern bureaucracy. Functionaries are forced

to look upward for the ultimate norms and rewards governing their actions. In doing so they must provide information to a higher office on which sanctions can be based; they thereby surrender the management of their actions. The structuring of offices into a pyramidal hierarchy in which the highest office is the ultimate judge and manager guarantees central control over all offices.

In summary, hierarchy means the clear delegation of authority descending through a series of less and less powerful offices, the clear status knowledge of where you are located in a hierarchy and the principle of supervision by the office next highest up.

In contrast, premodern organizations show an overlapping delegation of authority, with the higher office not necessarily more powerful, responsible, or authoritative. There is also uncertainty about what one's own place and authority and responsibility are from case to case. And there is a continuing struggle for power as a normal condition of office-holding, a continuous circumvention of higher-ups.

Most important, a psychology of dependence on hierarchy for guidance and reward in one's own actions, and therefore dependence as a psychology of survival, cannot develop in premodern organization. Without that development, premodern organization fails to develop a means of control that is reliable over a long period of time and can encompass the immense vastnesses of geographical or demographic space covered by bureaucracy.*

The interaction between the division of labor on rational grounds and the management of divided labor by hierarchy is the basis for the scope, intensity, and controlability of modern bureaucracy as the power instrument without compare.†

3. In bureaucracy management is "based on written documents."[29] Written records make visible both what bureaucrats are ordered to do and what they do. Rationally organized administration, suiting means to ends — including the correction of such administration based on written reports from below — thus becomes possible. In private business written methods of accounting are an example as are computer methods, which are equally visible because

---

*Charismatic authority, for example, can be more intense than bureaucratic legal-rational authority, but it is usually short-lived and yields to eventual rationalization. Traditional authority may encompass vast areas, but it is subject to fragmentation as office-holders develop their own power base on a psychology of independence from higher-ups ultimately demonstrated by force — knights vs. the emperor, feudal lords vs. their liege lord, etc.

†For further development of the psychological power base of bureaucracy developed through its peculiar social structuring of work, see chapter 3.

they are retrievable. Examples in public service include records and reports. Administration activities are recorded and survive personal willfulness, incompetence, dishonesty, and the departure and death of functionaries. Activities are at least potentially *open to supervision* from above — the hierarchy — and ultimately from outside — the public. There is here the promise of administration as a politically controllable enforcer of orderliness in those areas of human activity assigned to it.

In contrast, in premodern organization, communication and command tend to be by word of mouth and by humanly fallible memory. Personal control over bias of perceptions and understanding, personal determination to put personal interests aside — these guarantee reliability. Where such honesty is absent, administration breaks down.

Without permanent records, activities are difficult to inspect and analyze for the purposes of future correction and control. Control from one center becomes doubtful given the lack of formal regulation, evaluation, and feedback.

4. Bureaucracy's office management requires "thorough and expert training."[30]

Here Weber not only repeats his earlier observation that modern bureaucracy requires employes who qualify under general rules, but emphasizes that office management as an activity itself becomes specialized and rationalized.

In contrast, in premodern organization, the qualifications of employes are mainly the confidence and trust of the ruler — e.g., the boss, the machine. The question is not, "Can you do the job?" but "Can you be trusted?"

5. Bureaucracy requires the "full working capacity of the official."[31] Weber contrasts bureaucracy with the previous state of affairs in which the reverse was true: "Official business was discharged as a secondary activity."

Here Weber reemphasizes implicitly the primacy and continuity of administration over other personal interests and focuses, without developing it, on the psychology implicit in the officials who discharge administrative duties as their primary effort in life. This effort not only excludes time for personal or other interests, but suggests the development of an inner loyalty, and therefore inner dependence on the institution: bureaucracy becomes a way of life.

In contrast, in premodern organizations, the available work capacity of the individual is given primarily to private endeavors. The office is second, at best. Officialdom is a source of private or social honor and income, not of institutional status and identity. Given such orientations, we can hardly expect officials to favor the rationalistic ordering of society according to general rather than individual interests.

6. In bureaucracy, management of the office follows "general rules."[32] General rules are rules codified in the interests of all or of those in whose general interest a bureaucracy is set up. Specifically avoided are rules favoring some as against others. Thus management itself becomes predictable, expectations of functionaries become regular, and a general atmosphere of orderliness and predictability is fostered — even within the structure of bureaucracy itself — with an aim toward projecting this onto the outer world.

In contrast, in premodern administration, management tends to be *ad hoc*, guidance occasional and spotty, the expectations of functionaries uncertain, leading them to look outside of the office for security and support. A classic example of this is the type of administration that leads to corrupt police departments.

In summary, a restudy of Weber's brilliant analysis of modern bureaucracy should place the characteristics he cites in the light of the past and in the light of the purpose for which this form of administration was created. The ultimate imperative of control is reflected in each of the characteristics of structure, behavior, and implicit psychology he cites. In fact, the individual characteristics taken out of historical context make no sense at all and are apt to be understood only in a rote or ritual manner unless we ask ourselves: What purpose do they serve? What was modern bureaucratic administration trying to get away from? For what purpose did the first modern entrepreneurs and legislators, whose social and especially economic thinking was to be predominantly rationalistic, establish and foster this paragon of means-ends rationalism on which rests the calculability of our world today?

For each of the characteristics of modern bureaucracy above, there is a specific countercharacteristic in the inferior form of fatherly administration. Fatherly rule is personal rule. It consists of personal command downward. And it consists of personal trust, based on affection, upwards. The inner motivation for obedience is the individual's sense that obedience is "right and proper"; that is, the sense that commands are legitimate because of a higher explanation — theology, philosophy, ideology, or what Weber called "theodicee."*

---

*Theodicee literally means "God's way in the world." Traditionally all forms of domination have required an ultimate justification in a theodicee, Weber points out. That is, people universally want a transcendental explanation of why rulers should rule and why the ruled should obey.

The control imperative of modern bureaucracy, which demands visible behaviors and relationships because only such relationships are ultimately measurable and hence controllable, does away with the personal character of all fatherly administration. Out of this it promises greater exactness of behavior and a wider span of control which could potentially involve millions. All the characteristics of modern bureaucracy cited by Weber are designed to support the control imperative.* Managers who think they can be more human in using these subimperatives are actually threatening themselves with loss of control. Such loss of power over the bureaucratic imperative eventually means a failure to make bureaucracy's contribution to the overall imperatives of either private enterprise or public service. Ultimately such failure is punished by the collapse of institutions in both realms. †

These are the reasons why the imperative of bureaucracy is binding as an unavoidable norm. The manager who breaks that norm destroys the bureaucracy. Despite short-term exceptions, we are here arguing for an inexorable long-term tendency.

BUREAUCRACY WITHOUT CULTURE

Modern organization is *the* means to harness large masses of people into work aimed at achieving vast purposes. Initially, this focus on singleness of purpose had to bring bureaucracy into conflict with the multitude of individual purposes pursued by its recruits. Managers had to translate the organization's purposes into norms guiding the behavior of each functionary. Not only could the raw recruits be expected to resist this program of homogenization, but inevitably a culture conflict broke out between the means-oriented norms of bureaucracy and the ends-oriented norms of human beings. The substance of this conflict has been delineated in the preceding two sections. Much of the personal agony and recalcitrance of functionaries and many of what, from the management point of view, are disciplinary and morale problems can be thus explained.

However, there is a distinct further possibility. Such problems may, in the last analysis, stem not at all from a conflict between the cultures of bureaucracy and society, but from something much more serious — the possible absence of culture from bureaucracy altogether. Bureaucracy may be on its way to becoming an organization without culture.

That would make it the first organization without culture in the

---

*See also the list of norms contrasted at the beginning of this chapter. They are designed to contribute to the control imperative.

†The collapse of New York State's Urban Development Corporation in 1975 in which overemphasis on service brought about a loss of control is an example.

history of the world. After all, without norms to guide actions, how can people become organized? I believe it is the unprecedented nature of this possibility of organization without norms that has made us shy away from what experience and logic tell us is not only a likely prospect but already a partial reality.

The Loss of Purpose

For experiential evidence, there is the growing complaint of the individual in modern organization that his or her life appears to be *purposeless* and *meaningless*. I think we might do well, as scientists and human beings, to take such complaints seriously. In the sciences dealing with social life, there ultimately are no other reliable data than the self-reports of the organisms living such lives.

Nor should the paradox of the functionaries' experience of purposelessness as against bureaucracy's claim to purposefulness keep us long from the pursuit of that paradox's own implications.

We claim to live in "rational" organizations. Our forefathers, in contrast, were merely "traditional" in how they pursued their goals in their society. Since World War II we have even had several experiences with a third form of human organization — charismatic authority. The tendency is to think that what is new is superior to what is old. Rational authority does indeed rest, as Weber pointed out in his discussion of the three dominant forms of authority and organization, on the *possibility* of using reason to determine the legitimacy of orders from above. In contrast, traditional authority rested on habit, and charisma rests on affect.

Yet how much reason is used by a worker such as the following, by no means atypical of functionaries in modern organization, speaking of one of the infinite number of pieces of steel he handles:

> Sometimes, out of pure meanness, when I make something, I put a little dent in it. I like to do something to make it really unique. Hit it with a hammer. I deliberately fuck it up to see if it'll get by, just so I can say I did it. It could be anything. Let me put it this way: I think God invented the dodo bird so when we get up there we could tell Him, "Don't you ever make mistakes?" and He'd say, "Sure, look." (Laughs.) I'd like to make my imprint. My dodo bird. A mistake, *mine*.[33]

Actually, this man is quite sane. He can still reason. But his reasoning is not "rational" in the framework of the steel company. This is because he no longer sees the purpose of what he is doing in terms of the overall picture that someone at the top may have.

The tendency among personnel experts and human relations specialists is to ascribe this sense of purposelessness, which in the individual's frustrated search for purpose is experienced as meaninglessness, to a deviation from the norm. The man in question needs to be "reintegrated" and so on. At best, his sense of meaninglessness is "dysfunctional" or (moving a bit closer to a criticism of the organizational machine) a latent function, something you have to buy to get the benefits the machine so abundantly provides. We fail to admit to ourselves the possibility that meaninglessness or purposelessness is not an accidental outgrowth of modern organization but a logical, inevitable, and even intentional one.

Weber, whose description of the rationalized society is today used less for scientific analysis than for recitation of a ritual wisdom that keeps us from thinking, admitted this from the beginning. In a little-read analysis, he foresaw that in the rationalized world the masses would function fundamentally not on the basis of reason, but on the basis of faith and tradition.* Except that in this case it must be a faith in the overall rationality of the rationalized society on which habitual performance of everyday duties must be based. In exactly the same way, Weber points out, do children have faith in math without ever understanding the rational grounds behind the rules they habitually follow in adding, subtracting, and multiplying: "One determines whether one has calculated correctly, according to custom, not on the basis of rational considerations but on the basis of empirical proofs in which one has been trained (or which have been imposed on us)."[34]

If this means that even in such a rationalistic activity as doing math there is only a small elite of mathematicians who really understand math while the rest of us do it out of habit, this insight applies even more to rationalized society.

The Stratification of Meaning

Weber in fact proposes that any sense of the overall purpose and meaning of the rational society, of which bureaucracy is the logical successor, is unequally distributed through four levels of social strata: (1) the lawmakers, (2) the interpreters of law, (3) the users of law (those who use law for their own advantage), and (4) the mass of people who obey the law out of habit and simply because it provides comfortable channels for their everyday life. In Weber's words:

> The rational institutions of society, be it a compulsory or a voluntary association, are imposed or "suggested" by one group for specific

*His essay "Ueber einige Kategorien der verstehenden Soziologie" (On Some Categories of a Sociology of Understanding), in Max Weber, *Gesammelte Aufsätze zur Wissenschaftslehre*, 3rd ed. (Tübingen: J.C.B. Mohr, 1968), pp. 469 – 471.

purposes although individuals in the group may already differ on the intent. The institutions are interpreted more or less similarly and applied on a subjective basis by the second group, the "organs" of institutionalization. The third group, in turn, understands these institutions subjectively in so far as adherence to them is absolutely necessary in private dealings; this group converts the institutions into means serving as standards for (legal or illegal) action — because these institutions evoke specific expectations in regard to the behavior of others (the "organs" as well as the fellow members of the compulsory or voluntary association).* The fourth group, however, and this is the "mass," simply learns to behave according to "traditional" routines that approximate in some way the meaning of the institutions as it is understood on the average; these routines are maintained most often without any knowledge of the purpose or meaning, even of the existence, of the institutions in question.[35]

If very little of any overall purpose filters down to the "mass" level of rationalized society, bureaucracy's predecessor, then we can expect the filtering out of purpose to be even more serious in the more highly "rationalized" structures of bureaucracy itself.

One of the first to deal with this fact was sociologist Karl Mannheim. In bureaucracies, he wrote, as the rationalization of the overall organization increases, the ability of any given functionary to know the purpose of what he does decreases. Mannheim dealt with this paradox that increasing systems rationality produces decreasing individual rationality by distinguishing between the system's "functional rationalization" and the individual's "substantial rationality."[36]

Functional rationalization means the logical subdivision of an overall task into ever-smaller units of work, each tightly integrated with the other. Efficiency is the original goal of such rationalization. Substantial rationality refers to the individual's ability to know how his small task fits into the overall task. On this knowledge hinges not only his ability to use his own reason to better integrate his work into the overall activity of the system, but also his sense of purposefulness in the aim of his work and meaningfulness in the conduct of his work.

To the extent that Weber and Mannheim are right, it follows that purposelessness and meaninglessness are the unavoidable product, and not an accidental one, of modern organizations constructed on bureaucratic premises. But that means also that legislators and managers setting up or running a public or private bureaucracy face an almost insuperable task in trying to give workers a sense of the purpose of that institution and the meaning of their own work.

*In other words, "users" adhere to social institutions because they stabilize the behavior of others — individuals or organs of the state — making that behavior more predictable and therefore more manipulable.

For if meaninglessness at the functionary level is a direct, although undesirable, product of bureaucracy, then to attempt to reduce meaninglessness will have a reciprocal impact on the desirable characteristics of modern organization. Specifically, the manager, following Mannheim, will expect to lose efficiency in return for humane attempts on his part to let functionaries share in the overall purpose and meaning of the institution.

If to this the objection is raised that in some production enterprises — the classic example is the institution of teamwork in Volvo car production — meaningfulness has been raised through stimulating stronger personal relations, we need to be reminded what efficiency means. In modern organizations, efficiency tends to be process efficiency not output efficiency. Especially in public service, the manager, because of his need to be accountable to higher-ups and finally the public, must always be able to demonstrate that he knows at all times what behaviors his subordinates are engaging in. It is more important for him to show he is "in control" rather than to produce outputs. If this sounds absurd, which it is, the question can be asked what happens to a manager whose organization produces but who cannot tell anyone how it is being done. Surely, such a manager has just testified to the abolition of his own job. But more practically: public service by popular demand must always be conducted according to certain standards. To give away welfare without adherence to strict standards of the conditions under which taxpayers are willing to provide welfare to others is never managerially or politically defensible. The price that the functionary pays in terms of his sense of meaninglessness can thus be argued to be a necessary one, from the organization's point of view, in return for efficiency, control, and accountability.

Here we finally arrive at the original question asked above: Is it possible that the functionary's sense of meaninglessness and purposelessness reflects an absence of norms to guide his behavior? Weber has already suggested that, even in the rational society, what guides the behavior of the mass is not an understanding of norms but a copying of other behavior.

We have thus come to the point at which psychologist B.F. Skinner arrived some time ago. It is not ideas that guide the behavior of people, but other behavior. While this assertion may have been made in too generalized a way by Skinner himself,* his suggestion would certainly explain both the behavior and the experience of meaninglessness of the typical bureaucratic functionary. What the functionary does is not tied to norms as ideas that provide meaning,

*See the critique of Skinner in chapter 3.

simply because that is not the way he learns what he is supposed to do. He learns what he is supposed to do by doing it, quite as Skinner suggests. Systemically dysfunctional moves are punished or not supported, systemically functional moves are reinforced. Not ours to know the reason why . . .

In this sense, the progress of modern bureaucracy from its original collision with the norms of society, to which it counterposed its own inner norms, leads inevitably to the gradual development of the first human organization without norms. Bureaucracy becomes an organization without culture. This is especially true for those who look at it from the bottom up. Those at the top may have purposes in mind and may attempt to impose these downward as norms. But the distance is too great. Norms, as reasons why, are filtered out and only behaviors remain. Those below thoughtlessly model themselves on the pattern of those above and integrate their own behaviors into the behaviors of others at their own level. But this means not only the suppression of thought and of the connection of the individual human being to some overall saving grace of purpose in life, but, as will become apparent in the chapter on bureaucratic psychology, the restructuring of the human psyche altogether.

SUMMARY

Just as the new form of bureaucratic action separates actors from the actions themselves and from those on whom these actions impinge, freeing them of the implications of social ties and social obligations, the bureaucratic culture "frees" them from concern with ultimate values. Whether an action is "good" or "bad," from the viewpoint of the client or subordinate functionary acted upon, is no longer an issue. The standards against which conduct is now judged are all concerned with means not ends.

The question now becomes: Have I adhered to official rules or regulations in performing my duty? Not: Is the effect of my performance in keeping with generally recognized social norms of the type that evolve when human beings face one another as human beings?

This holds true even in the professions. As a doctor, I am ultimately judged not by the life or death of my patient — though these remain society's cultural standards — but by whether I have performed my duty using tools and procedures approved by my fellow doctors. Doctors, as aides to humankind, whose type arose out of a general human need for health and life, now become judges in their own cause, independent of the social beings who in a sense created them. The possessor of the means has become the ruler over ends.

As a member of a bureaucracy — whether I am doctor, lawyer, judge, cop, firefighter, welfare worker or multipurpose clerk in an interagency pool — I now know that I will be judged ultimately not according to any of the human values. No official will ask whether I have promoted the ends of justice over injustice, health over death, harmony over violence, well-fare over ill-fare. But they will ask whether, if I have promoted any of these, I have done so using officially sanctioned means.

As a judge or lawyer, the issue, should I ever face an administrative tribunal, is whether I have enforced the law and acted according to law, not whether I have administered justice. This is especially difficult to understand for those of us still living in society who expect the courts to reestablish a kind of equity and justice in human relationships disturbed by crookedness and crime.

The cop who has fired his weapon and killed a man, whether a criminal or an innocent bystander — by what is he judged? Not by the fact of death. Not by the fact that he has destroyed the value of life. But by the answer to the question whether he drew his weapon in a legally recognized and administratively prescribed situation allowing a weapon to be drawn. As a human being, the cop suffers as much as any of us when he takes a life. As a member of bureaucracy, he cannot but wonder that his own fate will ultimately be decided not by the value of the human being whom he killed, but by the abstract and often apparently arbitrary — because they are not understood — standards of the internal functioning of the police department.

Firefighters, when they act socially and risk their own lives to rescue another human being — something no bureaucracy can force them to do* — are given a medal, a social reward, not an administrative one. The medal proclaims their heroism before a social audience. Heroism is not an administrative category. † Further, the firefighter's lieutenant and captain receive at best an administrative wink of the eye to indicate that a superior will ignore the fact that a breach of officially prescribed conduct has occurred. And this only should the rescue succeed. Should the rescuer himself lose his life, his supervisors can be administratively held responsible for a breakdown of control and discipline.

---

*Not because bureaucracy has no need for such control, but because control over initiative action is difficult to supervise, especially in smoke-filled burning buildings.
†In fact heroism is, like charisma, the enemy of bureaucracy. All action above and beyond the call of duty breaks the tight rules upon which the very existence of bureaucracy rests.

Welfare workers are judged by whether they have followed the prescribed list of conditions under which an applicant may be admitted. If they see to the well-fare of the applicant outside "welfare" standards, they are engaged in corruption and may be prosecuted.

Most obviously, clerks succeed as long as they remain the means to someone else's goals. Asked to file a form, they know they are not going to be judged by their knowledge of whether the form contains a list of 200 enemies of the state to be delivered to a concentration camp or a requisition for pencils. The standard for their own survival is whether the form is so filed as to be retrievable on demand. Yet in principle the clerk's position is no different from anyone else's. Their powerlessness when it comes to doing anything positive in regard to society's cultural values is simply more apparent.

It is not surprising that people who work in an institution whose ultimate values are related to control and the maximization of power will themselves become mini-controllers and mini-maximizers. In situations that conflict with the cultural values of society, they can offer in the short-term defense of their own survival — and who does not like to survive? — nothing more than adherence to efficiency, precision, stability, discipline, reliability, and the various types of formal rationality. Theirs is not to reason why.

NOTES

1. Max Weber, *Economy and Society: An Outline of Interpretive Sociology*, 3 vols., eds. Guenther Roth and Claus Wittich, trans. E. Fischoff *et al.* (New York: Bedminster Press, 1968), p. 1002. Weber's emphasis.

2. Ibid., pp. 956 – 958, 224 – 241.

3. Jürgen Habermas, *Toward a Rational Society* (Boston: Beacon Press, 1971), p. 96.

4. "Morale of Justices in New York Is Low," *The New York Times*, May 21, 1976, p. 1.

5. Weber: "Office management, at least all specialized office management — and such management is distinctly modern — usually presupposes thorough training in a field of specialization. This, too, holds increasingly for the modern executive and employe of a private enterprise, just as it does for the state officials." (Max Weber, *Economy and Society*, p. 958.)

6. For a picture of the intent and ideal of this management approach see Peter F. Drucker, *The Practice of Management* (New York: Harper & Row, 1954), and *The Effective Executive* (New York: Harper & Row, 1968). The reality of MBO, especially in civil service where it penetrated last, is, of course, nothing like the ideal. It is especially difficult to cut through the morass of regulations to give managers the autonomy of action promised them so they may reach the measurable objectives to which they commit themselves in MBO contracts with their superiors.

7. Conversation with the author, June 1976.

8. "Klassen Told by a Senator That Mail Service Is a Joke," *The New York Times*, March 9, 1973, p. 14.

9. Letter from Edward J. Logue to Robert Moss, quoted in "Fiscal Collapse of U.D.C. Was Result of 3 Wrong Moves, Panel Concludes," *The New York Times*, May 27, 1976, p. 39. Compare Logue's attitude with that of the bureaucratic type whom Anthony Downs calls the "statesman." The fact that Logue was financially independent of his job may have to be considered in tracing the origins of the statesman type. See Anthony Downs, *Inside Bureaucracy* (Boston: Little, Brown, 1967), pp. 88, 110 – 111, 102 – 103.

10. *The New York Times*, May 27, 1976, p. 39.

11. "Rockefeller Backs U.D.C.; Says Audit Will Praise It," *The New York Times*, December 4, 1975, p. 45.

12. Ibid.

13. Interview with the author, June 1975. Anonymity requested.

14. Max Weber, *The Protestant Ethic and the Spirit of Capitalism*, trans. Talcott Parsons (London: Allen & Unwin, 1930), pp. 54 – 55.

15. Weber, *Economy and Society*, p. 164. My italics for emphasis.

16. These include the three-volume collected essays in the sociology of religion, *Gesammelte Aufsätze zur Religionssoziologie* (Tübingen: J.C.B. Mohr, 1920 – 21), which actually, in Weber's own words, constitutes "a universal history of culture."

17. Weber, *Economy and Society*, p. 162.

18. An initial recognition of such changing demands on administration is fostered by Dwight Waldo, ed., *Public Administration in a Time of Turbulence* (Scranton: Chandler, 1971). The response tends to be within the typical categories of existing problem-solving methods associated with bureaucracy itself. For my argument why existing dominant science is the problem rather than the answer, see chapter 6.

19. The standard source of reference for the essay on bureaucracy is Max Weber, *Economy and Society*, pp. 956 – 1005. But the essay is reprinted in numerous readers, especially in the areas of sociology, public administration, and management science.

20. Weber, *Economy and Society*, p. 956.

21. For classical cases relevant today, read Mario Puzo, *The Godfather* (Greenwich, Conn.: Fawcett, 1969), for patriarchal rule in the Mafia, and Mike Royko, *Boss: Richard J. Daley of Chicago* (New York: New American Library, 1971), for a thinned-down version of fatherly rule in a contemporary political machine.

22. Weber, *Economy and Society*, p. 956.

23. Ibid.

24. Ibid.

25. Ibid.

26. Ibid.

27. Ibid.

28. Ibid., p. 957.

29. Ibid.

30. Ibid., p. 958.

31. Ibid.

32. Ibid.

33. Studs Terkel, *Working* (New York: Avon, 1975), pp. 9 – 10, Terkel's italics. For recent research results on alienation at work, including work of nurses, bank employes, and industrial scientists and engineers in bureaucracy, see Ada W. Finifter, ed., *Alienation and the Social System* (New York: Wiley, 1972), pp. 138 – 179.

34. Max Weber, *Gesammelte Aufsätze zur Wissenschaftslehre*, 3rd ed. (Tübingen: J.C.B. Mohr, 1968), p. 471.

35. Ibid., pp. 472 – 473. Author's translation.

36. Karl Mannheim, *Man and Society in an Age of Reconstruction* (New York: Harcourt, Brace, 1940), p. 59.

3

The Psychology of Bureaucracy

. . . the bureaucratization of all domination very strongly furthers the development of . . . the personality type of the professional expert.

— Max Weber[1]

Psychologically, as in all other ways, the bureaucrat is radically different from the inhabitant of bureaucracy's precursor, society. If this is true, entry into bureaucracy should provide a shock for all concerned. For the newcomer the shock is one of stripping away the old psyche and donning the new. In such changes there is always considerable agony. But even the oldtime residents of bureaucracy must travel back and forth every day between bureaucracy and society. This means they must adapt to both environments. Are they able to slip in and out of two different psyches — each a necessary adaptation to different worlds?

Similarly, managers must learn new psychological techniques for guiding and coordinating the behavior of subordinates. If the psychology of bureaucracy is indeed radically different from the psychology of society, then the manager-subordinate relationship could be expected to be radically different from the power relationship that preceded it — that is, the leader-follower relationship. Successful managers would have to ask themselves: What are the rules of this new psychology?

Finally, if bureaucrat and citizen differ radically in their psychology, all the schools of psychology that have dealt primarily with the psychic structure of human beings in society must be superseded. The psychology of bureaucracy that supersedes them must deal primarily with the functionary, manager, and professional in the new organizational environment. To what extent are there organizational psychologies that consciously encompass the new realities of bureaucracy?

The following three sections explore these difficulties. First, we ask: What is the typical psychological experience of the bureaucrat? Second: How have the experts interpreted, or how would they interpret, this experience? Third: What conclusions can we draw for constructing a psychology of bureaucracy?

WHAT PEOPLE FEEL

A functionary:

> When I first joined the traffic department, I felt I knew my job. My job was taking out my crew — I had two helpers — , go out with the truck, and we'd see a street sign down, and we'd put it back up. We had all kinds of signs in the truck. We'd do maybe 40 signs a day, and when we got tired, we knocked off. Maybe an hour or two early.
>
> Then they said: Put it on paper. So we knocked off maybe three hours, did maybe 35 signs or so, and the rest was paperwork. I guess if it wasn't on paper, they didn't feel it was done.
>
> Then they brought in an efficiency expert. The section boss one morning hands me a piece of paper: "You will put up this and this many signs a day, or we'll know the reason why." I looked at the piece of paper, and took it out in the street to my crew. Then we rolled in the street for 20 minutes, laughing our heads off. Their quota was 20 signs a day. We'd been doing 30, 40 before they started screwing around. Paperwork, reports, efficiency experts. Now we do 20 signs, and knock off.[2]

A manager:

> I'm a banker. That is, I work for the ——— bank. We lend money. To big companies, too. When the company doesn't come through on a loan, we go in and take them over. I've fired an entire board of directors and the entire top management in one afternoon.
>
> Anyway, we go into this one company. There's me for my bank, and representatives for four other banks. This outfit really was stretched thin on loans. They hadn't paid off for almost a year. They made computers. We asked: What's your total output for the year? They said: Well, it varies. We asked: What does one of your units sell for? They said it depends on the market. These guys just didn't know what the hell they were doing. We fired them.

One vice president came in not knowing what was going to happen. He thought he was there to give the plan for the next year. We told him he was fired. He didn't even hear what we told him. He just went on giving his plan for the next year. I don't think it hit him 'til he got home.

The other vice president just put his head down and cried.

It makes you wonder. You feel you are somebody because you've got a lot of power. You've been running the lives of, say, maybe 300, 400, a thousand people. Suddenly you're out. You're a nobody. How could it happen to you? It can happen, though.[3]

These interviews illustrate three popular fallacies about bureaucracy. These fallacies are the direct result of a failure to understand the distinct psychology of bureaucracy.

The first fallacy is the "fallacy of the superego." Here the functionary assumes, because he has intimate contact with the work that needs to be done, that he is the best judge of whether that work is done properly or not.

The second fallacy is the "fallacy of the ego." This assumes that bureaucracy can and will allow an individual to achieve and maintain full mastery of a piece of work apart from other individuals.

The third fallacy is the "fallacy of identity." This leads the manager in the case above to confuse identity — what he is within the organization — with personality — who he is. Personality is a social product; identity, a bureaucratic one. When I become a member of a bureaucracy, identity tends to displace personality. All the things I was before entry that were not compatible with the organization's needs have had to be surrendered. Those psychological characteristics compatible with the organization take the place of personality through daily practice in my work. In the extreme, I give up my personality and accept organizational identity as a surrogate. Expulsion from the organization leaves me without identity or personality.

The fallacies are held by many. They are uttered in what amounts to typical folksayings among bureaucrats. What is the assumption of such sayings? How are they wrong? How does psychology explain why they are wrong?

The Fallacy of the Superego

In the case of the sign repairman, he presumed he could best judge what constituted an honest day's work. He knew the job. He presumed he could judge the standards for the job: you do as much as you can, when you get tired you knock off. His motivation was an inner motivation. So was his measurement of tiredness. So were his standards.

The Denial of Judgment

A typical folksaying among bureaucrats is: "As long as I do my job, nobody is going to bother me." In other words: "I know best whether I'm doing my job right; no one has a right to tell me what to do." Behind these arguments lies a hidden assumption: I am best capable of judging my own work.

Bureaucracy, because it is a control instrument, must deny that assumption. The reason for this has already been explored in our distinction between "invisible" and "visible" work* — that is, work actually done but not observed by control officers and work both done and observed. A modern organization is a control instrument par excellence. If that organization is to remain a control instrument, all actions taken by functionaries must be made visible, even, and especially so, if this means reduction of work not visible to control. Work not visible to control is work out of control. From the viewpoint of the organization, work out of control is a symptom of organizational pathology.

The assumption that I am best capable of judging my own work is therefore countered by what to many bureaucrats is a hidden reality that they would just as soon not consciously admit: in a modern organization, your superior is always the ultimate judge over your work standards — because ultimately he has the power to fire you. This is especially true when your actions contradict organizationally mandated actions. But it can also be true when your actions are in accord with organizational directives but are invisible to control.

What does this mean psychologically? In Freudian psychological terms, standards for behavior in society are stored in a structure of one's psyche called the superego. Let us for now define the superego as a structure of the psyche in which the individual stores, after some interpretation, society's norms of what is right and wrong. In society, where work you do for other individuals is very much tied in with how they will personally feel about you and your worth, the superego contains standards both for social relations and for work. Modern bureaucracy, however, is specifically a type of organization that intends to separate work from personal relationships. As a preformation of modern bureaucracy, the army, tells all recruits: you salute the uniform not the man. Or as Max Weber said about modern bureaucracy:

> An official who, according to his own view, receives an order that is wrong can — and should — raise protests. However, if the super-ordinated office persists in its instructions, then it is not only his duty

---

*See the discussion of visible versus invisible action, which parallels the distinction between rationally organized action and social action, in chapter 1.

but his *honor* to carry them out in such a manner as if they were in agreement with his own convictions, and thereby show that his sense of duty to office outweighs his own willfulness.[4]

While Weber seems here to speak in terms of a bureaucratic ethic in which even the term "honor" appears to contradict the personal meaning of the word "honor" in a social ethic, we can interpret his words not in terms of what should be but what must be. Officials who act otherwise simply are not promoted, may be reprimanded or otherwise punished, and ultimately open themselves up to dismissal.

To return to our psychological concerns, in bureaucracy the individual functionary is asked to surrender part of his superego to his superiors. He must not only, as Weber says elsewhere, "subordinate himself to his superior without any will of his own,"[5] but must subordinate himself to a superego that is not his own.

The functionaries in a bureaucracy, therefore, are individuals with externalized superegos. This term "externalized superego" expresses two thoughts. First, functionaries still act according to the norms and standards of a superego, but, secondly, the ultimate location of the superego containing these norms and standards, and possessed of a will to apply them, is not their psyches but the office of their superior.*

The fallacy of the superego is then the erroneous assumption on the part of subordinates that they are best suited to judge their own work. It divides into two subfallacies — the subfallacy of the individualist and the subfallacy of the professional.

The Subfallacy of the Individualist
The subfallacy of the individualist has already been discussed in the general discussion above. It rests on the functionary's carrying over from society a self-concept that has no place in bureaucracy. This will further be discussed below under the heading of the "fallacy of identity." For now only a few words of further explanation are necessary. The self-concept of the individual in society is that of a personality — those unique characteristics that make a person stand out from all others in society. The self-concept of the functionary in bureaucracy, however, is never allowed to develop in terms of separateness and uniqueness, but only in terms of integration and

---

*It would be a serious mistake to now see the superego of the subordinate placed personally in the psyche of the superior. The superiors simply carry out actions dictated to them by the job definition associated with their office. They are not their subordinate's personal superego; they are his official superego. Were the managers to be removed, others would carry out the dictates of the organization approximately in the same manner and certainly within the same definition of the function of the superego, which is that it is always the superior office that exercises the legitimate right of imposing and judging standards, not the subordinate within his own mind.

similarity (or functionality) in relation to the rest of the organization. What the individual functionary *is* the organization intends to design exclusively from above.

This is especially important to the question of norms and standards contained in the superego. In normal society, I, as an individual, judge myself, often harshly, according to my own standards of which the superego is comprised. My superego, it might be said, looks at what I do and, when I fail to measure up to its standards, punishes me severely through a variety of psychic pains — guilt, for example. My inner superego constitutes a sense of my own worth: it measures my self-esteem. There is, of course, the esteem of others. They have their norms and standards, and they often try to impose them on the lone individual who deviates.

There is, however, a tremendous difference between saying that in society others "occasionally" or even "often" correct the behavior of individuals and observing the reality in bureaucracy that ultimately all correction is carried out by an agency outside the psyche of the individual.

The difference becomes more clear when we consider the individuation process in society. Society exists before we are born into it. We learn, or internalize, its norms. But as we mature into individuals, as we go through the process of individuation, we adjust, change, and overturn much of what we have learned. Our superego, finally, is composed of learned norms and norms we ourselves have developed in our own experience with life. The new norms themselves are then again passed on or back to society as new generations come along who take their norms from us as parents, teachers, and fellow members of society.

In addition, social norms and individual norms always stand in a relation of reciprocity to one another; there is a chance that in my social relationships I can affect the norms of others.

Now consider what chance I have of doing so in a bureaucracy should my personal work experience lead to new work standards that I want to discuss with my superior in an open, social relationship. Here lies one of the great shortcomings of managers if not of bureaucracy itself as a concept. Managers often tend to view any correction of work standards suggested from below as a challenge to their control. This is a human failing. But ultimately, there is also an institutional failure in the bureaucracy concept — though never in terms of that specific bureaucracy looking at itself. The institutional failure becomes apparent when a particular bureaucracy has just recently reviewed its goals and its methods, found them in keeping with its overall purpose, and is then confronted with suggestions from below. If these suggestions contradict the just-reviewed goals and methods, they must not only be rejected, and if necessary suppressed and action stamped out, but the survival of the responsible subordinate is put in question. Functionaries know this well. The possibility of this kind of reaction to suggestions from below is always there. And because they have little experience in judging norms themselves and are subject to having their own work judged according to the norms of others by others, functionaries are likely to avoid the area of norms altogether.

All of which is to say that in bureaucracy norms are effectively dictated from above and accepted from below — all the time. There is a difference between the impact on the individual's superego of this situation and a situation in which he is not only allowed but expected to bring to his social relations, and to society at large, the benefit of his own norms and judgment — his own individuated superego.

The Subfallacy of the Professional

The subfallacy of the professional is best expressed in the folksaying: "I am a professional and must be judged on professional grounds." The hidden assumption here is that the professional, as distinguished from the functionary and the manager, is subject to internal norms, not to an externalized superego.

This assumption is wrong. It expresses a last attempt by a human being to retain both humanity and individuality as a professional. But such an attempt is not viable in the bureaucratic world. As a result it causes plenty of difficulties for the professional and those who have to work with him.

The assumption of professional independence is wrong for two reasons. First, it is wrong because professionals need institutions to work in: doctors, for example, the more specialized they are and the more they consider themselves professionals as a result, will need a hospital. But institutions are run by bureaucrats — by managers. Therefore managers, responsible for the existence and continuity of the institution, will either have the ultimate word over the professional's worth to the institution, or the institution will be threatened with organizational decay and untimely death. If these are to be avoided, professionals will have to adjust their inner norms to the dictates of the usual bureaucratic superego.

The professional's assumption of independence and psychological integrity is also wrong because of the existence of hidden superiors. The professional exists by the tolerance of a crypto-hierarchy of fellow professionals. If these cease to approve of his activities, he can be disbarred as a lawyer, expelled from the medical association with likely loss of license as a doctor, and defrocked as a priest. In other words, professional associations are bureaucracies in their own right, and they constitute the conscience for individual professionals who go astray. They also exercise the power of punishment.*

To summarize, in society, the individual must live up to his own inner standards, contained in his superego. A typical folksaying would be: "You've got to be able to live with yourself," or, "I've got to live with myself." The expression also indicates the limits the individual puts on willingness to accept social standards when these conflict with individual standards.

In bureaucracy, the individual must live up to external standards. If there is a conflict, he or she can be sacrificed — the strength of bureaucracy as a control institution cannot. Inner standards must be left at home before entering the office; office standards become a replacement superego for the human being during the eight hours a day he spends as a functionary on the job. But the fact is that many functionaries "become" their organization. They are the identity it gives them. They cease being private persons with private personalities. They internalize bureaucracy's external norms, thus displacing part of their private superego. In their public identity they become dependent on the organization because they internalize a set of norms the actual locus of which remains external. Only their superiors can change these norms or have power to maintain them. †
In the extreme, therefore, the functionary has an externalized superego, while the citizen has an internalized superego. In the case of the functionary, part of the psyche has been taken out and placed outside. ‡ Where? Not in superiors, for these may change, but in their offices. Together, these offices up and down the organization constitute what is called "hierarchy." Organizational hierarchy begins to perform for the bureaucrat the functions of the superego. Hierarchy is the bureaucrat's externalized superego.

The Fallacy of the Ego

The sign repairman in our case study complains about two demands typically made by bureaucracy. The first is for information from below: "Then they said: Put it on paper. So we knocked off maybe

---

*Professionals do present a special case, if only because of their infinite capacity for self-deception.

†This unidirectionality in the construction of norms and the superego exactly parallels the unidirectionality of rationally organized social action observed in chapter 1. There is a striking difference between superego formation under the influence of both external authority and the inner psychic experience of the unique individual in his specific environment, on the one hand, and superego formation from above only.

‡This is the origin of the psychology of dependency that characterizes the organization man.

three hours, did maybe thirty-five signs or so, and the rest was paperwork. I guess if it wasn't on paper, they didn't feel it was done." The second demand was for obedience to control from above: " 'You will put up this and this many signs a day, or we'll know the reason why.' "

The Denial of Mastery

Aside from the fact that each demand reduced the amount of work done in the putting-up-signs department, as experienced by this particular sign repairman, what was the basis for the repairman's objections?

Psychologically, a demand for information and a demand for control mean that an individual surrenders mastery over a piece of work. Someone is saying to him: You are no longer master over your fate. Give us the information about the challenge you face. We'll judge what is the proper response, and we'll tell you what to do.

Such instructions are seen as a direct attack on the individual's ego. The ego is a structure of the psyche charged with exactly the functions that our sign repairman's superiors now arrogate to themselves. The ego receives information from the individual's environment in the form of a challenge. The ego judges how the challenge relates to the organism's ability to handle it. The ego designs responses that take into account both environmental demands and human needs.[6] Ultimately, the ego is master over the individual's survival within an environment.

How can an attack on such mastery be justified? The fact is that the power of a modern organization to cope with challenges larger than any challenges ever met before rests exactly on its assuming mastery over the actions of all its employes. The organization handles huge tasks; an individual handles limited tasks. The organization has a vast horizon; the functionary has a limited horizon.

The sign repairman's complaint about the denial of mastery stems directly from his limited horizon. Within that limited horizon he sees it as his task to put up signs, as many as he can, as well as he can. Any order from above that reduces his sign output, he sees not only as an attempt to supersede his mastery but as bad mastery. Yet, from the viewpoint of the organization at large, less work from him might actually mean more work overall from all departments of the organization. This is especially true when less work from him means less uncontrolled work.

For example, imagine our hero presses happily ahead day after day putting up as many signs as the strength of himself and his crew will allow. One day, a Friday, they put up forty signs. On "Blue Monday," when the crew is tired and hung over, they put up fifteen and knock off at noon. On Tuesday, stirred by guilt they make it up: they put up a total of sixty-five signs.

Now assume there is a section of signpost painters that scrapes and paints signposts from which signs have fallen. To let the paint dry, they are always one day ahead of the repairmen.

Two problems can arise if the repairmen are allowed to set their own quota. If the painters' quota is smaller, the repairmen will be falling over painters while putting up signs. Signs are likely to get splattered with paint, and so are the repairmen. Motorists can't read the paint-covered signs. No one will like it. And the repairmen will put in for an additional uniform-cleaning allowance.

Secondly, the problem will not arise in a predictable fashion. Let us say the quota for painted posts is thirty a day. On Friday, collisions between painters and repairmen might occur at a maximum of ten posts. On Monday there will be none. And by Tuesday the repair crew will have caught up with the painters again and be exactly a day behind. The reader who intends to be a manager can himself envision further complications, beginning with the day when the repair crew comes into the garage demanding a gallon of cleaning fluid for their clothes and extra wash-up time.

Even at this simple level of coordinating two crews, each crew's horizon, their view of how work is best to be done, does not extend to encompass that of both crews together. Once labor is divided and becomes specialized, it must be coordinated. Such coordination is best done by an office superordinated to both crews. In this way the function of evaluating work to be done — the environmental challenge — is shifted from the level of those actually doing it up to the supervisory level. So is the ultimate decision of striking a balance between organizational capacity to respond and the demand of the environment for a response. And so, finally, is the task of designing the response.

Because workers on the scene are intimately involved and acquainted with the nature of the immediate work at hand — which means they have more detailed and close-at-hand information than anyone else can have — the removal of the final decision-making power from their egos to the "organizational ego" of a superior office is always perceived by workers as a psychological insult.* Yet, if bureaucracy survives as the most successful of control institutions yet invented, it does so exactly because it does not leave mastery to each and every individual employed — especially not to the individual on the line.

---

*I use the term "insult" here in both the popular and the medical sense. In the medical sense it signifies an injury or impairment of an organic function.

This is a major paradox of working in bureaucracy from the functionary's point of view: if I know more about my work than anyone else, why is it that I cannot be allowed to manage my own work? The problem, of course, is that the functionary's definition of the work is circumscribed by a limited horizon and that the organization's definition of work, with its larger horizon, must supersede the individual's if the organization is to remain what it is — an organization.

The individual worker always misperceives what life in the organization is all about. It is never about getting the job done. It is always about integrating yourself with the rest of the organization so that the organization can get the job done. When there is a conflict between getting a job done individually and the demand for integrating one's self with the organization, the primacy of the latter is and must always be asserted — again, if the organization is to survive as a control instrument.

Frederick W. Taylor

In the psychology of modern organizations, this conflict was recognized and dealt with as early as the late 1800s, when Frederick W. Taylor, perhaps the most memorable of "human engineers," attempted to modernize the Bethlehem Steel Company works in Bethlehem, Pa. Part of that modernization program included preparing for the men the tools they used, on the assumption that engineers and managers knew which tools should be used and how they should be applied better than the men themselves. It was a clearcut case of an attempt by the superior offices in the organization to arrogate mastery and to deny mastery to the men. The struggle between the men's psychology of mastery over their work and the psychology of management was an epic one. Taylor's goal was:

> To render the management of the shop entirely independent of any one man or any set of men so that the shop will be in a position to run practically as economically if you were to lose your foreman, or if, in fact, a considerable body of your workmen were to leave at any one time.[7]

This goal is strictly in keeping with the characteristics that make the bureaucratic form of organization strong in industry or business as well as in public service — the impersonalization of tasks to be achieved, the assignment of expertise to offices instead of men, the emphasis on control from above by management. What was the workers' response to this attempt? They resisted the denial of mastery just as many workers resist it today.[8] Taylor himself bemoans his difficulties:

An illustration of a particular case may perhaps more fully explain my meaning in this regard. If, in the ordinary machine shop, a foreman were to order any one of his men to do a certain job on Piece Work [getting paid by the piece made not by the hour put in] and attempted to tell the man what cutting speed and feed to use, the result would be in nine cases out of ten that the man would grind his tools so that they could not do the work. If the foreman were then to put another man onto the machine he would probably find that the first man had either hidden many of his best tools belonging to the lathe or transferred them to some friend in the shop, so that the new man coming onto the machine would have to spend perhaps two or three days in getting tools dressed and ground before he could start to do the work, and even then unless he were skilled in the art of designing machine shop tools, which not one machinist in a thousand is, he would probably have tools that would fail to do the work economically on this particular machine.[9]

Now, anyone who has seen machinists work, or who has a craftsman in his family, as does the present author, has had experience with the pride and competence of such workers. Taylor's diatribe about the inability of workers to take care of their own tools rings wrong not only for this reason, but because presumably someone somewhere must be found to learn the competency involved. Taylor, who was a great believer in the ability of "good men" to learn the competencies required by management, was grinding a different ax. He was attacking the resistance of a generation of masters against the first onslaught of the succeeding generations of managers. When work at Bethlehem Steel was so organized and subdivided as to deny the individual machinist at his job the "privilege" of sharpening his own tools, the psychology of mastery ended.

The Hawthorne Experiments

Another classical example is presented by F. J. Roethlisberger in his evaluation of the famous Hawthorne Experiments undertaken at the Western Electric Company plant of that name in the 1920s and 1930s. In one of the experiments, group piece work was introduced for the wirers and solderers, as well as their foremen, involved in the assembly of an electrical relay. The more they produced as a group, the more they would get paid. "In such a situation," wrote Roethlisberger, then associate professor of industrial research at the Harvard Business School, "one might have expected that they would have been interested in maintaining total output and that the faster workers would have put pressure on the slower workers to improve their efficiency."[10] This was not the case. What happened was that the workers agreed among themselves to keep output at a certain comfortable level, and they proceeded to punish rate breakers by appropriate devices of social pressure and ostracism. This result was generally interpreted to indicate that social relations on the job were more important than work conditions themselves, including pay. This conclusion was supported by several other experiments in which, for example, lighting conditions were radically altered while work output remained the same.

What do we get to see, however, when we put the Hawthorne workers' emphasis on social relations in the context of what Taylor told us about the workers he encountered? If Taylor's observations were not totally wrong, then his workers were much more individualistic than the Hawthorne workers. Taylor's workers hid their tools not only from management, but from their fellow workers. They did not seem to be protecting the overall output of the work through a conspiracy: each protected his own individual mastery over the tools he had to work with and consequently over the way he did his work. One might suspect that something had happened between 1898 and the 1920s to change the psychology of individual mastery to a psychology of dependence. Of course, American industry itself claims that what has changed is that business and industry have become modernized. Could it be that Taylor and other industrial "human engineers" had in the meanwhile succeeded? Could it be that the "sociability" the Hawthorne workers were displaying was nothing more than a social version of something they had learned in bureaucracy — namely, that interdependence comes before independence?

What in fact happened to anyone's independence in that group? Roethlisberger himself gives us the answer:

> One man in this group exceeded the group standard of what constituted a fair day's work. Social pressure was put on him to conform, but without avail, since he enjoyed doing things others disliked. The best-liked person in the group was the one who kept his output exactly where the group agreed it should be.[11]

Thus, in one single paragraph has modern management psychology recorded the demise of the last individualist.* Having dis-

---

*To tell a worker he should give up personal mastery in favor of sociability with his co-workers is to lie to him. The organization is concerned with having him give up independence in favor of *organizational* interdependence. Under this rule, even the group resistance of the Hawthorne workers *against* higher production is a plus in organizational terms. The resistance is evidence of worker acceptance of the idea of interdependence. As pointed out so many times before, when there is a conflict between control and production, control emerges as the prime value of bureaucracy. Here interdependence is a measure of control.

covered the effect of group pressure, a perfectly normal component of prebureaucratic social life, management psychologists ever since have disguised the need of a modern organization for integration and interdependence of its individuals under the terms of the sociability needs of the functionaries themselves. The result has been the inability of management specialists to distinguish in their own minds between the needs for specialization and integration of the production or control processes of modern organizations and the needs of living people for social relations. On the basis of this confusion, it has been impossible to explain to individual workers, who themselves quite clearly distinguish between personal relations and role relations (especially when their co-workers commiserate with them on management's denial of individual mastery), the actual reasons why management must insist on taking from them mastery over their own work.

It is not, as Roethlisberger said, that "most of us want the satisfaction that comes from being accepted and recognized as people of worth by our friends and work associates."[12] That is a desire of society and life in society. The need of bureaucracy is to make functionaries understand the built-in necessity of modern organizations that they surrender their ego, not to the immediate work group of social beings (to which such a surrender is at times normal), but to the cold and impersonal machine that cannot exist without such surrender at all times.

The Fallacy of Identity

The vice president of an organization is fired.* The man who fired him comments: "He thought he was there to give the plan for the next year. We told him he was fired. He didn't even hear what we told him. He just went on giving his plan for the next year." Another vice president in the same situation "just put his head down and cried." A federal civil servant at the G-16 level discusses with friends the possibility of applying her fifteen years of top management experience to the private sphere. Then she admits she probably will not take the leap: "I am afraid that outside the office I won't have any identity at all."[13]

Psychologically, something very serious is going on in all three instances. In the first case, there is an inability to even admit the reality of the firing; in the second, a breakdown; in the third, a sense of dependency on the institution and fear of other institutions despite

---

*See the case study at the beginning of this chapter.

a clear display of superb competence within one's institution.* Are these atypical cases?

Personality and Role

We are all dependent on our environment to some extent, especially on the environment of family, friends, and co-workers. F. J. Roethlisberger, the man who made sense out of the Hawthorne Experiments, concluded this about the "sociability" findings of the original research group headed by Harvard's Elton Mayo:

> Most of us want the satisfaction that comes from being accepted and recognized as people of worth by our friends and work associates. . . . We all want evidence of our social importance. We want to have a skill that is socially recognized as useful. We want the feeling of security that comes not so much from the amount of money we have in the bank as from being an accepted member of a group.[14]

And Roethlisberger concludes:

> A man whose job is without social function is like a man without a country; the activity to which he has to give the major portion of his life is robbed of all human meaning and significance.[15]

In other words, Roethlisberger sees no difference between the need for sociability in society and the need for sociability in bureaucracy. To him both institutions provide the member with human meaning and significance. Without either of these institutions, the individual is dead.

Somehow Roethlisberger's conclusions, to the extent that they see organization as just another extension of social life, ring false both in terms of our daily experience and in sociological terms.

Any American, especially, must be offended when told he or she is nothing without society. The belief in individualism on which the nation was founded tells us just the opposite: I am most free, I am most me, when I am not being pressured by others in society. But even if this American emphasis on the individual *versus* society should exaggerate the importance of the individual, there is another experience each one of us has in daily life which makes nonsense of Roethlisberger's confusion between the kind of dependence fostered by society and the kind fostered by bureaucracy.

In a former career, I was a copy editor for *The New York Times* foreign desk. My first question on arriving at work each day was to inquire who would sit "in the slot" of the copy desk that day; that is,

---

*The resumé of the civil servant in question reads like the life history of an Horatio Alger. Contrary to popular assumptions about civil service bureaucrats, many of these climb to the top through a display of considerable energy, initiative, and even courage within the institutional framework — as was the case in this instance.

who would be the boss. The question for me was, "Who is the slotman today?" — a question very similar to an autoworker asking, "Who is the foreman today?" or to the secretary of state asking, "Who is the duty officer?"

In other words, in our workaday world we distinguish between who a person is in and of himself (personality) and the role the person plays in an institution (identity). There is a difference between who I am for myself — my personality — and what I have to be for others — my institutional role identity. Furthermore, each one of us knows that in society I am much more free in determining who I am than I am in bureaucracy.

I recently was asked by an IBM repairman for directions to an office within which I worked. "Oh, the so-and-so office," I said. "Well, you go down this hall to the right, make the first left, and you'll be there." As he walked away, I noticed that along with his dark suit, he was wearing gym sneakers. I ran up to him and said, "Your shoes, your shoes!" "Yeah, I know," he said, "they can tell us what to wear at the office, but when I'm out on my own and they can't see me, I wear what's comfortable for me."

Now, there are social pressures in society as to what kinds of clothes are proper at what time. But when IBM tells you what to wear, it is not just a social pressure: at the end of that dictate lies the very distinct threat that unless you wear what you are told you will lose your job with IBM.

In society, the eccentric is a distinctly allowable type. You are allowed to express your own personality, whether it is in what you wear or in what you do and who you are. Within bureaucracy, whether private or public, deviance from institutional expectations is calculated as a measurable cost to that institution. When the cost gets too high you are fired. In brief: in society, you have personality; in bureaucracy, you have identity.

Identity in Bureaucracy

In terms of the other two fallacies, the agonies of the individuals cited at the beginning of this section become understandable in an entirely new way.

First, while both society and bureaucracy make demands on the individual, society tends to be much more flexible on who you can be than is bureaucracy. To be rejected by society is not to cease to exist altogether, especially in a culture in which individualism is a central and prized characteristic of the person. But what about identity in bureaucracy? Who I am is to a large extent determined by the standards I have for myself and by my self-perception of how I measure up to these standards. Another measure of "being somebody" is the extent to which I am allowed to exercise control over a challenge and derive a sense of mastery over it and a feeling of satisfaction with my own powers from the experience.

For the individual the first measure is a matter of coming to terms with the standards stored in the superego. The second measure is a matter of the exercise of mastery by the ego over both the external world and inner impulses and needs in relation to that world. From the study of the fallacies of the superego and ego, however, we know that in bureaucracy superego standards and control are external to the individual while the ego and its need for mastery are fragmented among the individual and many co-workers.

This means that, in contrast to the individual in society, the functionary in bureaucracy has essential parts of identity located in persons and structures outside the self. Specifically, the superego, as a resource for identity, is located in organizational hierarchy. And the ego is so fragmented in terms of exercising mastery over a task as to be at least partially located in those organizational structures that express the institution's division of labor.

To the extent that functionaries at all levels — whether at the street level or in managerial regions — have accepted this evisceration of their psyches, to that extent separation from the institution specifically means leaving their superegos and parts of their egos behind. Those dismissed or threatened with dismissal from bureaucracy are not simply threatened with physical dislocation, but with being sent out into a new environment without the necessary psychological equipment — their superegos and their egos. In a very real sense, then, did our civil servant above speak of her fears of "not having any identity at all." Bureaucrats who have permitted the substitution of an institutional identity for their individual personalities face a world outside the institution in which they must suddenly operate without an inner sense of who they are or who they should be (superego), and without the experience of mastering a challenge all by themselves (ego).

Finally, to the extent that bureaucrats are typically unconscious of the externalization of their superegos and the fragmentation of their egos — as reflected in the fallacy that they assume they are still possessed of these — they also commit the ultimate fallacy of identity. While they are institutionally employed, bureaucrats assume they have personal identities, or personalities, in the same way that they had personalities when still within society. That is the fallacy of identity.

This fallacy is two-fold. The first part we commit when we assume that we are someone independent of bureaucracy. Bureaucracy is what ultimately dictates our norms and assigns us our jobs. We are deprived of self-judgment (superego) and mastery (ego) and we refuse to acknowledge it for the simple reason that it is too painful to do so. The fallacy expresses itself in the typical folksaying heard again and again at social parties in answer to the question, "Who are you?" Typically, those of us imprisoned in the fallacy of identity reply: "I am a professor at New York University," or "I am an autoworker at the Ford Rouge plant," or "I am the secretary of state." What is wrong with all these statements is that we may "be" all these things while we are in our office or on the assembly line. We are not any of these things outside our office or away from the line. For without the institutional environment, we cannot know what we are to do, whether what we do is right or not, and worst of all we lack the power that only institutional structures can give us to exercise the quasimastery that our role entails. The secretary of state vacationing in a mountain cabin and away from a telephone is not the secretary of state.*

Secondly, the fallacy of identity involves a further confusion. It is the confusion between personal personality — the patterns of behavior we have learned and that remain at our beck and call no matter where we go — and institutional identity — the patterns of norms and behavior that have meaning and can be exercised only within and through cooperating institutional structures. Identity in this sense is not personality. The individuals who surrender their personalities, who they are, to institutional identity, what others make of them, give up something that can never be recovered. Bureaucracy empties the successful functionaries of two essential inner resources for being somebody independent of others, for individuation — their private superegos and their personal egos. To send a well-conditioned functionary out into the world of society, which was originally formed and continues to be formed by the interaction between autonomous individuals, is akin to amputating a man's head and sending him off to fend for himself.

WHAT THE EXPERTS SAY

The bureaucrat's psychology is radically different from that of the man or woman in society. This assertion stands supported by two groups of experts. First, the picture painted of normal people in society by leaders of traditional psychology does not mesh at all with the reality of the bureaucrat's psyche. This point is made below in

---

*Identification with office — and the status that office carries — exists even at the highest level. Former presidents of the United States continue to be addressed as "Mr. President," and it is not atypical to read a report that a former governor, William W. Scranton, "likes to be addressed as 'Governor'," even though having assumed the office of U.S. Ambassador to the United Nations. ("Scranton's 2-Month Report Card at the U.N. Shows High Marks," *The New York Times*, May 22, 1976, p. 8.)

surveys applying two traditional psychologies to the bureaucratic reality — Freud's individual psychology and existential psychology. Second, entirely new psychologies have had to be constructed to match the new reality. "Organizational psychology" now treats the institution itself as possessed of a psyche, in which case human beings become mere subcomponents that must be integrated into the organizational psyche. And as bureaucracy penetrates into society, Skinner's behaviorist psychology tries to explain behaviors inconsistent with earlier models of an integrated psyche standing apart from the conditions that surround it. The new psychologies, whether of bureaucracy or society, emphasize the two characteristics most striking in our discussion of bureaucrats in the preceding section — their lack of personal psychic integration and their psychic dependence on the environment.

Freud and Individual Psychology

The most striking event of the bureaucratic age is the disappearance of the individual. This becomes clear when we juxtapose Sigmund Freud's image of humans against today's reality.

Elevating the Ego
As Freud saw the history of the psyche, it developed through two stages. In the first, the communal stage, the individual was submerged in the mass. From the viewpoint of ego psychology, we might say that his psychic structure, to the extent that separate components could then be considered as already differentiated, consisted of a dominant superego, a weak ego, and a repressed id. Graphically the constellation might be depicted in this way:

Superego

Ego   Id

This constellation asserts the supremacy of communal norms through the superego. The ego, as autonomous integrating center for the individual to adapt to reality, is correspondingly weak: all the allowable patterns of adaptation have already been worked out by the community and are dictated through the superego. Similarly, the superego, at this stage almost entirely congruent in its norms with the will of the community, sharply represses or punishes any asocial attempts by the instinctual drives to assert themselves. The id is repressed. It can gain satisfaction only through tightly circumscribed, culturally approved social channels.

In contrast, we may observe, as Paul Roazen has done, that in applying his psychology to the people of his time, "Freud's whole therapy is aimed at liberation and independence."[16] The concern of Freud's ego-dominant psychology is with the maturing of the individual into an autonomous source of intelligence and power from whom society in turn draws its strength. Gone is the communal idea of each member's subjection to the community. Here also lies the difference between society and community, the form of social life that preceeded it.[17]

The psychology of the single human being is restructured. It places the ego on top, pushing the superego aside when its socially derived norms get in the way of individual survival. And it frees the id to expression in channels approved by the ego in its attempt to mediate between the outer and the inner world. This is not total freedom, as is psychosis in which the id runs wild, but in contrast to the restraint and submission to both the laws of nature and of men characteristic of the communal world, individuals in the modern social world did radically make over the world in their own image. We need think only of the vast destruction wreaked on nature and the vast construction of both material and social empires. The structure of individualist man, psychologically, can be depicted as follows:

Ego

Superego   Id

Here ego is dominant. "The ego has a unifying function, ensuring coherent behavior and conduct. The job of the ego is not just the negative one of avoiding anxiety, but also the positive one of maintaining effective performance."[18] And what Freud did not do for the dominance of the ego, having developed his ego psychology late in life, his successors did.[19] With the ego dominant in adapting the individuals' needs to their environment, society's standards, as enshrined in the superego, were subject to revision and adaptation to the needs of individuals. In contrast to the communal era, the superego itself now becomes dominated by the ego. The id remains often repressed, but when its needs are fulfilled these now tend to be channeled through the ego and not as likely through the superego.

Freud considered the growth of the individual not only crucial to the individual himself but essential for society at large:

> The liberation of an individual, as he grows up from the authority of his parents, is one of the most necessary though one of the most painful results brought about by the course of his development. It is

quite essential that that liberation should occur and it may be presumed that it has been to some extent achieved by everyone who has reached a normal state. Indeed, the whole progress of society rests upon the opposition between successive generations.[20]

Exactly for the reasons that politically Freud was a liberal and that scientifically he made the individual his unit of analysis,[21] his later ego-dominant image of man stands in stark contrast to our age. There, man as individual created himself in the company of other men. Often he would be, in the words of Thomas Hobbes, alone, alive, and afraid. But then freedom was defined exactly in terms of being left alone by others to work out one's own fate. On this definition both the political philosophy and the theology of liberalism met.[22] Here the prevailing political and social reality is that of the corporation. The unit of analysis now is the situation encompassing a disindividualized individual at best, as in the works of B. F. Skinner, or the organization itself, as in the works of Edgar H. Schein.[23]

Fragmenting the Ego
With the separation of the superego from the rest of the psyche, and with the fragmentation of the ego, the possibility of the individual itself resubmerges into the eons from which it had only recently emerged. The concept of the individual derives from the Latin word *individuus* — "indivisible." The individual as such did not exist in the world of community; he was molded too much by his social environment. The individual arose only with the development of modern society. He owed his existence to the idea that man could grasp hold of his world, including the social world, and reshape it in his own image. This was the idea of early science, technology, and industry. It carried over into the early social sciences.

By the time Freud formed his psychology, it was, despite its group context which he did not at all deny, an "Individual Psychology."[24] The task of Freudian psychoanalysis and therapy to this day remains, at least avowedly, the reestablishment of the functioning individual. If analysts or therapists are asked to whom they owe their direct obligation, it is to the individual whom they analyze or heal.

But man the indivisible is now no longer so. Especially not in bureaucracy. He is man the divisible. Whether or not he is still a human being in some absolute sense need not be asked here. All we require is an understanding of why bureaucratic man looks so inhuman to us as outsiders. He looks inhuman from our perspective to the extent that we still operate under the definition of "individual" that emerged with the rise of society, the form of social organization within which we still perceive ourselves to live apart from working hours. Similarly, the less surprised we are at divisible man, the more our own perceptions reveal the penetration of bureaucracy's man-concept into society at large.

The cutting edge of that penetration is revealed in a recent television commercial in which a young woman who feels she is in fact three women is regarded as perfectly normal — and requires the "normal" equipment of such a fragmented individual, i.e., three types of watches to go with all her incarnations. How recent this acceptance of the split personality is, is reflected in the fact that in the 1950s a young woman was subjected to considerable psychiatric treatment when she had a similar experience. The story is told in *The Three Faces of Eve.*[25]

In contrast to both preceding pictures of the structure of the psyche in other eras, perhaps the best that can be done for the image of bureaucratic man might look like this:

Externalized Superego

Fragmented Ego

Id
(in the service of the organization)

While this image has a faint resemblance to the communal psyche, under the dominance of a superego, it has no resemblance to the structure of individualist man at all. The individual has simply disintegrated under the immense power of bureaucracy and his need to make a living in it because he cannot make a living elsewhere in the shrinking arena of society.

Existential Psychology: Ernest Keen

The crisis of the individual penetrates all traditional psychologies — that is, those psychologies that either have not sold out to organizational masters and distorted themselves or those that recognize the new organizational reality and voluntarily abandon the concept of the individual.* While it is not possible here to survey the scope of that crisis, it is possible to take specific problems of individualistic psychologies in the face of the bureaucratization of the world.

*The psychology of Abraham Maslow is of the first type, although its distortion was accomplished by others. For an outline of Maslovian "third force" psychology, see Abraham Maslow, *Motivation and Personality* (New York: Harper & Row, 1954). For examples of the second types, the behaviorism of B. F. Skinner and the organizational psychology of Edgar H. Schein, see below.

Presenting a False Self

Existential psychology is concerned overall with what it considers three faces of being[26] — the faces an individual turns onto his existence. A very conscious concern of existential psychologists is that at least one of these faces of being is so overemphasized by the pressures of the modern world that the individual's essential integrity is permanently damaged. The three faces of being are:

1. Being-in-the-world. This is the way I experience myself as actively engaged in the world. It is my direct experience of the world through my involvement in it. I am the active subject working my way out in the world. Maslow might say that this is the me that is actualizing itself in the world. What is important is that my experience in the world is, in this state of being, direct, not reflective. I am not looking back at myself in action from a detached distance. I *am* in action.
2. Being-for-oneself. This is the way I see myself by doing what I did not do in the state of "being-in-the-world" — through reflectively looking at myself as an object. "Out of this experience of oneself 'as object' comes the notion of 'self-concept' and the casting of oneself into substantive terms so that there is some kind of solid 'me' or definition which one can use to make decisions about what to do, how to act, etc."[27]
3. Being-for-others. This actually means how others see me as an object. But since I can never directly experience how others actually perceive me, being-for-others means presenting myself to others in terms I expect will be acceptable to them. As Keen states, "Oneself is experienced through the eyes of others, and one becomes the object of 'the other'."[28]

In a well-integrated individual, there is a balance between these three states of being. But life in bureaucracy forces me to over-emphasize an aspect of myself that others — specifically co-workers and superiors in the hierarchy — will like. When this presentation of a face to others is in conscious conflict with what I know myself to be, I am said to be "lying-for-others." The first experience of lying-for-others occurs when I, as a child, discover that I can present myself to my parents in a way that differs radically from what I perceive I am. This is an important stage in growth because I previously believed, as Jean Piaget among others has pointed out,* that my parents could read my thoughts. The problem becomes serious because "there comes a time in the life and lying of the child when he comes to believe his own lies."[29] It is this problem that modern man faces in

*Jean Piaget, best known for his cognitive psychology emphasizing child development. For typical examples among a large array of works, see Jean Piaget, *The Language and Thought of the Child* (Cleveland: World Publishing Co., Meridian Books, 1955), and *The Construction of Reality in the Child* (New York: Basic Books, 1954). For an introduction to Piaget's concepts, see Barry J. Wadsworth, *Piaget's Theory of Cognitive Development* (New York: David McKay, 1971).

bureaucracy: he must so much be what others expect him to be that he loses his own self. Keen gives a specific example:

> Suppose, for example, that a salesman is encouraged by his company to be aggressive. His supervisor is aggressive and this supplies a model for the salesman. Because of the power structure, satellization around the supervisor occurs and the individual internalizes the value "aggression = good" as a criterion against which to measure himself. He comes, then, to see himself as aggressive (whatever that might mean to him) and to feel that he is not being the "real him" when he is not. Idealization of one's self around this concept and guilt for not living up to the idealized image grow together in the vicious circle of lying-for-oneself. The guiltier one feels, the more adamant is the affirmation of the standard, and vice versa. Soon the salesman has identified with the role to such an extent that his immediate perception of the world is changed. Neutral persons become potential sales targets; relationships are subordinate to the goal of sales.[30]

It is easily understood how an organization might be very happy with such an employe, but anyone concerned with what might happen to him in his journey from society into the world of bureaucracy can only shudder. Keen here asserts what within Freudian analysis we have understood as a loss of integrated self — through the absorption of external superego standards — but foreshadows what below we describe as the dynamic of the bureaucratic psychology. That is, he answers the question: Why do bureaucrats, though they suffer in bureaucracy, feel forced to return again and again? Keen's answer is that once I have absorbed for my state of being the external standard set by bureaucracy, I cease to have a state of "being-for-myself" — cease not only to "be" myself, but cease to "have" a self. For this reason, the bureaucrat cited in the last section expresses the constant fear: "I am afraid that outside the office I won't have any identity at all."

Existential Therapy

The fact that most people in today's world live in bureaucracies creates serious professional problems for the individualistic psychologist, as Keen observes. In a special section of his book, entitled "Therapy and the Bureaucrat,"* Keen takes up one such problem among others:

> To call the bureaucratic style "lying" is to imply that the therapist's job is to help him to be "honest," which may indeed be a maladaptative

---

*This is one of the few such treatments of bureaucracy available in psychological literature of the individualist type.

stance to take given the social and political contingencies of bureaucratic life.[31]

In other words, not only the individualist but the individualist therapist's role seems to have become an anachronism. However, there is worse to come. "The question is not . . ." Keen continues, "whether a behavior is adaptive within a social system but whether it violates the ontological structure of being."[32] In other words, it is not whether an individual is to be fitted by the therapy into "being-for-the-world," but whether he can be made to develop an integration of all three states of being that is in accord with basic human potential. But here the therapist's options are limited: "The attempt to force overt honesty in a patient may subject the patient to the wrath of his bureaucratic context and do him a great disservice." This leaves the therapist with only one task: "The goal must be, therefore, to open up for the individual the *option* of honesty."

> If he decides to run the risk of honesty in a system built on lies, he does so presumably in the service of other than bureaucratic values. To become aware of his own experience of self-as-subject may enlighten latent values. This may put him into agonizing conflict between his personal values and his bureaucratic values,* and the therapist must be willing to accept responsibility for his role in bringing that conflict to a head.[33]

Given such a dilemma for the therapist, it seems no more than responsible to again ask the question whether an individualist psychology that both sheds light on this dilemma and exacerbates it should not be replaced by a new psychology that specializes in individual-organizational relations.

To the extent that existential psychology sees the individual as, in essence, the only valid unit of both analysis and being, its practitioners can strike no compromises with the new bureaucratic reality that destroys individuals as we have known them.† The dilemma that Keen raises for the therapist remains unresolved except through a declaration of war against bureaucracy waged on the grounds of ontological necessity — what Abraham Maslow called man's need to be what he must be. If man is man only as the

---

*Here Keen returns us to our discussion of the "norms of society" versus "norms of bureaucracy" in chapter 2, for what he calls "personal" values are likely to be the values of the person raised in society who now enters the new world of bureaucracy. In bureaucracy itself there are no opportunities for the development of personal values, except incidentally.

†Rollo May questions whether freedom — and therefore the "option" of honesty, for example, of which Keen speaks — is not illusory in our present bureaucratized world. For May's discussion of the dilemma of the therapist in a world of constraint, see his *Love and Will* (New York: Dell, Laurel Edition, 1974), pp. 194 – 199.

existentialists define him, then he must be defended by all means. This, however, is a problem not only for the existentialists but for all individualist psychologists that claim an "essence" of manness.

Behaviorist Psychology: B. F. Skinner

The problem that psychology has had in centering its explanations on the individual, in a time when bureaucracy abolishes the individual, is effectively dissolved through behaviorism.

Dissolving the Individual

"A concept of self is not essential in an analysis of behavior," states B. F. Skinner, the major representative of behaviorist psychology. This may or may not be true for psychology. The trouble is that for living people, forced to make the voyage from society to bureaucracy, giving up the concept of being or having a self is extremely painful if not impossible.

To make this point, let us look at a recent news report of bombs exploding in suitcases at Jerusalem's Ben-Gurion International Airport. "A few seconds after the first blast today," the report said at one point, "a young woman rushed out of the front of the terminal with her hair ablaze, shrieking: 'What's happening? What are you doing to me?' A police officer threw her to the ground and rolled on top of her to smother the flames."[34]

The fact is that in society we are used to taking everything personally. The fact that Palestinian terrorists, who took credit for the attack, were assaulting an entire nation regardless of who the individuals injured might be was irrelevant to the young woman. To her, the attack was an attack on her by *someone* else, not an anonymous group of technologists making ever smaller and more effective bombs. That the woman merely happened to be the intersection of a worldwide battle between immensely powerful systems was not of the slightest interest to her; to her, she was the center of the world at that moment. More accurately, in her own view and agony she was *the* world, and everyone else was "you" — "What are *you* doing to *me*?" — an alien world.*

In the words of another inhabitant of an outdated world, for which modernity no longer has time: ". . . don't let anybody kid you. It's all personal, every bit of business. Every piece of shit every man has to eat every day of his life is personal. They call it business. OK. But it's personal as hell."[35] Bureaucracy, as the form of modern

---

*Here even the policeman who saves her becomes part of that alien world outside the self.

organization based on impersonality, cannot tolerate such personal world views. A psychology that attempts to explain the psychic pressures of such organization must either overlook or effectively disintegrate the legitimacy of having individuals look at the world from the inside out instead of accepting it from the outside in. Behaviorist psychology chooses the latter route.

The major contribution behaviorist psychology makes to a realistic understanding of life in a bureaucratic world is that is recognizes the technological environment as the prime mover of behavior. "By questioning the control exercised by autonomous man and demonstrating the control exercised by the environment, a science of behavior also seems to question dignity and worth," Skinner writes in *Beyond Freedom and Dignity*.[36]

> A person is responsible for his behavior, not only in the sense that he may be justly blamed or punished when he behaves badly, but also in the sense that he is to be given credit and admired for his achievements.* A scientific analysis shifts the credit as well as the blame to the environment, and traditional practices can then no longer be justified.[37]

At another point, Skinner half-approvingly and half-critically cites an anonymous writer as saying, "We are prodded and lashed through life."[38] Skinner amends this to say, "The environment not only prods and lashes, it *selects*."[39]

> Its role is similar to that in natural selection, though on a very different time scale, and was overlooked for the same reason. It is now clear that we must take into account what the environment does to an organism not only before but after it responds. Behavior is shaped and maintained by its consequences.[40]

Skinner draws great hope from this discovery because it has what he calls a "practical" result: "the environment can be manipulated." In other words, if we recognize that people are what the environment makes them, we can shift our attention onto that environment and construct an environment that will make people into what we would have them be. The individual — or what Skinner derogatorily calls "autonomous man" — vanishes in the process, although the term "individual" survives, as in the following statement in which Skinner raises the hope of effecting radical changes through environmental manipulation:

> It is true that man's genetic endowment can be changed only very slowly, but changes in the environment of the individual have quick

---

*Skinner considers such a view of a person unscientific and invalid.

and dramatic effects. *A technology of operant behavior** is, as we shall see, already well advanced, and it may prove to be commensurate with our problems.[41]

What Skinner argues is entirely compatible with how a bureaucratic world sees itself. Our problems are huge and involve the massed efforts of many people tightly organized into bureaucracies. Just because some bureaucracies produce painful results is not sufficient argument for abandoning the idea of designing environments to manipulate people because without such design our king-size problems will not go away. The task simply is to design technologies for conditioning operant behavior on *scientific* grounds rather than on prescientific ones.[42]

Exactly what problems does Skinner dissolve that had previously arisen in our portrayal of the agony of the social individual in the new bureaucratic environment?

Hierarchy, Conditioning, and the Superego
The first problem that Skinner resolves on behalf of bureaucracy is its imperative demand for subordinating the individual's sense of what is right and wrong to the dictates of the hierarchy. Hierarchy is an essential part of the control mechanism that turns modern bureaucracy into a power instrument without compare. Bureaucracy's power is unstable unless the use of hierarchy — and its position of absolute dominance over the individual's sense of right and wrong, proper and improper — can be justified.

Skinner provides exactly this kind of justification. Here he proceeds in two steps. First, he discredits the idea that there ever was a superego with which modern organization could come in conflict. Certainly, he suggests there never was such a thing as an inner superego particular to an individual:

> . . . the controlling behavior engendered by the community [in pre-bureaucratic days] consists of a selected group of practices evolved in the history of a particular culture because of their effect upon antisocial behavior. To the extent that this behavior works to the advantage of the community — and again to this extent only — we may speak of a unitary conscience, social conscience, or superego.[43]

---

*My italics. Skinner here recognizes that modern organization can be so designed as to become the institutionalization of technique — technology — for converting social or premodern man into man compatible with the general "advance" of science and material technology. The literature of earlier psychologies, for example that emphasizing "dignity" of man, he argues, "may oppose advances in technology" and "thus stands in the way of further human achievements." (B. F. Skinner, *Beyond Freedom and Dignity* [New York: Bantam/Vintage, 1972], p. 55).

Here Skinner invents what we have called earlier in this chapter the externalized superego as distinct from the inner superego of which Freud spoke. The sources of right and wrong, he argues, have always lain in the adaptive value that certain behaviors have for the community at large. The community, through punishment or reward, conditions individuals to repeat adaptive behaviors and shun maladaptive ones. From this position it is not even a small step to arguing that hierarchies in modern organizations are simple transmission channels for informing functionaries of behaviors adaptive to the survival of the institution as a whole and for reinforcing these. Skinner sees no difference between the process of conditioning performed in bureaucracy and the process of socialization performed on individuals in society — except that the former is conscious, rational, and hopefully scientific whereas the latter process is automatic, guided by premodern dependence on emotions and anti-rationalistic fallacies, and sometimes leads to mistakes.*

Earlier such techniques of control were mere "rules of thumb." "The scientific study of behavior has reached the point where it is supplying additional techniques. . . . the effect upon human affairs will be tremendous."[44] Specifically, these techniques include what Skinner calls "operant conditioning." What is operant conditioning?

Contrary to popular impression, operant conditioning is not a simple "stimulus-response" process. Skinner argues vigorously to distinguish his process from Pavlov's famous experiments with dogs that were taught to salivate at the sound of a bell:

> Pavlov himself called all events which strengthened behavior "reinforcement" and all the resulting changes "conditioning." In the Pavlovian experiment, however, a reinforcer is paired with a *stimulus*; whereas in operant behavior it is contingent upon a *response*. Operant

---

*Elsewhere, Skinner argues that any supposed inner superego has always been the kind of externalized superego of which he speaks here and which we, in contrast, suggest has developed only with the rise of bureaucracy. Speaking critically, he says that "one kind of control said to be internalized is represented by the Judeo-Christian conscience and the Freudian superego." But, he argues, the conscience and the superego are merely "the vicars of society, and theologians and psychoanalysts alike recognize their external origin." In part, then, the concept of an internalized superego simply comes into being when external punishers are not visible. (*Beyond Freedom and Dignity*, pp. 64 – 65.) This view of the superego as the direct delegate of the community misrepresents at least Freud's concept of the superego. The latter concept is based on the premise that each individual both receives cultural norms from the society and then modifies these in terms of his or her personal experience, all of which results in a "feeding back" into society as a whole of the aggregate or the synthesis of the experience of all its individuals. Skinner's in-formation, on the contrary, is only a one-way street. But this simplification makes it possible for him to argue that there is nothing new going on with the appearance of bureaucracy's control mechanisms as an externalized superego.

reinforcement is therefore a separate process and requires a separate analysis. . . . In operant conditioning we "strengthen" an operant [behavior] in the sense of making a response more probable or, in actual fact, more frequent. In Pavlovian or "respondent" conditioning we simply increase the magnitude of the response elicited by the conditioned stimulus and shorten the time which elapses between stimulus and response.[45]

The appeal of "making a response more probable" or "more frequent" should be obvious to anyone acquainted with the nature of modern bureaucracy. The strength of control of a bureaucracy depends on making the activities of functionaries as predictable as possible. A method of training them that promises to make more probable a desirable response to orders, standing operating procedures, or specified qualifications on the basis of which a client becomes "a case" is clearly attractive to all those charged with managing bureaucracy. And there are other attractions.

"Operant conditioning," writes Skinner, "shapes behavior as a sculptor shapes a lump of clay."[46] What an exciting prospect for a manager, to use a phrase borrowed from John Dean.* If human beings are lumps of clay, resistance to bureaucratization is really no problem, and all the manager has to learn is the process of conditioning if he wants to exercise control. The techniques of this process are complex — as the complexity of Skinner's writing demonstrates — but one or two characteristics may be singled out. In operant conditioning, the individual engages in a behavior that is immediately reinforced, whether through reward or punishment, so that it may be made persistent or "extinguished" altogether.†Skinner:

> The reinforcement which develops skill must be *immediate*. Otherwise, the precision of the differential effect is lost.‡ In many practical areas skilled behavior is encouraged by arranging a quick report of accomplishment. In rifle practice, for example, extremely small-scale properties are differentially reinforced by a hit or a miss. Properties of this sort can be selected only if the differential reinforcement is immediate.[47]

The environment selects; the individual responds. The bureaucracy

---

*John Dean, self-confessed Watergate conspirator, commented in response to a vow by then President Richard M. Nixon that, "This is a war . . . I want the most comprehensive notes on all those who tried to do us in . . ." by saying, "What an exciting prospect." (*The New York Times*, May 1, 1974, p. 27.)

†The term "extinguished" is used in learning theory in general.

‡The term "differential effect" refers to distinguishing between producing "a relatively new unit [of behavior] and making slight changes in the direction of effectiveness in an existing unit." (Skinner, *Science and Human Behavior* [New York: The Free Press, 1965], p. 95.)

determines; the functionary acts out. This is the promise that behaviorism holds for modern management.

The Division of Labor, Mastery and the Ego

Much of the power that bureaucracy has over its members comes from the division of labor which so specializes and fragments work that mastery over a piece of work has to be handed over to a coordinator who becomes the master of the members. The experience of labor in a bureaucracy eventually runs afoul of the expectations raised by the experience of work in society. Work in society means designing logical means to achieve known ends. Often such work is also socially approved and carries social rewards, such as honor and status. Above all, there is in individuals the sense that they know what the work to be done is and how their contribution relates to the final goal. This is the sense of mastery. This sense of mastery is denied in bureaucracy because it is in the interest of bureaucracy as a control instrument to divide and subdivide work. The reasons are numerous. Divided work can lead to the application of individuals' refined skills to segments of extremely complex tasks. Divided work also makes possible, however, the reduction of the level of skill required so that it no longer matters who fills a specific role because the low level of skill required makes it possible to quickly train and replace any specific individual in any given role. The power that is handed over to managers, mentioned above, is another reason. Because of the distance between the ultimate piece of work to be done and the fragment of labor he contributes to it, the functionary ceases to know the meaning of activity. He loses his sense of individual accomplishment, of satisfaction derived from logically integrating his skills into an overall project. He loses the sense of mastery.

In daily experience, we miss the sense of accomplishment that allowed a medieval stone mason to chip into his finished work the words "Ioannes Paulus Fecit" — John Paul Made This. Studs Terkel in his interviews with working people recalls the words of a stone mason of our day:

> I can't imagine a job where you go home and maybe go by a year later and you don't know what you've done. My work, I can see what I did the first day I started. All my work is set right out there in the open and I can look at it as I go by. . . . The people who live there might not notice it, but I notice it. I never pass that house that I don't think of it. I've got one house in mind right now. (Laughs.) That's the work of my hands.[48]

Days of such work and such a sense of mastery are gone by when the Advertising Council of America has to try to instill pride in

American workers by showing a picture of a hot dog "signed" by its maker and arguing that America needs more people who are willing to sign their work.

The reality of work on the assembly line and in the office is such today that it sounds incongruous to hear a steelworker say of the forty to fifty thousand pounds of steel he helps handle a day:

> I want my signature on 'em, too. Sometimes out of pure meanness, when I make something, I put a little dent in it. I like to do something to make it really unique. Hit it with a hammer. I deliberately fuck it up to see if it'll get by, just so I can say I did it.[49]

But those of us born into society and its ways, as against bureaucracy, can empathize with the same steelworker's sense of distance between what he does and what gets done: "It's hard to take pride in a bridge you're never gonna cross, in a door you're never gonna open."[50]

Traditional psychology took account of such desires for mastery.* Skinner himself well understands traditional psychology's linkage between mastery and the ego. "The ego," he says in a summary of Freud's structures of the psyche, "besides attempting to reach a compromise between the id and the superego, also dealt with the practical exigencies of the environment."[51] But, while Skinner states that "the facts which have been represented by such devices" as ego, superego, and id "cannot be ignored," he proceeds quickly to abolish the idea of "any analysis which appeals to a self or personality as an inner determiner of action."[52] This leaves the field wide open for bureaucracy and its masters to arrogate unto themselves not only the power to be determiners of action, but to claim a kind of legitimacy based on Skinner's concept of human nature as wide open to external manipulation.

In regard to mastery, Skinner specifically attacks the assumptions of traditional psychologies that specific types of action are discrete units in the psychological sense, a violation of which would raise heavy psychic costs. Such discrete units simply don't exist, Skinner asserts. Referring to work among pigeons, the kind of experiment that represents the staple for his generalizations about human nature, he notes:

> An operant [a piece of behavior] is not something which appears full grown in the behavior of the organism. It is the result of a continuous shaping process.
>
> The pigeon experiment demonstrates this clearly. "Raising the head" is not a discrete unit of behavior. It does not come, so to speak, in a separate package. We reinforce only slightly exceptional values of

---

*See "The Fallacy of the Ego" in the first section of this chapter.

the behavior observed while the pigeon is standing or moving about. We succeed in shifting the whole range of heights at which the head is held, but there is nothing which can be accurately described as a new "response." A response such as turning the latch in a problem box appears to be a more discrete unit, but only because the continuity with other behavior is more difficult to observe. In the pigeon, the response of pecking at a spot on the wall of the experimental box seems to differ from stretching the neck because no other behavior of the pigeon resembles it. If in reinforcing such a response we simply wait for it to occur — and we may have to wait many hours or days or weeks — the whole unit appears to emerge in its final form and to be strengthened as such. There may be no appreciable behavior which we could describe as "almost pecking the spot."[53]

We have cited this section at length to make the point that, with Skinner, what previous observers had thought to be clearly defined behaviors or pieces of behavior first become very fluid and secondly come to be determined not from the inside but from the outside.

From this position, it is only a small jump for Skinner to suggest that humans are so flexible in their behaviors that organizations can divide and subdivide their labors in almost any arbitrary way — just as long as each fragment of labor is properly and promptly reinforced.

With this suggestion Skinner not only produces a justification for the division of labor which both workers and traditional psychologists have criticized in modern life, but he manufactures a rationale for the necessity of having personal mastery taken away and reassigned to supervisory levels of the hierarchy. Only if the hierarchy — instead of the individual worker — exercises mastery over the total work to be done can it hand out rewards and punishments based on a rational and scientific analysis of how any given piece of labor integrates with the overall product or service.

In summary, we can add only a few words. Organizational changes in recent years have been of such quality that central concepts defining who man is were put in question. Either man was being distorted or the concepts were out of date. Traditional psychologists opted to attack modern organization as a distortion of man. Those of us who were raised in prebureaucratic areas and eras experienced a similar attack: when we entered bureaucracy we *felt* distorted. B. F. Skinner is the first psychologist to develop an entirely new system of psychology, internally coherent and cogent, that at least theoretically lifts the contradictions between the man of society and the man of bureaucracy. Eventually we must judge the accuracy of his vision. Nevertheless, his achievement temporarily remains in having resolved contradictions where other psychologies, both theoretically and practically, fell short. If Skinner's solution does not please us, then at least he has set a model of the kind of thing that must be done if the encounter between bureaucracy and society, with all its conflicts and agonies, is to be made easier for living people caught in the middle.

Organization Psychology: Edgar H. Schein

B. F. Skinner is by no means the last word on bureaucratic psychology. Beyond Skinner and Skinnerisms, there are actually scientists who still call themselves psychologists but who speak of the "psyche" of the organization. With these organization psychologists, the abandonment of the individual as possessed of a psyche is complete. Shorn of his autonomy and treated as devoid of any competence in choosing his fate, the individual is now treated as a fragment, a constituent part of the larger "psyche" of the bureaucratic organization. Instead of speaking of a human being's need to survive and adapt, organization psychologists now speak of the system's need to survive and adapt. Bureaucratic man must adjust to the survival needs of the system, the implication being that without the system he also dies.

Elevating the Machine as Psyche
The major paradox of organization psychology is that, as a component part of the organization mechanism, the individual is actually dead *within* the system — without a life of his own that he is permitted to live — yet is warned against an even more dire fate — death *without* the system. Increasingly, man in the bureaucratic system is therefore asked to choose between various kinds of death just as man in the concentration camp was forced to choose between varying gradations of evil. To what extent such paradoxes can be maintained over a long period of time has not yet been tested, but we can be sure it will be.

What do organization psychologists actually say?

Organization psychology is the "psychology" of the organization. It is the study of how the *organization* deals with the tension between internal needs and external challenges of adaptation.

Traditional psychology is the study of how individual *human beings* deal with the tension between internal needs and external challenges of adaptation. The "psyche" was the cognitive and emotional mediator between such needs and tensions. It was presumed to operate in a pattern or patterns. The "psyche" had a "logic" — a *psycho-logic*. Through this psycho-logic, each individual designed patterns of meeting adaptive challenges to himself as an organism. Among these patterns were social arrangements, such as engaging other people in a relationship for mutual protection, and eventually material arrangements — tool patterns, or *technologies*.

Technologies were extensions of psychologies. They provided tools, whether human or animal or material, through which the *psyche* could extend its *logic* of survival beyond the body. Yet, if we are correctly reporting the work of organization psychologists, the new "psychology" now deals with the logic of the *techne* to allow it to adapt to an environment *by using human beings as tools*.

If so, not only has the meaning of the term psychology been turned inside out, but what once was internal to man is now external to him. Psychology of old assumed that all action and meaning originated with man. Organization psychology, if we accuse it correctly, assumes that all action and meaning originates with the machine. As the old psychology loses its object — man — so man is lost to himself as an object of study for purposes of survival.

To the extent that psychology has always studied patterns people use to survive and is now studying patterns machines use to survive, the survival of man has ceased to be the central issue in the sentient universe.

Has psychology *really* become techno-psychology, or, more accurately, "technology" itself? Are we exaggerating?

Let an organization psychologist speak for himself. "Two examples," announces one textbook, "will highlight the difference between the traditional concerns and the 'new' questions which organizational psychology is raising." Let us see what these questions are: "First, given a rapidly changing technology which requires a great adaptive capacity on the part of organizations, how can an internal environment be created for the members of the organization which will enable them to grow in their own unique capacities?"[54]

The underlying assumption is that the major problem at stake is the requirement for "a great adaptive capacity." On the part of whom? The author is straightforward and unashamed: "on the part of organizations." Yet the human-centered psychologists among us might still detect a fundamental concern for the human organism in the question that follows: "How can an internal environment be created for the members of the organization which will enable them to grow in their own unique capacities?"

But the author of this text on techno-psychology has no intention of misleading us. His next sentence reveals what all this concern for human uniqueness is about: "The underlying assumption is that unless such personal growth takes place, the organization will not be prepared to cope effectively with an unpredictably changing external environment."[55] Human development stands exposed as a subordinate condition of organizational survival — *for the sake of* organizational survival.

The only parallel between this new science, which intends to learn how the organization can adapt, and what used to be known as psychology is in the concern for the integration and differentiation of subfunctions for the purpose of allowing the entire system — once organism, now organization — to survive.

The techno-psychologist gives this advice to the machine: you must pull all your parts together — especially the human parts — if you hope to survive! Can there any longer be any question but that the organization will now command its human components into order for the sake of its survival? That exactly this is the purpose of the new techno-psychology is affirmed by our author's very next statement:

> Second, how can organizations be designed to create optimum relationships between the various subgroups which tend to develop within them? For example, how can intergroup competition be converted to intergroup collaboration? The underlying assumption is that intergroup collaboration will be related both to over-all organizational effectiveness and to individual productivity and morale.[56]

Errors in the Model
The mechanistic model is here complete. The differentiation of the subsystem into groups and its integration of groups that collaborate here become the equivalent to psychology's ego, id and superego functions, if we choose the Freudian model. These functions must be both differentiated for healthful balance and integrated if the organism is not to be held back by internal resistances in its adaptive day-to-day efforts. What the new psychology, of course, misses is the difference between an organic and a mechanistic model. This becomes evident in an assumption that intergroup collaboration will necessarily favor overall organizational effectiveness.

Here the new techno-psychologist commits one certain error and a possible second one. First, he assumes he can pick up rules from an *organic* psychology and translate them into rules for the "psychology" of a machine. The integration of different functions in organic psychology, however, does *not* necessarily mean that the functions smoothly "collaborate" — i.e., without conflict. On the contrary, it often means that the organism is put onto a level of special adaptive alertness and capacity exactly because internal psychic functions working against one another have produced that state of tension that produces alertness. Thus ego-desires and superego rules may result in a strongly felt guilt propelling the individual into social action that is especially sensitive to the social rules and norms of others while optimizing the individual's adaptive position. To carry over, and mistranslate, rules from the psychology of organisms to the psychology of organizations is to commit certain error.*

The possible second error may lie in the assumption that that machine works best that works most smoothly. This may reflect ignorance, on the part of the psychologist involved, of factors that would not escape a real expert on the "technologic" of machines. An engineer would be thoroughly aware that stress and strain are as essential to the turning of the gears of a machine, which the "techno-psychologist" here appears to take as his model for organization, as the lubrication that ensures that the wheels and gears will turn. A machine, in other words, is an engineering compromise between load and mobility. Without load being placed on the parts, nothing will be conveyed from one end of the machine to the other; without mobility and smooth functioning of the parts, nothing will move. Load ensures *work* will be done; mobility ensures work will be *done*.

To assume therefore that there is no conflict in a machine, which is to say no stress or strain, is to assume the machine produces no work output. Now, while that may be true for some of our bureaucratic organizations, it is never true for a machine — unless Rube Goldberg invented it.

Since the present writer is not himself an engineer, he will content himself with the accusation of *possible* error in this case. But it can be suggested that words like "competition" and "collaboration," humanly defined, have no place in a machine model, and it is a machine model that the author attempts.

At the very least, we can conclude from this examination of one organization psychologist that a number of certain and possible errors underlie his conception that what he is doing is psychology.

First, since he admits that organization psychology deals with the logic necessary for the adaptative enterprise of organizations, not humans, and since organizations have no "psyche," he is *not* dealing with *psych*-ology. Where there is no psyche there can be no psychology.†

*Such error might possibly be avoided if an organic adaptive model were carried over into the analysis of large groups of human beings, treated as a survival enterprise in which individual capacities and population expansion were regarded as ultimate norms — that is, in a paradigm that puts the survival of human population groups in environmental *niches* at the center. Such a paradigm has been suggested in the biological sciences.

†Since the precursor of organization psychologists, B. F. Skinner, has already abolished the concept of psyche even as it applies to man, and replaced it with machine-made stimuli and responses, the organization psychologist can hardly develop at this point a "fall-back" position that argues his ultimate concern for the "psyche" of the organizational employe. Where the survival of the organization is the *sine qua non* of all else, humans cannot develop a psychology.

Second, to the extent that the organization of which organization psychologists are enamored is a "system" in the very same sense that a machine is, they had best surrender the field to those who know mechanical systems — systems theorists, engineers, mechanics, and technicians. None of these has of late, even jokingly, suggested that he is a "psychologist" of the machine.

Third, to the extent that an organization is not a machine, organization psychologists would be well advised to stop treating organizations as if they were anything more than tools to help human beings meet environmental challenges, tools the purpose of which every employe has a right to know and to approve, tools that can have no metaphysical purpose of their own.

To do otherwise is to continue to enshroud the purposes of those whom organizations still do serve — those who control them — and to disguise the point at which organizations serve no one.*

THE BUREAUCRATIC DRIVE

What drives people to continue to work in bureaucracy? Bureaucracy tears from them their conscience. It fragments their ego. It punishes and satisfies them at their lowest level by titillating the craving for power of the id or by threatening psychic identity. In contrast to the integrated personality of the nineteenth-century individual in the center of Sigmund Freud's psychology — with the ego as the mediating center between organism and environment, dominating superego and id† — the bureaucrat's personality is devastated. It is no longer possible to easily speak of the individual's personality as

*It should be noted that Schein's organization psychology is not the only one making the organization itself the unit of analysis. Where Schein indicates that the organization has a kind of psyche or that, at the least, it has its own psychology, Herbert Simon, for example, suggests the organization has a kind of biology: "A biological analogy is apt here, if we do not take it literally or too seriously. Organizations are assemblages of interacting human beings and they are the largest assemblages in our society that have anything resembling a central coordinative system. Let us grant that these coordinative systems are not developed nearly to the extent of the central nervous system in higher biological organisms — that organizations are more earthworm than ape. Nevertheless, the high specificity of structure and coordination within organizations — as contrasted with the diffuse and variable relations *among* organizations and among unorganized individuals — marks off the individual organization as a sociological unit comparable in significance to the individual organism in biology." (James G. March and Herbert A. Simon, *Organizations* [Pittsburgh: Graduate School of Industrial Administration — Carnegie Institute of Technology; John Wiley and Sons, 1958], p. 4.) This vision is of interest because it signifies that, for analytical purposes at least, the organization is being placed alongside living organisms. Such originally scientific models have a habit of filtering into the general populace and becoming an ideology, especially when there is a strong group of people in whose interest it is to promulgate such an ideology — the functionaries themselves.

†The free enterpriser is the model of the individual who in that reality actualized that personality, but we all strove for the ideal.

"belonging" to him. It is more accurate to say that instead of a personality, which the individual carries with him wherever he goes, there is a role identity. The individual slips into his role identity when he enters his office — and desperately tries not to let this cloak slip from his shoulders when he leaves at the end of the day.

The Bonds of Bureaucracy

To an outsider, who can understand such clinging to office because of the status and class position it brings, the bureaucrat's intense devotion to office and duty is incomprehensible. To us it must seem clear that his office is his prison, his duty his chains. As Max Weber mourned in a related work: "But fate decreed that the cloak should become an iron cage."[57]

To what fundamental human need could the cold machine of bureaucracy possibly appeal to find perennial recruits to scrape and paint the rusting structure, to grease the cogs, to put their shoulder to the very same wheels destined to run over them?

It is easy to understand the bonds that tie us to other social orders. In fear of chaos, we flock to the charismatic leader.[58] Bound by loves and routines first experienced in the family with our father and mother, we submit to the traditional authority of societies and subsocieties in which the head or the institutions symbolize the father.[59] But what could possibly be the emotional need that is satisfied by the most impersonal of orders — bureaucracy?

If we take Weber's famous characteristics of bureaucracy, we are confronted with amazing preferences manifest in the behavior of bureaucrats. While historically we can still have empathy with the motivations of our forefathers, who deserted traditional farms to flock to the cities — escaping the often arbitrary rule of fathers for the sibling egalitarianism of modernity — we can only wonder why free men would willingly subjugate themselves to a rule a thousand times stricter than any father's — the dominion of bureaucracy.

In the family and in traditional society, where the sons owe everything they have to the father or the subjects and vassals to the lord, we can understand the sense of personal obligation that commands the sons or vassals, like an inner voice, to come to the aid of the father or lord. But in bureaucracy, as Weber points out, "official duties" replace personal obligation.[60] Yet duty is always to an empty office, not to the person occupying it. We salute, as the saying goes in armed forces all over the world, the uniform, not the man. How, possibly, could the cold and impersonal sense of duty be as intense and effective a loyalty to an organization as the sense of obligation was a safe and certain guarantee for the life of traditional society? All affect, has by definition, been formally removed from the relationship between subordinate and superior; in fact, the relationship between persons has been replaced by a relationship between offices. If there is nothing more binding than affect, how is it that nevertheless we find the bureaucrat bound more strongly to the organization than was any other subordinate at any other time?

Weber sheds some light on this matter. In bureaucracy, he states, "The authority to give commands required for the discharge of these duties is distributed in a stable way and is strictly limited by rules concerning the coercive means, physical, sacerdotal, or otherwise, which may be placed at the disposal of officials."[61] We can understand that bureaucrats may prefer a bureaucracy where "authority . . . is distributed in a stable way" over the ad hoc and unsystematic — and therefore unpredictable — exercise of authority in traditional society. Similarly we can empathize with a preference for "authority . . . strictly delimited by rules concerning coercive means." It is nice to know what one is being punished for, what the limits of punishment are, and to have the rules and limits set before the act that brings punishment or reward down on us. In contrast, familial authority, especially in the psychological sphere, is to this day often willful and arbitrary, and rules are ex post facto — which gives us some idea what things were like under the paternal rule of a medieval lord or an absolute monarch, two examples of domination in premodern times.

But why the dedication to hierarchy* and jurisdiction? † Why the incomparably desperate need to know where one resides in a bureaucracy, what one's place is in the chain of command, and the nearly territorial and definitely aggressive defense of jurisdiction — the officially defined area within which the bureaucrat is able to practice his competence? And, finally, why are the "good" bureaucrats never satiated with what they have?

There is a near-hysteria in the activities of most "personality types" which Anthony Downs, then of the Rand Corporation, observed among bureaucrats. In these descriptions, we are inundated with a vast outpouring of energy by officials on behalf of their officialdom: "The peculiarities of zealots' behavior spring from two characteristics: the *narrowness* of their *sacred* policies, and the *implacable energy* they focus solely upon promoting those policies." They *"trample* all obstacles," they are *"tremendously desirous* of procuring

---

*Weber, *Economy and Society*, p. 957. Point II: "The principles of office hierarchy and of levels of graded authority mean a firmly ordered system of super- and subordination . . ."

†Ibid. Point I: "There is the principle of fixed and official jurisdictional areas, which are generally ordered by rules, that is, by laws or administrative regulations."

more resources," they "*agitate* for *extremely intensive expansion* of a few policies."[62]

Another type, the climber, "seeks to *maximize* his own *power, income,* and *prestige,* he *always desires more* of these goods." "If a climber cannot *aggrandize* by creating wholly new functions, he will seek to '*capture*' functions performed by persons whose power of resistance is low."[63]

And so on through several more types. Even the "conserver" displays a personal intensity shocking to anyone who like Weber sees bureaucracy as a place where officials behave "*sine ira ac studio*" — without hatred or passion. Conservers "seek to *maximize* their *security* and *convenience,*" they are "essentially *change avoiders,*" and they pursue this goal with a vengeance: "many conservers *eschew* even the *slightest deviation* from written procedures unless they obtain approval from higher authority." They are characterized by "*extreme rigidity.*"[64]

It is impossible, even in the most negative and defensive of these personalities — to say nothing of the aggressive ones — to avoid the sense that we are experiencing an inner intensity behind action or inaction that can only appear as strange in this structural paragon of rationalistic organization.

In sum, the bureaucrat seems constantly to be running a race for survival. Even the conserver cannot stand still, though he merely wants to remain what he is. All are involved in a struggle that ceases only in death. How did this become so?

A career in a bureaucracy, especially under the protection of formalized civil service commissions and officials' rights enshrined in law, seems the most secure of professions. The most often cited reason for entering the police force and the fire department of New York City, mentioned always with great shock during the layoffs of 1975 – 1976, was security.[65]

Yet on what does that security depend? It is in effect a substitute security that can be only institutionally maintained. It is not an inner security. In fact, any "good" bureaucracy in its recruitment, selection, and training programs will attempt to dissolve the personal inner security that stems from an integrated personality based on ego-centrism, a private sense of conscience, and strict personal control of urges of the id. Only if the recruit can be separated from his "private" superego will he reliably yield to the norms of the bureaucracy. Only once separated from the need for an integrated ego will he accept the division of labor as a way of life. Only if his self-control over urges of the id is loosened, does his id become "freed" — for manipulation by outsiders.

What is at issue always in the rite of passage from society to bureaucracy is the paramount need of the bureaucracy for reliable officials. To satisfy that need, bureaucracy restructures personality. The questions we have asked so far all revolve around the nature of this personality.

The Bureaucratic Personality

There is a distinct "bureaucratic personality" that cuts across the various "role identities" associated with different tasks and different office levels in different bureaucracies. We have already suggested what it does: bureaucracy tears people from their conscience. It fragments their ego. It punishes and satisfies them at their lowest level — through the id.

One striking characteristic of the "bureaucratic personality" however is that it does not "belong" to the individual, but is a set of relationships with subordinates, superordinates, and peers and is therefore achieved only in that situation in which these relationships are brought to life — at the office.

What does this mean? Contrast the personality of the bureaucrat with the personality of the individual familiar in Freudian psychology. The three main personality structures of the individual personality are the ego, the superego, the id. The ego serves as the integrating center of the psyche. It receives pressures for adjustment and adaptation from the individual's environment. Its range of response is limited on the one hand by the norms and mores contained in the internalized library of cultural patterns — the superego. Its need to respond is pressed upon it by the various biological drives of the id.

In the role of the free enterpriser in industrial society, this personality type finds its utmost fulfillment. Ego-dominance over the other structures is clearcut there. The self as ego is foremost in all decisions of adjustment and adaptation to the environment, and the devil — the superego and id — take the hindmost. This is not to say that the individualist is amoral, but as John Stuart Mill regretfully had to conclude, when there is a final conflict between the ego and society, ego comes first.[66]

The task of the psychologist, as healer in a culture that thus defined the psyche, was always to reintegrate the three structures where they had been torn apart, with the ego on top. The task of the construction of a bureaucratic personality is the exact opposite.

Let us ask ourselves what has happened to the dominance of ego when the individual turns bureaucrat. First of all, specialization and the division of labor make certain that there shall be no one complete psychic structure in any single official that can possibly integrate all the various environmental pressures impinging upon the issue of his or her survival. The bureaucrat knows that his job is part of a team task and that only with other individual bureaucrats will he be able to fulfill his assigned mission. If there is an ego to do any integrating of an adaptive task, it is always a series of fragmentary egos, each belonging to a different individual, all of which must combine their specialized and divided skills to accomplish the task.

Next we can ask where bureaucrats take their norms from. The individualist could still conform to an internalized superego where immediate ego advantage to himself was not easily apparent. Where is the bureaucrat's superego, his reference system of values? All those acquainted with bureaucracy understand that they are supposed to leave their personal biases, values, and beliefs at home when they enter their offices. Certainly we cannot expect to find a "private" internalized superego within the bureaucrat. Further, the very nature of bureaucracy requires, as Weber said very clearly, "the supervision of lower offices by higher ones."[67] An office may possess its own delegated authority, and in fact its own code books and rules.[68] But the sources of the norms for official acts are always outside the individual bureaucrat: they lie structurally embedded in the office in which the bureaucrat works or they reside in the office directly above his. Even the professional, who may have the illusion of individuality based on an internalized professional code, is a member of a profession exactly and only so long as other members of that profession agree that he is following *externally* arrived at rules — that is, rules on which there is agreement by the community of scientists, engineers, doctors, or other professionals.

In this sense, if we can still speak of the existence of a personality structure called the superego, it is an *externalized* superego. In a seeming miracle of making the invisible visible, bureaucratic organization has taken a psychic structure of mere conceptual existence,* but nevertheless invisible, residing inside an individual's head, and made it material and open to the inspection of all outside the individual in the structure of the organization. What used to take the skilled probing of the in-depth psychologist now is written clearly into rule- and code-books as information available even to those least skilled in psychology.

Unless the administrative efficiency and the vastly increased probabilities of control, as the central values of bureaucratization, are

---

*The three components of the human psyche — ego, superego, and id — can be conceived as structures only for theoretical purposes. It is not possible, obviously, to find a physical location in the brain that could be called the location of the superego. On the question of a structural paradigm of the psyche, see also Paul Roazen, *Freud*, pp. 66, 71 – 73, 222.

themselves to be vitiated — and the need for a bureaucracy thereby reduced to zero* — then the official must be trained and conditioned to accept the essential precondition of efficiency and control, that is, acceptance of the rules of the office and of orders from above.

So far we have made three points about the bureaucratic personality:

1. An integrated personality exists for the bureaucrat only to the extent that each shares his or her "self" with others.

2. Specifically, the bureaucrat's ego is fragmented in that he or she is allowed to bring to bear on questions of official response to outside stimuli — demands from clients, for example — only those ego characteristics officially relevant to an acquired specialization and assigned division of labor. Only together with ego fragments provided by other bureaucrats can the overall environmental challenge constituted by such tasks be resolved.

3. Specifically also, the bureaucrat surrenders his or her internalized superego to domination by an externalized superego. The latter is a superego only in the sense that it constitutes the reference library of norms for an entire team or office or even bureau. It is never a private or personalized superego, relevant only to the individual bureaucrat. †

The bureaucratic drive that makes the entire machinery of bureaucracy tick on the basis of hidden affective motivations, quite aside from any dedication to rational goals such as efficiency, springs from the integration of the bureaucrat into structures that at one and the same time constantly deprive him of *personal identity* and supply him with *institutional identity*. Bureaucracy, in other words, has plugged into the most basic of drives — the drive to be. The bureaucratic drive is a fight for identity and existence.

How do bureaucratic structures accomplish the ongoing mobilization of the bureaucratic drive?

From Ego-Dominant Psychology to Id Psychology

Bureaucracy, in sum, appears as the instrument that replaces ego-dominant psychology with id psychology. Having externalized the

---

*If bureaucracy does not give us these main advantages, which are its claim to fame, why have it at all?

†The question whether the terms "individual" and "bureaucrat" are semantically compatible will have to be raised elsewhere. For now we can suggest that functionally speaking the individual organism acting as bureaucrat can no longer be a unit of analysis. The unit of analysis in bureaucratic situations, if we are to understand the behavior of bureaucracies, will always have to be, as Mary Parker Follett saw early on, the "situation" or, more accurately, "teams" of bureaucrats in situations. See Mary Parker Follett, "The Giving of Orders," in D. S. Pugh, ed., *Organization Theory: Selected Readings* (Baltimore: Penguin, 1971), pp. 147 – 165.

superego through the replacement of private norms with official ones, and having fragmented the ego through the division of labor, thus denying the possibility of individual adaptation that is autonomous and apart from the collaboration of others, bureaucracy is a structure that directly commands the id.

In general, bureaucratic structures, such as hierarchy and separate roles that reflect the division of labor, directly appeal to, and become the means for satisfying, the human organism's urge to live as comprised in the id.

Specifically, we can now understand why ego-dominant psychology has been decisively defeated within the confines of industrial and organizational psychology. There the concern is understandably with the relationships between organizational structure and the id. The time is past when one could say with Freud that "all our social institutions are framed for people with a united and normal ego, which one can classify as good or bad, which either fulfills its function or is altogether eliminated by an overpowering influence."[69] The institutions that dominate the bureaucratic world promote no "united and normal ego." The choice between ego function in the sense of an autonomous, self-directing individual and the elimination of ego by "an overpowering influence" has long been made.

Id psychology already has a long and well-defined history within the area of bureaucratic organization, ranging from those who focus on the direct manipulation of the id through stimulus-response behaviorism;[70] to the application of old socialization techniques to elicit distinct id capacities, conceptualized as "motives";[71] to the situational psychologists who focus on finding organizational structures that promote work output;[72] and finally to those abandoning concern with the individual altogether in an attempt to group individual ids into a component of an organizational "psyche."[73]

Despite the association with industrial humanism of some of these writers, their dominant theme is always the adaptation of the individual to the organization and, ultimately, with organization psychology, the adaptativeness of the organization to its environment.

Their underlying theme is that the individual is, in the end, infinitely moldable if only the right kind of organizational structures can be discovered, designed, and applied. For them all, the bureaucracy itself has become the ego. Its structures exert a legitimate claim to a normative monopoly replacing the individual's superego. The individual merely continues to provide the energy to live; it is the organization's task to translate that energy into the energy to work.

These assumptions have become so ingrained that they are no longer made explicit. Yet for the manipulator and the manipulated alike, their rediscovery means the recognition of the basic psychological principles on which continues to rest the bureaucrat's "voluntary" imprisonment in his "iron cage."

SUMMARY

The personality of bureaucratic man emerges from psychological analysis eviscerated and fragmented. Specific organizational structures take over the role of what in society were "inner" psychic structures. In denying the individual a sense of mastery over his work, the division of labor both fragments and externalizes his ego. To constitute something resembling an ego, the collaboration of several individuals now is necessary.* There can be an "ego" of the team, but never an ego of the individual. † Secondly, the division of labor makes necessary supervision by the next higher office in the hierarchy; only so can we achieve the integration of the fragmented work processes according to central norms. Hierarchy therefore takes over and externalizes the functions of the formerly internalized superego. This means externalization of ultimate knowledge of what is right and wrong. With it disappears the inner psychic dynamic capable of enforcing such knowledge. The functionary is stripped of his conscience. He becomes more pliable to direction from outside and above. We can speculate at this point that the development of the conscienceless or guiltless generation associated with the recent "hippie" subculture reflects the penetration of the new bureaucratic psychology into the social realm. The dilettantism prevailing in a generation lacking competence for mastery over any craft is not at all incompatible with the ever-increasing division of labor that makes possible the employment of morons for ever more moronic jobs. The freeing of libido from the controls of conscience further provides,

---

*The desperate socializing activities on the job of people thus fragmented was mistaken by the researchers of the human-relations school as authentic "social" activity. In reality it was nothing of the sort. It was an attempt at saving identity long after the conditions for true social relationships had long been destroyed by the new structuring of work.

†The recent choruses of praise that have accompanied the official emergence of the "team" to spur production in situations where fragmentation *ad absurdum* has wrought disaster needs further investigation. For one thing, it is doubtful, on the basis of bureaucratic psychology, that the productive or administrative team in any way constitutes a return to the humane voluntary associations that existed in society. Rather than constituting self-actualization, what is being actualized is the team, and what is being confirmed thereby is the division of labor that made the team necessary to begin with. For several examples of "substituting closure for a linear division of labor," see the excellent text by George E. Berkley, *The Craft of Public Administration* (Boston: Allyn and Bacon, 1975), pp. 468 – 469.

during off-duty hours, a handy outlet for those energies of the id that the bureaucracy cannot utilize.*

The neutralization of ego and superego finally makes accessible to direct outside control the energies reposing in the individual's id. The psychology of bureaucracy is an id psychology. The psychology of society, with its emphasis on self-control and mastery, was an ego psychology. The psychology of community, with its emphasis on the internalization of communal norms and their primacy in guiding individual behavior, was a superego psychology.

Finally, initial investigation into the dynamics of the new bureaucratic psychology shows that bureaucracy is able to control its functionaries for the simple reason that, having stripped them of their inner resources of mastery and conscience, it supplies them with a reason for continuing to live. By replacing personality with an institutional identity, bureaucracy seizes the ultimate power of determining whether or not any functionary will have any being at all.

What motivates the bureaucrat is the basic drive to assure himself of existence and identity. He pursues this drive by clinging as tightly as he can to the externalized structures of his psyche. Because these structures happen to coincide with the structures of bureaucracy, his being is essentially dissolved into the being of bureaucracy itself.

This development strictly follows the logic of a form of administration that from the beginning insisted on a tendency toward absolute integration of the functionary for the sake of maximizing control. † Therefore the ultimate psychology should not surprise us.

---

*That this penetration is not merely a passing fad is supported by a Daniel Yankelovich survey taken in 1974 which reported that "working-class young people in the United States are taking on many of the attitudes on sex, politics, patriotism, religion, the family, morals, and lifestyle that marked college student thinking of five years ago." Reflecting the spread of new values to noncollege youth, the following changes were recorded between 1969 and 1973 [corresponding figures for college students in brackets]: Number of noncollege youth between 16 and 25 who "would welcome more acceptance of sexual freedom": 1969 — 22%; 1973 — 47% [43%; 61%]; number feeling "casual premarital sexual relations are morally wrong": 1969 — 57%; 1973 — 34% [34%; 22%]; number feeling "relations between consenting homosexuals are morally wrong": 1969 — 72%; 1973 — 47% [42%; 25%]; number believing "having an abortion is morally wrong": 1969 — 64%; 1973 — 48% [36%; 32%]; number feeling "living a clean moral life is a very important value": 1969 — 77%; 1973 — 57% [45%; 34%]; number feeling "religion is a very important value": 1969 — 64%; 1973 — 42% [38%; 28%]; number feeling "patriotism is a very important value": 1969 — 60%; 1973 — 40% [35%; 19%]; number believing that "hard work always pays off": 1969 — 79%; 1973 — 56% [56%; 44%]; number who would welcome "less emphasis on money": 1969 — 54%; 1973 — 74% [73%; 80%]. ("Survey Finds Young U.S. Workers Increasingly Dissatisfied and Frustrated," *The New York Times*, May 22, 1974, p. 45.) One does have to wonder, of course, about just what is being measured when "attitudes" are said to change so radically. At least there is evidence here that *something* is very pliable in the way people report their orientations toward values representing the absolutes of a by-gone social world.

†See chapter 2, the section on the bureaucratic imperative.

Indeed it should endow us with an understanding leading to both an empathy for the bureaucrat and the insight that the psychological difference between society and bureaucracy is not merely a matter of variation on the human theme. It is the termination of the theme.

NOTES

1. Max Weber, *Economy and Society: An Outline of Interpretive Sociology*, 3 vols., eds. Guenther Roth and Claus Wittich, trans. E. Fischoff *et al.* (New York: Bedminster Press, 1968), p. 998. Professional expert here is a general term that includes professionals, managers (professional of management), and functionaries specializing in some substantive or procedural expertise. See the entire section of "Bureaucracy and Education," pp. 998 – 1002.

2. Interview with the author, May 1975. Anonymity requested.

3. Interview with the author, May 1975. Anonymity requested.

4. Max Weber, "Parlament und Regierung im neugeordneten Deutschland," in *Gesammelte Politische Schriften* (Tübingen: J.C.B. Mohr, 1958), p. 323. This essay appears as "Parliament and Government in a Reconstructed Germany," in Max Weber, *Economy and Society*, pp. 1381 – 1469. I have here preferred my own translation.

5. Weber, *Economy and Society*, p. 968.

6. In Freud's own words, the ego is "an intellective activity which, after considering the present state of things and weighing earlier experiences, endeavors by means of experimental actions to calculate the consequences of the proposed line of conduct . . ." (Sigmund Freud, *An Outline of Psychoanalysis* [New York: W.W. Norton, 1936].)

7. Frederick W. Taylor, "Letter to Mr. Rob't P. Linderman, Pres., Bethlehem Iron Co., Jan. 19, 1898," reprinted in Frank Barkley Copley, *Frederick W. Taylor: Father of Scientific Management*, vol. 2 (New York: Harper and Brothers, 1923), pp. 10 – 12.

8. See Studs Terkel, *Working: People Talk About What They Do All Day and How They Feel About What They Do* (New York: Random House, Pantheon Books, 1974).

9. Taylor, in Copley, *Frederick W. Taylor*, p. 11.

10. F.J. Roethlisberger, *Management and Morale* (Cambridge, Mass.: Harvard University Press, 1941), p. 24 – 25.

11. Ibid.

12. Ibid., p. 24.

13. My thanks to Professor Charles Hayes of the Department of Government, Seton Hall University, who shared with me the preliminary results of a survey on bureaucrats' fears about seeking a career outside bureaucracy.

14. Roethlisberger, *Management and Morale*, pp. 24 – 25.

15. Ibid.

16. Paul Roazen, *Freud: Political and Social Thought* (New York: Knopf, 1968), p. 247.

17. For an understanding of what communal life is like psychologically, see the example Bruno Bettelheim draws from the kibbutzim of our contemporary era in *Children of the Dream: Communal Child-Rearing and American Education* (New York: Avon Books, 1970). See especially his concept of the "collective superego" in contrast to the individual superego of man in society, pp. 142 – 143.

18. Roazen, *Freud*, p. 234.

19. Ibid., p. 233 ff.

20. James Strachey, ed., *The Standard Edition of the Complete Works of Sigmund Freud* (London: Hogarth, 1955), vol. 9, p. 237.

21. Roazen, *Freud*, p. 248.

22. For the definitive work on the meaning of modern liberalism since Hobbes, and on the elective affinity of Hobbesian-Lockean politics and Lutheran-Calvinist theology, see H. Mark Roelofs, *Ideology and Myth in American Politics: A Critique of a National Political Mind* (Boston: Little, Brown, 1976).

23. See B.F. Skinner, *Science and Human Behavior* (New York: The Free Press, 1965), and Edgar H. Schein, *Organizational Psychology* (Englewood Cliffs, N.J.: Prentice-Hall, 1965). See also the section on Skinner and Schein below. Thus, for example, psychiatrist Gregory Zilboorg, in commenting on "this sacrifice of the individual, " speaks of a "disindividualized concept of the human personality" and the "rather sickening phenomenon of the disindividualization of man in favor of his serving the social, or mass machine." (Gregory Zilboorg, "The Changing Concept of Man in Present-Day Psychiatry," in Benjamin Nelson, ed., *Freud and the 20th Century* [Gloucester, Mass.: Peter Smith, 1974], pp. 31 – 38.)

24. Freud, *Group Psychology and the Analysis of the Ego* (New York: Boni and Liveright, undated), p. 1.

25. Corbett H. Thigpen and Hervey M. Cleckley, *The Three Faces of Eve* (New York: Popular Library, 1957).

26. I am taking this phrase from the title of Ernest Keen's summary of existential psychology, *Three Faces of Being: Toward an Existential Clinical Psychology* (New York: Appleton-Century-Crofts, 1970).

27. Ibid., p. 59.

28. Ibid.

29. Ibid., p. 46. Keen continues: "This is a highly subtle and yet very important phenomenon. When the child presents himself to his parents as 'good' and knows he is 'bad,' that is not a lie-for-oneself. But when a child invests so much in the being-good-for-his parents that it becomes an overwhelming concern, then his honesty in confronting himself is likely to suffer. Extremely punitive parents, therefore, undermine the child's honesty with himself. The experience of guilt can be so threatening that one effectively loses control with what one really feels or desires. In the place of this honest reckoning of oneself emerges an 'idealized self,' as Horney (1950) has called it, which may come to dominate one's entire being." Keen here refers to Karen Horney, *Neurosis and Human Growth* (New York: W.W. Norton, 1950). An interesting application of this theory of child development would be an investigation of the childhood of former President Richard M. Nixon, with whom the press experienced the great difficulty of finding the "real" Nixon.

30. Ibid., pp. 330 – 331.

31. Ibid., p. 331.

32. Ibid.

33. Ibid., pp. 331 – 332.

34. "Bomb Kills Two at Israel Airport," *The New York Times*, May 26, 1976, p. 5.

35. Michael Corleone, son of a Mafia Chief, in Mario Puzo's *The Godfather* (Greenwich, Conn.: Fawcett, Crest Book, 1969), p. 146.

36. B.F. Skinner, *Beyond Freedom and Dignity* (New York: Bantam/Vintage, 1972), p. 19.

37. Ibid.

38. Ibid., p. 15.

39. Ibid., p. 16. Here Skinner distinguishes his model from the simple stimulus-response models of Pavlovianism.

40. Ibid.

41. Ibid., p. 16.

42. Ibid. My summary of chapter 1 of *Beyond Freedom and Dignity* entitled "A Technology of Behavior," pp. 1 – 23. See especially p. 197.

43. B.F. Skinner, *Science and Human Behavior* (New York: The Free Press, 1965), p. 287.

44. Ibid., p. 437

45. Ibid., p. 65.

46. Ibid., p. 91.

47. Ibid., p. 96.

48. Studs Terkel, *Working: People Talk About What They Do All Day and How They Feel About What They Do* (New York: Avon Books, 1975), pp. 21 – 22.

49. Ibid., pp. 9 – 10.

50. Ibid., pp. 1 – 2.

51. Skinner, *Science and Human Behavior*, p. 284.

52. Ibid.

53. Ibid., pp. 91 – 92.

54. Edgar H. Schein, *Organizational Psychology* (Englewood Cliffs, N.J.: Prentice-Hall, 1965), p. 4.

55. Ibid.

56. Ibid.

57. Max Weber, *The Protestant Ethic and the Spirit of Capitalism*, trans. Talcott Parsons (New York: Scribner's, 1958), p. 181. Weber is equating the entire modern economic order with his "iron cage."

58. The point is made in regard to heroes by Freud in his *Totem and Taboo*. The relationship of Freud's analysis to the study of charisma is pursued in R.P. Hummel, "Psychology of Charismatic Followers," *Psychological Reports*, 37 (December 1975), 759 – 770.

59. This original Freudian point is developed in Eric H. Erikson, *Insight and Responsibility* (New York: W.W. Norton, 1964), p. 206, and in *Gandhi's Truth* (New York: W.W. Norton, 1969).

60. Max Weber, "Bureaucracy," in *Economy and Society*, pp. 956 – 1005. A most striking passage: "It is decisive for the modern loyalty to an office that, in the pure type, it does not establish a relationship to a *person*, like the vassal's or disciple's faith under feudal or patrimonial authority, but rather is devoted to *impersonal* and *functional* purposes." (p. 959) Weber's italics.

61. Ibid., p. 956.

62. Anthony Downs, *Inside Bureaucracy* (Boston: Little, Brown, 1967), pp. 109 – 110. (All italics in the citations from Downs are mine for emphasis of the degree of affectivity evident in the motivations of bureaucrats.)

63. Ibid., pp. 92, 95.

64. Ibid., pp. 96, 97, 100.

65. Personal conversations with 250 New York City policemen and firemen, spring 1975 through winter 1975 – 76.

66. John Stuart Mill, *On Liberty*, various editions.

67. Weber, *Economy and Society*, p. 197.

68. Ibid.

69. Sigmund Freud, *The Standard Edition of the Complete Psychological Works of Sigmund Freud*, ed., J. Strachey (London: Hogarth and Institute of Psycho-analysis, 1961), vol. 20, p. 221.

70. The focus on behaviorism can be traced as far back as J.B. Watson's famous aphorism asserting his ability to turn a child into a being capable of exercising any role identity — as long as the child was given to him at an early enough age. In *Beyond Freedom and Dignity* Skinner dismisses ego and ego autonomy as illusions, calls social norms like freedom and dignity irrelevant to actual behavior and its manipulation, and zeroes in on specific techniques of evoking from what is left of the psyche — the id — responses desired by external structures.

71. David C. McClelland specifically concerned himself with the forms of socialization that could evoke the id's orientations toward "achievement" and "power." See, for example, his well-known *The Achieving Society* (Princeton: Van Nostrand, 1961). McClelland's propositions boil down to a form similar to the behaviorists though the terminology of socialization literature is retained: any child if placed under the proper stimulus can become power-oriented or achievement-oriented. Superego and ego resistance are irrelevant if the child is "stimulated" or "socialized" young enough.

72. Mary Parker Follet in Henry C. Metcalfe and Lyndall Urwick, *Dynamic*

Administration (New York: Harper & Row, 1940); Fred E. Fiedler, "Leadership — A New Model," *Discovery*, April 1965; for a collection: C.A. Gibb, ed. *Leadership* (Baltimore: Penguin, 1969).

73. See Warren G. Bennis, "Toward a 'Truly' Scientific Management: The Concept of Organizational Health," *General Systems Yearbook*, 1962, vol. 7, pp. 269 – 282; David M. McGregor, *The Human Side of Enterprise* (New York: McGraw-Hill, 1960); and Edgar H. Schein, *Organizational Psychology*.

4

The Language of Bureaucracy

Bureaucratic administration always tends to exclude the public, to hide its knowledge. . . . The treasury officials of the Persian Shah have made a secret science of their budgetary art and even use a secret script.

— *Max Weber*[1]

Language used to separate countries. Today it separates bureaucracy from its clients in society, functionaries from one another, and even managers from employes.

HOW PEOPLE TALK

One-Directional and Acausal Language

The language of society was causal ("You started it.") and two-directional ("But let's talk this over."). The language of bureaucracy is one-directional (Manager: "Just follow the orders!") and acausal (Manager again: "And don't ask questions why!"). Try to talk back. Try to find somebody to talk back to.

Clients and customers feel this one-directionality most acutely when they try to talk back to a computer; they don't know computer language and even if they did the program would not allow them to be heard. The complainant who asks after the identity of the miscreant who set up the program is effectively blocked by that very program from pursuing the question. The computer, through its requirement for specialized language knowledge to operate it, protects its operators from attempts by laymen to find the cause of their discomfort and powerlessness. Once programmed, the computer talks only one-way, from the top down. Its language is one-directional. The fact that the language itself contains no clues as to why the program was set up in one way and not another means it is also acausal.

One-directionality and acausality are the two major characteristics not only of computer language but of bureaucratic language in general, of which computer language is an advanced case. One-directionality as a language characteristic permits the functionary to receive a message from the top of the bureaucracy and pass it on in only one direction, down. For the client, one-directionality means he cannot talk at all, only listen. Acausality as a language characteristic manifests itself in structuring what is said in such a manner that the message itself can never be subjected to analysis as to its *bona fides*: Who sent it? Has the person who sent it a right to send it? Is the content in keeping with ultimate social norms of right and wrong?

The typical bureaucratic order is, "In case of reality No. 1003, do prescribed action No. 112!" There is no clue here as to origin or legitimacy of the order (acausality). The only choice left to the recipient is to engage in the action commanded; such action is always action down the hierarchy (one-directionality). The typical computer-language equivalent is, as we shall see later, "If ———, then go to ——— ."

Just as one-directionality and acausality in computer language guarantee the one-way unfolding of the predetermined program without unscheduled delays by subcomponents asking undue questions, bureaucratic language in general guarantees one of the chief characteristics of modern bureaucratic institutions: top-down control.

Functionaries: Police and Firefighters

Employes experience bureaucratic language always in the imperative voice and bureaucratic communications as always coming from the top, that is, as one-directional: "When the orders come down, you can't talk back." Or in terms of the favorite gripe of the policemen I used to teach: "We're the guys who know what's going on in the street better than anybody. You'd think they'd want to know about that upstairs. But the hardest thing for us is to try and get to talk to them." Employes often tend to attribute causality to the commands they receive; that is, they assume there is both a reason and a person behind them. This assumption is erroneous to the extent that the officer in charge does not act on behalf of the office and the organization at large in personal terms. Nevertheless, the favorite line in a large East Coast fire department undergoing painful management changes is: "If it weren't for ——— [the fire commissioner] all these changes wouldn't be happening to us."[2]

Ironically, the habit of one-directionality — being talked to from above or talking to others from a power position that forbids back talk from below — also makes it harder for functionaries to talk to one another. "It's hard to talk with people in other specialties in your own company," observes a personnel officer of the General Electric Company. "It's as if you have different vocabularies."[3]

But in answering his own question by observing one fact of bureaucratic life — different specialties have different vocabularies — the personnel officer here overlooks a much more important question. Why is it that people in bureaucracy persist in having this difficulty? Why don't they just start talking to one another and explain what the language of each specialty means? The answer is that once a technical language has been set up, it is no longer subject to redefinition, especially by outsiders. The language of a specialty is an imperative language. You learn it or you never will be able to talk to the man or woman practicing that specialty. The practitioners are not free to redefine their vocabularies in a two-way exchange with you. To do so would be to weaken their knowledge of their own field and their capacity to talk with fellow specialists. This is the professional answer. There is also the bureaucratic answer: because specialists are also bureaucrats, they are not in the habit of allowing two-way conversation on such essential tools of their power as the language they use.

Thus there are two reasons for the linguistic separation of people. To open up a specialized language to outsiders means to weaken a professional's ability to speak with fellow insiders. One-directionality also is so ingrained that insiders see no reason to open up, especially as long as staying closed in their vocabulary forces outsiders either into ignorance or into the submissive posture of having to learn the language and as long as keeping a closed system is rewarded by peer relations.

Managers are ultimately paid off in the coinage of the language they use. They talk through power; employes pay them back through resistance. One-directionality and acausality may be essential characteristics of bureaucracy as an ideal control instrument, but many modern bureaucracies are mixed organizations, not yet quite perfectly bureaucratized. Their inhabitants often make social demands: they insist on being able to talk back and they want to know to whom they can trace an order. In the same fire department mentioned above, a high-level manager complained, after having instituted a special program for improving manager-functionary communications: "We just can't be sure at our level that anything we say will get past the battalion chief level. There seems to be a breakdown there." The breakdown in this case was not the fault of subordinate managers who might have failed to push communications on down the line, but the result of resistance thrown up by oldtimers in the lower ranks against a new managerial system imposed from the top.

Clients: A Man on Social Security

The client is the ultimate victim of the language barrier that bureaucracy erects — and not necessarily an unconscious one. In the client all the conflicts between bureaucracy and society come to rest. Listen to Pasquale Plescia, who went by bus from California to Washington, D.C., to find out about delays in his Social Security checks:

> Well, I'll tell you something about this town. They got a secret language here. You know that? Bureaucratese. Same thing we used to call double-talk. These government people, they don't hear you. They don't listen. You start to say something and they shut you out mentally, figuring they know right away what you're going to say before you say it.
>
> I knocked on doors here for two weeks but everyone's so busy with paperwork, they got no time for nothing else. I go to see one Congressman — a priest, so I figure he's got humanitarian interests — and his aide says I got to write him a letter first. Another one won't let me in cause I'm not in his constituency. Another gives me a press release and says, "This is the Congressman's position on Social Security." No kidding, that happened. So I go down to HEW. They've got 180,000 people working for HEW, and you know what? They've got nobody to make a complaint to.[4]

The client's misunderstanding of bureaucracy is classical. He assumes bureaucrats are people, but finds they can treat him only as a "case." He assumes a priest-congressman's values might include humanitarian ones, but the priest in congressional "office" — the priest as bureaucrat — must carefully apportion his time, and efficiency demands a written letter first. He assumes that bureaucrats are people like himself — personalities with a head on their shoulders, able to respond to human complaints, able to make decisions — but he finds no one in Washington corresponding to that personality type. The bureaucrat's self has been castrated.

And finally, although he recognizes that bureaucrats speak a different language, he commits the error of interpreting the language they use as double-talk, a deliberate attempt to mislead him.

The Function of Bureaucratic Language

Indeed the function of bureaucratese is fundamentally to make outsiders powerless. But that is a secondary function. The fact is that the people who speak bureaucratese do not design what they say and how they say it with Pasquale Plescia in mind at all. As he correctly perceives: "These government people, they don't hear you. They don't listen." Bureaucratic specialized language is specifically designed to insulate functionaries from clients, to empower them not to have to listen, unless the client first learns the language. For a client who has learned the language is a client who has accepted the bureaucrat's values. Language defines both what problems we can conceive of and what solutions we can think of. Once a client uses the bureaucracy's language, the bureaucrat may be assured that no solutions contrary to his interests and power will emerge from the dialogue.

Once we recognize this function of language, it is only one further step toward recognizing the ultimate function of bureaucratic language: a bureaucracy's language is usually so constructed as to prevent both bureaucrats and outsiders from ever formulating questions that might attack the underlying assumptions of the bureaucracy itself. A bureaucracy's language hides the questionability of that bureaucracy's own existence.

In summary, everyday experience raises in us the sense that, just as bureaucracy differs from society in all other ways, it differs from society in the use of language. This difference presents itself in two aspects:

First, based on our use of language in social life, we often would like to talk back in bureaucracy, but can't. This is the phenomenon of one-directionality.

Second, because we are trained to do so in society, in our attempts to talk back to bureaucracy, we naturally look for a *person* to talk back to. In bureaucracy, because of the way it is designed, communication is naturally not personal, but impersonal. That means if there is anything to talk back to at all, it is a *structure*, not a person.

Pasquale Plescia finally found the office of the secretary of HEW and in it a responsive administrator over the entire bureaucracy. But normally bureaucracy is so designed as to make unavailable or invisible from below who is the cause of a citizen's discomfort. In the last section of this chapter, I shall argue that not only is bureaucracy structurally designed not to reveal its causes of action, but the language it uses is itself couched in terms that dissolve the concept of responsibility. The result is a language that is acausal because it is impersonal.*

In the following section, experts on the question of language in general and bureaucracy in particular give their explanations of the language difference between bureaucracy and society. The point of this second section is to see what support exists for our perception that we feel at odds with the language of bureaucracy because it is a radically different language. Attention will also be paid to the special problems of one-directionality and acausality.

WHAT THE EXPERTS SAY

Wittgenstein: The Abolition of Language

In bureaucracy, we may be moving in a direction where language is not language at all. One of the strongest arguments on behalf of the death of language can be drawn from the philosopher Ludwig Wittgenstein. Language is communication, this argument runs; what goes on in bureaucracy is not communication, but information. Communication is two-way exchange between at least two human beings; information is literally the molding and shaping of one human being by another. Information, as we shall see, does not necessarily involve human beings: machines can "inform" one another.

Communication and Information
Language originates in the common life that human beings share as members of a community, Wittgenstein seems to argue.[5] Within this communal context, we engage in "language games."[6] That is, we engage in mutual interaction through language that is based on taken-for-granted rules silently agreed upon between ourselves. The fundamental agreement of the game is agreement in "what we do."[7] We might think of such agreement as a result of convention: "Okay, Joe, let's agree on not killing each other in this game by calling this a head and we all know heads are easily injured." But before I can even begin to agree with you on such definitions, I must already have an understanding of what a head is and what it means to be injured.

*The experience of acausality in bureaucratic language is fostered by the structure of that language itself. Bureaucratic language is functionalist; that is, it is so constructed as to make easy and clear to read what functions or activities have to be going on together at any given time. It is not constructed to reveal which activity *causes* the next activity. More of this in the last section of this chapter. For now it may be sufficient to refer you to your own inability to gain access to the cause of your financial embarrassment when Macy's sends a computer-printed statement canceling your credit.

That is, I must share with you my humanity. "If language is to be a means of communication there must be agreement, not only in definitions, but (queer as this may sound) in judgments."[8] As one Wittgensteinian commentator said, "Unless people agree in their reactions to colours they will not have the concept of colour they need to have to see certain behavior as 'agreement in reactions to colours'. Unless they agree in their expressions of, and reactions to, pain, they will not have the concept of pain they need to see behavior as pain behavior'."[9]

In summary, what makes language as a means of communication possible is the shared experience of being human. This shared experience Wittgenstein called "forms of life" [*Lebensformen*]. Forms of life are literally specific expressions of behavior among human beings that rest on the organic peculiarities of the species. In the words of another Wittgensteinian commentator:

> Language, and therefore the higher forms of consciousness, depend, logically, for their existence on the possibility of common 'forms of life . Hence, also, they depend, as an empirical matter of fact, on the existence of human beings regarded as members of a (fairly gregarious) species. To assert the existence of *such* forms of consciousness is in part to assert the existence, not of a single person, nor even of several separate persons, but rather, of people, that is to say of groups of individuals having not only common characteristics but also common (mutual) responses, interactions, etc.[10]

The relevant question to be asked about life in bureaucracy is whether such life still maintains the characteristics of human "forms of life" based on mankind's biological characteristics as a species.

Specifically we can address this question to two kinds of "communication" within bureaucracy: (1) "communication" between bureaucratic structures and individual functionaries; (2) "communications" between computers and individual functionaries or clients.

One of the leaders in modern organization theory, Herbert Simon, considers bureaucratic structures to be frozen decisions.[11] In other words, the office of the sales manager in a vacuum-cleaner company is set up to perpetuate the decision that whenever a customer comes in to buy a vacuum cleaner there will be adequate sales staff to effect the sale. Setting up this structure once — the structure of the sales manager's office — for all time hence, or until another decision is made, obviates the need to have unassigned personnel run around, when a customer comes, searching desperately for vacuum cleaners, price lists, and the proper procedures for recording the sale so that inventory can be brought up to date, new machines produced, and so on. In this sense, the office structure is not simply one frozen decision — the decision to sell — but many decisions: the frozen decisions on how to sell, what price to ask, how and when to reorder.

Nonhuman "Language"

The question that arises here is: Are the instructions contained in the frozen decision — i.e., the sales manager's office — really communication? That is, are they language? Or are they something else?

Let me tentatively suggest that the instructions so frozen are neither communication nor language in the traditional sense, but information. That is, for the very good reason of achieving predictability of behavior by the sales staff, the instructions encoded in the sales office are not subject to mutual agreement from below. They are one-directional. They shape behavior from the top down. As soon as, and because, it becomes detached from the original decision-makers, who then become inaccessible to communication from below, information of this technical sort loses an essential characteristic of human language. The office in question is not a living thing, although it might be argued that it is usually inhabited by a living thing, the sales manager. But what characterizes the bureaucratic office is that its frozen decisions exist no matter whether there is a sales manager or not and no matter who he or she is. Even when the office is temporarily empty because the manager has been fired, the office "exists" and even "talks." It "talks" because many of its frozen decisions are encoded in price lists and work rules, which serve me as external guides to my behavior as sales clerk.

But does it talk and exist the way human beings do? As a sales clerk, I am quite aware I can never talk back to it to inquire after the original decisions under which it was structured. One of these decisions was to have an office that would talk to me without having back talk. But, more importantly, in bureaucracy the office is specifically not the human being that fills it. Rule is impersonal. This means that even if I were to try to engage in back talk, I would be addressing a "partner" of intended communication that very specifically, and by design, lacks experience in the human condition. The office, after all, is the attempt to mechanize and automate both perceptions of what goes on in the sales process and instructions based on such inputs. Lacking human experience, the office as such can never become, under Wittgensteinian concepts of language, a partner for mutual agreement about a language-game called "sales." Because the office is inhuman, it can only treat me as a thing like itself. I, who think of myself as a human being, am "thought of" and treated as an analog to the machine — another machine. I can understand it only to the degree that I accept the rules it imposes on me, that is, to the extent that I become mechanical not only in my behavior, but in my conception of what language is. At this point whatever "talk" goes on between me and the office is no longer "language" in the Wittgensteinian sense. As Vesey notes, with tongue-in-cheek, about similar such situations: "Arguments from analogy haven't a leg, even *one* leg, to stand on."[12] This is, of course, because offices, unlike humans, do not have legs. Given such a handicap we might, under Wittgenstein's premises, have assumed from the beginning that neither communication nor language is possible between human beings and the structures of bureaucracy.

But something does go on between the two, and if it is not language in the traditional sense, what is it? Here we may look to what Herbert Simon considers the ideal structure of modern organization, the computer, for an answer.[13] Don't computers speak to us? Don't programmers "program" — that is "speak" to — computers?

Before proceeding to an answer, let us emphasize that the above argument on the linguistic relation between office structure and functionaries already demonstrates our main point: even language is radically different in bureaucracy than it is in society. Wittgenstein's argument in fact suggests language is not only different, it is abolished.*

Nowhere does this become more clear than when people freeze business or public service decisions into a computer and then make other people subject to the computer's instructions. For exactly the reasons pointed out in the relationship between organizational structure and functionary, the relationship between computer and functionary is not one of communication. The computer provides us with an especially clearcut example of the difference between communication and information exactly because the last human element has been squeezed out of the computer, seen as an organizational structure into which decisions are frozen. An office, on the other hand, still seems to be occupied by a human manager, giving the impression of a man-machine symbiosis. In general, computer-man relationships can no longer be understood in terms of how language used to link humans because the computer is not part of the human species.

A computer is as different from humans as humans are from dogs or stones. As one Wittgensteinian put it: "Why can we not intelligibly say of a dog or an infant that it is hopeful? Or of a stone

---

* *Similarly, Jenny Teichman on the concept of "inaudible" language: "He [Wittgenstein] seems to be saying . . . that a language which cannot be used in communications is not a language at all (any more than infinity is a number)." (Teichman, "Wittgenstein on Persons and Human Beings," in Royal Institute of Philosophy, *Understanding Wittgenstein* [New York: St. Martin's, 1974], p. 145.)

that it is in pain? Why can we not say that a computer calculates?"[14] Pointing out that Wittgenstein himself asked this last question,* the same author summarizes Wittgenstein's reply:

> A computer can reel out unimpeachable answers to the questions we feed into it. It may be tempting to think that here is exemplified the kind of competence that makes us speak of thought and intelligence in a mathematician. If the mathematician differs from the computer in *other* respects why should that undermine the similarity in their mathematical performance? Certainly if a man or a child writes down the answer to a mathematical problem this, in *itself*, does not prove that he has intelligence. To think of him as having mathematical ability we want him to be able to solve *other* mathematical problems. Whether or not his present performance exhibits ability and intelligence depends on what he does on *other* occasions. But when we call a man who solves a wide range of difficult mathematical problems intelligent, we take it for granted that the symbols, formulae and simple operations he uses have meaning for him, that he understands them. We cannot take this for granted in the case of the computer. Merely responding to the problems fed into it with the correct answer does not show that the computer understands what it prints. . . .
>
> In short, if the computer is to calculate it would have to have something like the human body, with arms, face, eyes, and enter into various activities in which the symbols and formulae it prints play a role. It is their role in these many activities, in shopping, measuring, accounting, engineering, that gives them the sense they have.[15]

In other words, without participation in the human experience, the computer is not capable of something like understanding. For the same reason, we can argue that the interaction between people and computers can never fully partake of the characteristic of communication, because one of the basic requirements for communication, the capacity for understanding on ultimate grounds of sharing the human condition, is not available to the computer.

Similarly, the more human beings, who are dependent for their very lives on employment by modern organization, adjust to the machine, the less likely they will remain capable of communication. As Wittgenstein himself points out, if a human responded to mathematical questions with the quickness of a computer and always came up with the correct answer, could carry out complicated formal transitions, work out involved mathematical proofs, but were "otherwise perfectly imbecile," then he or she would be "a human calculating machine."[16]

In yet other words:

---

*In *Remarks on the Foundations of Mathematics* (Oxford: Basil Blackwell, 1956), Part IV, Section 2.

A person who produces such answers, whether in words, writing or print, is performing an activity in which thought and intelligence are displayed *only* if he lives a life in which this activity has a point and a bearing on other things he does, *only* if he has other interests — interests independent of producing these answers. In the absence of such a life even a being who is alive is not a human being.[17]

As we move from the society of human beings to the bureaucracy mix of functionaries and machines, we thus experience a sense of strangeness in the kind of language spoken there. According to the Wittgensteinian explanation, this is because structures of the bureaucratic type are incapable of producing human language, human communication, and human understanding.

Searle: The Separation of Language from Meaning

There is a very basic experience in bureaucracy in which we sense that speech spoken there is radically different from speech spoken in society. We reflect this when we call an institution's press spokesman a "mouthpiece." And we encounter a similarly strange experience when we see computer specialists "talk" to their machines. In both cases we sense that something strange is going on, but we don't understand why. In both cases we are right.

Detaching Meaning from Message
What we are observing when bureaucrats or bureaucratic structures (including computers) speak, or are spoken to, is often something unparalleled in human history — the separation of meaning from the message. Marshall McLuhan may glibly tell us that the "medium *is* the message," that the form of message is its meaning; and he may be right: all communications media shape what they are capable of saying. But what is happening in bureaucracy is very specifically the separation of the message from both its content and its context.

The press secretary of a government institution is very specifically understood by listening news reporters *not* to be involved in what he is saying. He does lend, as the derogatory but very descriptive appelation of "mouthpiece" suggests, his mouth to the conveying of the institution's message, but his personal meaning is detached from what he says — the impersonal message. This is the function of the "good" bureaucrat's impersonal detachment from his acts. It is a sign of insufficient bureaucratization that news reporters held then President Richard M. Nixon's press secretary, Ronald Ziegler, personally responsible for the misinformation he distributed on behalf of the office he held. On the other hand, Ziegler showed he understood the function of his office in purely bureaucratic terms when he chose to characterize previous statements exposed by the press as falsehoods as "inoperative" instead of as "lies." A lie is a concept that belongs to the world of social language in which individuals are held responsible for what they say, and their intentions are expected to be congruent with their words. Within the world of bureaucratic language, "inoperative" is a perfect term for a statement that no longer functions in the overall attempt by the bureaucracy to remain adaptive to its environment — that is, in a world where means and meanings no longer matter but results do.

Nevertheless, those of us coming to bureaucracy from society are right in feeling there is something very strange going on in the way bureaucrats use language — though perhaps our sense of strangeness should be resolved through understanding rather than outrage. What can explain our sense of strangeness when confronted with bureaucratic language? For something to be strange it must differ from what we are used to. How does bureaucratic language differ? If we could answer this last question, we could also understand our sense of being strangers in a strange land.

But first another example. Our sense of strangeness reaches a peak when we are spoken to by computers. Computers interest us here because they have replaced large segments of bureaucratic structures, are in fact often used *as* bureaucratic structures. A computer can, for example, replace a large section of a business's or civil service institution's accounting and payroll office. To a large degree it is, in effect, the accounting or payroll office, and it is more bureaucratic in Max Weber's sense than any structure that preceded it. Precomputer structures are mixtures of people and machines in which people still visibly dominate even if, for the sake of bureaucratic control and stability, they are supposed to act like machines. For the segments that the computer takes over, this duality has been resolved: the structure in which formerly twenty accountants performed calculating operations on a payroll now is a computer; the computer *is* the structure.

When such a structure speaks, as we have said, such speech seems very strange to us — because all human components have been removed from the speaker. What is left is myself and the IBM card, myself and the printout.

Here, because the computer presents us with an extreme or "pure" example, we begin to see clearly for the first time the nature of bureaucratic talk — machine language — as against people talk — human language.

The difference, as we have already indicated, is that in bureaucratic talk the message has to be so encapsuled and protected against the personal interests of its human carriers that it can stand by itself — apart from, and even despite, these human carriers. With the machine language of the computer, the designers of bureaucracy have finally reached that goal. There now is an impersonal language. And it is free from human interference. It is this fact which is unique in human history. No wonder we feel strange!

At this stage we may call upon the services of an expert linguist, John R. Searle, to deepen our understanding of just how serious this difference is.

A Retreat from Language

In ordinary human language, Searle argues, what is said — language — is never separate from the intentions of the person who says it — the speaker. The purpose of language, in fact, is to have the listener recognize the intention or meaning of the speaker.

Now, one of the strangest things about observing people who program computers — that is, who construct what computer specialists call "machine language" — is that they "utter speech," or construct speech, which the machine will then be able to use, without having in mind anything specific that they want to communicate. They are simply laying down the *means* of communication without reference to any specific *meaning*. Someone who wants to use the computer to communicate will come along later and use the means laid down — I hesitate to call it language for it is nothing of the sort in traditional terms — by attaching a meaning to it. Aside from the obviously strange characteristics of the computer, its storage capacity and its swiftness, this process of attaching meaning to the means of a language is one of the strangest experiences in which humans have ever engaged. Not that definitions have not been imposed from above for millenia. But the permanent, and very visible, separation of what is said, the signs and symbols, from what is meant has been experienced at best only for short spans, as when a child or a newcomer to a country learns the meaning attached to a strange word. In the past such separation has always been a handicap, a barrier to communication; the computer promises that separating means from meaning will encourage communication and make it more certain.

Some further exploration of Searle may deepen our understanding of this difference. Searle writes:

> Human communications has some extraordinary properties, not shared by most other kinds of human behavior. One of the most extraordinary is this: If I am trying to tell someone something, then (assuming certain conditions are satisfied) as soon as he recognizes that I am trying to tell him something and exactly what it is I am trying to tell him, I have succeeded in telling it to him. Furthermore, unless he recognizes that I

am trying to tell him something and what I am trying to tell him, I do not fully succeed in telling it to him.[18]

That is, in ordinary human life the act of telling and the meaning attached to the told are usually inseparable.* In contrast, the computer, and to a lesser degree the thoroughly bureaucratized bureaucrat, separates the two. Computer "language," as a pure example of an ideal bureaucratic "language," is really not fully language until it is applied *by someone* to a *particular case*.† That is, it requires someone to come along and put what is a highly abstract and detached system of signs into a human context.

Such "language" is strange to us, because most language we are acquainted with ordinarily appears in some sort of context related to a problem, interest, or meaningful activity in which we are engaged. Computer language, and to a large degree bureaucratic language in general, is in this sense "context-free." It lacks a context in the same way that a tongue would lack a context if I suddenly saw it going for a walk unattached to a head. And bureaucratic language thus unattached appears strange to us users of attached language in much the same way.

Linguists, who take language apart as part of their day-to-day work, have of course encountered language in this amputated form before. But, as Searle says, in real life, "speaking a language is everywhere permeated with the facts of commitments undertaken, obligations assumed, cogent arguments presented, and so on."[19] Those of us toying playfully and naively with computer "language," and the "language" of bureaucracy in general, might well be forewarned by the caution Searle addresses to his fellow linguists:

> . . . the retreat from the committed use of words ultimately must involve a retreat from language itself, for speaking a language . . . consists of performing speech acts according to rules, and there is no separating those speech acts from the commitments which form essential aspects of them.[20]

---

*In social life having meaning attached to what is told us is best achieved by having the speaker remain personally attached to his or her words. For example, juries apparently tend to lend more credence to words uttered by a witness in a narrative style than to the same information presented in a non-narrative manner, according to a research group headed by anthropologist William O'Barr of Duke University. (As reported in "Verdicts Linked to Speech Style: Anthropologists Say Subtle Patterns Influence Juries," *The New York Times*, December 14, 1975, p. 88.) Contrasting mock juries' reaction to narrative versus non-narrative information, the report concluded: "The result: The juries considered the narrative form of testimony to be more authoritative and stronger, even though the substance presented in the two varieties was indistinguishable." The narrative style, of course, is *social* speech. In contrast to bureaucratic speech, it allows speakers to become directly involved in what they say.

†I am putting the word "language" in quotation marks here to indicate that these kinds of "languages" are not language in the traditional sense.

While Searle does not address himself to what we have observed — that people in ordinary bureaucratic life are now playing games with a language that involves the same separation he fears — it is perhaps not too impertinent for us to read into his specific caution a general warning for ourselves as speakers, listeners and, above all, as human beings. The fact is that in everyday life we have begun to use "language" in a way that only linguistic analysts have encountered in their scholarly studies. And I am certain we are dealing with such "language" without being aware of its truncated nature and without a single thought of its consequences — except the vague sensation that something strange is going on.

THE NATURE OF BUREAUCRATIC LANGUAGE

Bureaucracy separates man from his language. This is the major conclusion to be drawn from the Wittgensteinian and Searlean analyses of the nature of bureaucratic language and of computer language as its logical extension.

A Language of Functions

Both experts specify that language is not language unless what is spoken is attached to the intentions of the speaker and addressed to the understanding of the hearer. In Wittgenstein's judgment, a person who speaks outside this human context "is not a human being." Searle similarly comments that human language is never separated from the meaning of the speaker and that "the retreat from the committed use of words ultimately must involve a retreat from language itself . . ." But it is the pride of designers of bureaucratic systems that the individual functionary is in the anomalous position of not being personally committed to his words.* The bureaucratic

---

*In contrast to society, where a man's word is his bond, in bureaucracy it is exactly the *lack* of personal attachment to his words that guarantees the reliability of the functionary — especially in cases in which there is a danger of conflict between his personal values and the values contained in the words he must officially use.

The vocabulary of the Vietnam war is an example. Soldiers carefully separated in their mind's eye the social and human world in which they preferred to live and the field of operations in which they were to fight: the first was "the world," the second "the boonies of Nam." Personally unpleasant activities are given bureaucratic cover names that defuse their emotional potential: murder of an enemy spy becomes "termination with extreme prejudice" and defoliation becomes "resources control program."

On the other hand, soldiers converted the officialese of "winning the hearts and minds" of the enemy to the more descriptive "WHAM." When bureaucracy devalues ordinary human language, the act of abbreviating, itself borrowed from bureaucratese, may become an ironic act of human liberation. (See "The Uses of Vietspeak," *Time Magazine*, November 6, 1972, p. 36.)

language — always unique in its systemic definition of terms and in its structural echoing of the bureaucratic processes it enshrines — is designed before the first functionary ever arrives at his place of work. It is protected by underlying cultural imperative against the process of ordinary dialogue which changes and amends meanings. It also exists apart from the speaker and will continue to exist long after the speaker is gone. It is in this sense a dead language. If it were a living language it would be subject to modification by every user. But the terms that define what operations a bureaucracy may and may not engage in must not be so amendable, otherwise the certainty of having the lowest functionary do what the highest echelons command is gone and with it the raison d'etre of bureaucracy. It is for these reasons that the problems with language that we have cited at the beginning of this chapter exist.

At the boundary between the two linguistic communities, functionaries must not be allowed to change the meaning of the term "welfare mother" one iota from the legal and administrative pre-definition of the term — females of a certain age, with a certain number of children, unemployed, and husbandless.

Similarly, the term must be encapsuled through administrative and legal sanctions against attempts by a potential, but not quite qualified, client to engage in the normal dialogue usual in human relations and to persuade the functionary to amend what he "means" when he uses the term "welfare mother" in the officially defined way. The functionary's only survival strategy is to teach a potential client to learn the meaning of official language — its categories and procedures — in the same way that he had to learn them. And the central tactic of that strategy, especially if he has personal sympathies with the client, is to separate what he says officially, including his choice of terms and grammar, from his private intentions. Only if the functionary and the client both understand that in bureaucracy it is never a human being speaking — to whom intentions, empathy, or responsibility of a human sort might, after all, be prescribed — will bureaucracy work. The client who blames the functionary personally for what he officially utters commits the serious misunderstanding of associating speech with the speaker. Such an expectation is reasonable only in social life. How else are people ever to trust one another? Why else, except that you mean what you say, should I pay attention to you? How else, but with such mutual willingness to listen and talk back, can we ever hope to communicate and act together on a problem? But in bureaucracy such two-directionality of speech is forbidden for the simple reason that whatever the problem with which we approach a bureaucracy, the solution has already been predesigned for us. The "language" through which bureaucracy speaks to us is not a language designed for problem solving. Bureaucratic language is a language for passing on solutions in as precise and efficient a manner as possible. As such it is a language of functionality: in content as well as in form, bureaucratic language consists of fragments of information. These fragments each describe actions that the client has to carry out if he or she is to become a part of the system of administration which the bureaucracy represents — that is, if he or she is to become "functional." The language bits passed on by functionaries to clients are descriptions of functions the client has to perform, in exactly the same way that the functionary's work sheet or code book is nothing but a listing of functions the functionary has to perform.

It is for this reason that the client, much to his surprise and often irritation, hears himself spoken to predominantly in the imperative.

At the New York State Motor Vehicle Department:

1. CHECK if you have your Registration, your Insurance Form (F-1), and your Completed Application for Renewal!
2. Go to Line 1. Get your Application Form checked, stamped and fees calculated.
3. Go to Cashier's Line. Pay fees.

These instructions are not only designed to reinforce the division of clerical labor, but to shorten lines to a physical length the building can handle, separate evaluation and money-handling functions to ensure honesty — or at least make collusion between evaluator, cashier, and client difficult — and so on.

What is most striking about this language of functionality is that its content and structure coincide: it is a series of imperatives stated in the imperative.

"If . . . then" Language of Computers

The parallel to computer language can hardly be overlooked. A simple program to average a large number of figures printed on computer cards might read:

```
CALL PROGRAM
PROGRAM: AVERAGE
```

This section of the program tells the computer in imperative terms what functions it will be asked to perform, in this case averaging. The term "AVERAGE" here is predefined by the computer engineers to describe a number of mechanical functions that the machine will perform when the cue "AVERAGE" is given. It is predefined and immutable in its meaning in exactly the same way that the terms "Registration," "Insurance Form (F-1)," and "Application" are in the case of the car-registration bureaucracy. Misinterpretation by the user of the term "AVERAGE" will have exactly the same results in the case of the computer as misinterpretation of the term "F-1" will have when the client tries to have the bureaucracy work for him: the machine — mechanical/electronic or human — will not work for him unless he understands its terms *in* its terms.

The program continues, probably with some further definitions that translate social language into machine language. For engineering and programming reasons, some computer languages limit the use of certain letters to certain functions. Therefore certain social terms have to be translated into computer language, as follows:

CARD=KARD
COUNT=KOUNT

This is likely to be followed by instructions for the first function to be performed in averaging a number of cards; that is, to count the number of cards:

KOUNT KARDS

Without previous translation — or from another point of view, adaptation — of social language to computer language, this simple instruction could not be "processed" by the machine.

Further instructions would then follow, narrowing the functioning or further specifying the functioning of the machine. For example, if the user wants to have the machine skip a card on which the number is smaller than 1.01, he or she would write into the program:

IF NUMBER .LT. 1.01 GO TO 100

I have purposefully introduced this complication into the averaging operation in order to bring out the importance of a standard form that both computer and bureaucratic language takes. This is the "if . . . then" form.

In exactly the same way that the computer is instructed to go to the next card if a card has a number smaller than 1.01, the welfare case evaluator is told by rules and regulations to go on to the next case if a "welfare mother" candidate has fewer than the requisite number of children or more than the requisite maximum number of dollars.*

In other words, when they act officially, functionaries engage in exactly the same kind of operation as a computer: they draw analogies between reality and predefined categories and operations.

---

*Such procedure is becoming formalized. In the New York State welfare system, some clerks now must, in judging applicants' eligibility, follow a series of preprinted if-then statements based on Decision Logic Tables derived from computer language.

And they proceed by using exactly the same kind of language that the computer uses, language I would characterize by its central element as "if . . . then" language.

Functionaries may even express this in their "communication" to a client: "If you have more than the maximum amount of money allowed, then I can't consider you as a case." What is just as important, their mental operations are "if . . . then" operations. Here begins what further research may consider one of the key characteristics of bureaucratic language as distinguished from social language.

It cannot be my task here, since I initially intended to do no more than demonstrate *that* bureaucratic and social language differs, to describe exactly all the key positive characteristics of the bureaucratic language of functionality. I want, however, to make one further point before simply leaving this exploration with a suggestion of some future directions of research.

What is especially striking about the "if . . . then" structure of both the bureaucratic thinking and working process and the language that usually encapsules these is that the "if . . . then" structure is not causal. Exactly as does the computer, functionaries either think or act through the use of analogy — comparing an event in reality to a relevant fragment of the code of operations. Their thinking and speaking are therefore analogous thought and analogous speech, not causal speech or causal thought.

This then is a second distinguishing characteristic of bureaucratic language. In social speech we tend to give our reasons for our projected actions because only by doing so can we make clear to others what our intentions are, what drives us to act, and how seriously we are committed to it. Clients typically complain, when trying to communicate with bureaucracy, that bureaucrats give no reasons. "If only they would explain why I have to stand here for hours," a client in line might say. But the bureaucracy does not explain for the simple reason that explanations are not essential to its operations — its actions, thoughts, or speech. Again, as in most things bureaucracy does, the client and even the bureaucrat must learn to understand that there is no malice here. The lack of performance of an explanatory operation is merely a reflection of bureaucracy's inherent lack of a need to explain itself to itself, much less to others. No more do rocks explain themselves, though I must explain either the rock or myself when I stumble over it.

SUMMARY

We have reached the point at which we can reiterate the key distinctions between bureaucratic language and social language.

These distinctions explain much of the language relations and barriers between bureaucracy and society that have hitherto been left incomprehensible or explained only in a fragmentary fashion by behavioralists who draw simple correlations without looking for underlying principles or causes. The chart below outlines these distinctions:

Social Language	Bureaucratic Language
1. causal	1. analogous (acausal)
2. two-directional	2. one-directional

The analogous, or acausal, nature of bureaucratic language is mainly responsible for the resistance by bureaucracy to penetration by outsiders. A language that lacks causal paths and consists merely of lists of conditions against which reality must be tested by the user — i.e., the functionary — is not a language that lends itself to having questions asked as to why a certain operation exists, why it is exercised just so, and what the justification might be for the sum of operations of the entire bureaucracy. Such questions can be asked only by those who designed the instrument, and from their viewpoint the answer is often merely that things are the way they are because they were laid down that way.

Secondly, a language that does not allow mutual definition and redefinition by speaker and hearer is admirably designed to maintain a one-way power relationship from the top down, especially in situations in which people are dependent on the bureaucracy for their very survival. The client's only choice is to learn the language of the agency from which he or she seeks service or the control of others and accept the kind of help that is codified into its vocabulary, whether it fits a need exactly or not. Functionaries themselves bow the more easily to the absurdities and inhumanities of such language for the simple reason that bureaucratic language is so designed as to surgically separate the speaker from involvement with, and often understanding of, what he or she must say.* One-directionality makes bureaucratic language impenetrable to attempts to understand from below the principles of its ultimate sources. The division of labor is already paralleled by the analogous structure of the available grammar, and one-directionality parallels bureaucracy's hierarchical social structure. Thus the language, because of its one-directional nature, is also immune to action from below. Each level of the hierarchy becomes a new barrier against changing the meaning of definitions and processes from below.

---

*This separation is ultimately maintained by the exercise of a special kind of coercive power over the functionary. See the chapter on politics and power as well as the description of psychological dependency in chapter 3.

Further research may show that many of the communications difficulties in and with bureaucracy can be traced to these two characteristics of acausality and one-directionality. But these difficulties face those trying to buck the system from below. From above, the two characteristics — one-directionality, by guaranteeing a monopoly over the definition of reality, and acausality, by discouraging casual thought as the only method through which the validity of orders can be questioned — constitute a control instrument without compare.

NOTES

1. Max Weber, *Economy and Society: An Outline of Interpretive Sociology*, 3 vols., eds. Guenther Roth and Claus Wittich, trans. E. Fischoff *et al.* (New York: Bedminster Press, 1968), p. 992.

2. For the same reason that the police officers behind the composite quotation here must remain anonymous, I am extending the same courtesy to the fire commissioner in question, although in his case personality plays a strong role in creating animosities that extend beyond the necessary severities of bureaucratization.

3. "Shifted Workers Miss 'Stimulation' of City," *The New York Times*, November 4, 1975, p. 39.

4. Reported in *The Los Angeles Times*, reprinted as "He Forces Bureaucrats to Hew to the Line," *The New York Post*, July 29, 1975, p. 62.

5. The representation of Wittgenstein attempted here follows closely the work of Jenny Teichman in "Wittgenstein on Persons and Human Beings," in Royal Institute of Philosophy, *Understanding Wittgenstein* (New York: St. Martin's, 1974), pp. 133 – 148. The other major source is Wittgenstein, *Philosophical Investigations* (Oxford: Basil Blackwell, 1953).

6. Wittgenstein, *Philosophical Investigations*, Part I, paragraph 241.

7. Godfrey Vesey, "Foreword," in Royal Institute, *Understanding Wittgenstein*, p. ix.

8. Wittgenstein, *Philosophical Investigations*, Part I, paragraph 207. In this case judgment as to what a head is, when I see it on someone else's shoulder. Such judgments can, according to Wittgenstein, only be based on shared concepts. And shared concepts, according to him, can emerge only out of a shared human nature and the behaviors that nature leads man to share. See also R.M. White: "The fact that human beings do in general react in the same way . . . is a contingent anthropological fact, but one without which language could never get off the ground . . ." (White, "Can Whether One Proposition Makes Sense Depend on the Truth of Another? (*Tractatus* 2.0211-2)," in Royal Institute, *Understanding Wittgenstein*, p.26.)

9. Vesey, "Foreword," p. x.

10. Jenny Teichman, "Wittgenstein on Persons," p. 145.

11. See for example his widely read article, "Decision-Making and Organizational Design: Man-Machine Systems for Decision-Making," in D.S. Pugh, ed., *Organization Theory: Selected Readings* (Baltimore, Md.: Penguin Books, 1971), pp. 189 – 212.

12. Vesey, "Foreword," p. x.

13. Herbert Simon, "Decision-Making and Organizational Design," especially p. 194.

14. Ilham Dilman, "Wittgenstein on the Soul," in Royal Institute, *Understanding Wittgenstein*, p. 165.

15. Ibid., p. 166. Dilham's italics.

16. Wittgenstein, *Remarks on the Foundations of Mathematics* (Oxford: Basil Blackwell, 1956), Part IV, Section 3.

17. Dilman, "Wittgenstein," pp. 166 – 167. Human beings who behave like machines have been analyzed in modern psychology as early as Freud. Machinelike functionaries are no strangers to anyone who has visited a bureaucracy.

18. John R. Searle, *Speech Acts: An Essay in the Philosophy of Language* (London: Cambridge University Press, 1969), p. 47.

19. Ibid., p. 197.

20. Ibid., p. 198.

5

Bureaucracy
as
Polity

*In a modern state the actual ruler is necessarily and
unavoidably the bureaucracy . . .*

— Max Weber[1]

In bureaucracy, administration replaces politics. Not politics as the
decision-making center of society — bureaucracy increasingly makes
the central decisions that govern public and private life — but politics
as the participatory activity of citizens cooperating and fighting with
one another to work out solutions to public problems.*

Politics of this sort is replaced by purportedly "apolitical" decision-making of the managerial few. The only thing apolitical about
such decision-making is that the public is excluded from the process.
The rest of this bureaucratic "apolitics" is as political as traditional
politics used to be in the sense that through it are determined the
ways in which we live our lives. Apolitics, in short, is hidden
decision-making which decides the fate of the public but excludes the
public from the process. †

*This definition of politics dates back to the ancient Greek concept of the political
system as political community: politeia or polity.
†I first coined the term in Robert A. Isaak and Ralph P. Hummel, *Politics for Human
Beings* (North Scituate, Mass.: Duxbury Press, 1975). The term "apolitical politics"
was previously used to encompass a variety of political phenomena marking the
transition of public decision-making from the polity to bureaucracy. See Charles A.
McCoy and John Playford, eds., *Apolitical Politics: A Critique of Behavioralism* (New
York: Crowell, 1967).

HOW PEOPLE COMMAND AND OBEY

Apolitics of this sort has, of course, long existed within bureaucracies. Public politics used to require a public. That meant citizens recognizable as individuals, each with identifiable needs providing motivation from within and each possessed of a will to express that motivation. In bureaucracy, it is exactly this foundation of a public politics that is dissolved: the individual is psychologically fragmented; personal motivations are considered illegitimate; and if any will is to be expressed, it is the will of the system not of the individual. Within bureaucracy, in short, the public has long been replaced by the system and the citizenry by the corps of functionaries.

This conversion is made the more interesting by two questions that it raises: First, how does bureaucracy exercise its apolitical power apart from the usual motivations that bind people to obey in traditional politics? Second, what is the impact of bureaucratic apolitics on the surviving remnants of the polity that is officially established outside bureaucracy's borders but which bureaucracy increasingly penetrates?

The present argument seeks to demonstrate that bureaucracy subverts politics in two arenas — within and outside itself. This is achieved through two methods:

1. Through the conversion of practical questions, turning around social norms, into technical questions purportedly solvable only by experts, bureaucracy takes on an apolitical appearance. This hides the fact that it continues to make political decisions, though these are now handily removed from public participation.

2. Through the very structuring of bureaucracy, specifically through the concepts of hierarchy and the division of labor, this modern form of administration transmutes the nature of power from authority to psychological coercion, a subtle but effective form of force.

What characterizes the apolitics of bureaucracy is not only that decisions made on behalf of the public are no longer open to participation by the public, but that these decisions are enforced by a new form of power. Traditional political power rests at least minimally on the citizens' belief that orders given by government are just and proper because they were arrived at through just and proper means, generally approved by the citizenry. Political power of this sort rested on legitimacy; it was authority. The power of enforcing bureaucratic decisions, however, rests ultimately on the psychological dependency of subordinates on superordinates and on the system at large. Such power is the power of psychological coercion, resting not on ideas, but on mere survival impulse. Just as bureaucracy reduces citizens to functionaries, it reduces authority to force.*

In short, what characterizes bureaucracy politically is *apolitics* and the replacement of *ideology* by *psychology*. This conversion, and in effect termination, of politics takes place both inside bureaucracies and at the point at which they penetrate the polity.

The conflict between bureaucracy and polity can be viewed as it was in the chapter on psychology as a confrontation between the power of the individual to create his or her own life and the power of the system to control their choices. In Max Weber's words, uncannily predictive:

> Given the basic fact of the irresistible advance of bureaucratization, the question about the future forms of political organization can only be asked in the following way: . . . How can one possibly save *any remnants* of "individualist" freedom in any sense?[2]†

Just what this means can be understood by looking at the everyday experiences of four kinds of people — the citizen and the politician, on the one hand, and the manager and the functionary on the other. Specifically we are trying to demonstrate here, through examples, how the citizen and politician experience the bureaucratization of politics, that is, its replacement by administration. Further we are trying to show how the new character of power affects the experience of the manager and the functionary within bureaucracy. These experiences fall under two headings — the bureaucratization of politics and the bureaucratization of power.

The Bureaucratization of Politics

Citizens

In trying to follow the previous format of this book in which people themselves express the strangeness of their experiences with bu-

---

*I am here arguing that psychological coercion constitutes the use of force as much as physical coercion.

†Weber raises two other points: two "In view of the growing indispensability of the state bureaucracy and its corresponding increase in power, how can there be any guarantee that any powers will remain which can check and effectively control the tremendous influence of this stratum? How will democracy even in this limited sense be *at all possible?*" [Weber's italics.] And: three "A third question, and the most important of all, is raised by a consideration of the inherent limitations of bureaucracy proper." Here he argues that the mentality of the bureaucrat is radically different from the mentality of the political leader and that bureaucratic decisions cannot properly solve the problems of public life. I believe we have since had the answer to Weber's last concern: bureaucrats will exercise their irresistible power simply because they have it, whether or not it is competent to provide solutions for the well-being or survival of a society.

reaucracy, I have here encountered some difficulty. When it comes to the realm of politics, people seem to be less able than in the social, cultural, psychological, and linguistic spheres to put their finger on exactly what it is they find strange.

Nevertheless estrangement from the political system is endemic in the United States today.[3] Tracing public confidence in American political institutions and leaders from 1966 to 1973, Louis Harris found a rapid decline.[4]

CONFIDENCE IN THE U.S. GOVERNMENT

Percentage of people who have a "great deal" of confidence in:	1966	1973	Percentage Change
U.S. Supreme Court	51	28	−23
Executive Branch	41	27	−14
Congress	42	21	−21

Source: Louis Harris, The Anguish of Change (New York: W. W. Norton, 1973), p. 12.

Another study, looking at three attitudes toward government and politics — the sense of distrust, sense of personal powerlessness, and sense of meaninglessness of politics — came up with startling results[5]; see the chart on page 169. Such figures give powerful, if only mute, testimony of the estrangement of Americans from government and politics.

Politicians
From politicians, who could be expected to be most sensitive to change and most capable of expressing its meaning, comes more direct testimony. Pollster Lou Harris quotes President John F. Kennedy as having said at one point:

> Sooner or later it seems that every problem mankind is faced with gets dumped into the lap of the president right here in the center of it all. But by the time it reaches here, the problem has been dissected, sanitized, and cast into a series of options* — almost as though they were engraved in stone. What is missing is the heart behind them, what they mean in human terms.[6]

Earlier, in analyzing the disastrous invasion of Cuba at the Bay of Pigs, Arthur Schlesinger, Jr., a Kennedy advisor, pointed his finger even more sharply at bureaucracy. As political scientist James David Barber reports, "The Bay of Pigs muckup, he [Schlesinger] suggested,

---

*By whom? This is a classical case of apolitics in which experts and administrators claim the right to make technical *predecisions* on the options that can then safely be left to mere amateurs — the politicians and the citizens.

Percentage Change in American Feelings of Political Distrust,[a] Powerlessness, and Meaninglessness,[b] 1956 – 1972[c]

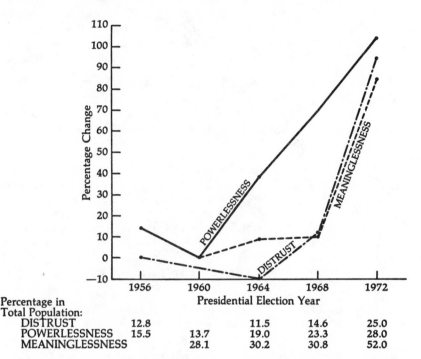

Percentage in Total Population:	1956	1960	1964	1968	1972
DISTRUST	12.8		11.5	14.6	25.0
POWERLESSNESS	15.5	13.7	19.0	23.3	28.0
MEANINGLESSNESS		28.1	30.2	30.8	52.0

Source: Robert S. Gilmour and Robert S. Lamb, Political Alienation in Contemporary America *(New York: St. Martin's, 1975), p. 17*

[a] Questions on political *distrust* were asked of the 1956 ISR panel,[d] but they were not repeated in 1960.

[b] Only one of the three political *meaninglessness* questions was asked in the ISR survey in 1972.

[c] 1960 is set as the base year in calculating percentage change.

[d] ISR refers to the Institute for Social Research at the University of Michigan. The "panels" referred to are groups of 2,000 to 2,500 Americans surveyed in samples drawn for the years indicated.

had stemmed in large part from 'excessive concentration' on military and operational problems and the wholly inadequate consideration of political issues."[7] If by this Schlesinger meant an overemphasis on means and a neglect of considering ends and overall purpose, we are on familiar ground. It is the typical problem that arises in any attempt to solve human problems when bureaucracy gets involved.

In a more clearcut example, also involving Kennedy, the president discovered in the midst of delicate negotiations with the Soviet Union during the Cuban missile crisis, which would determine whether the two nations would go into a nuclear war, that policy was snagged by bureaucracy. The Russians suddenly demanded that the

United States remove its missiles from Turkey. An order for such removal had been given by the president eighteen months earlier.

> Much to his chagrin, Kennedy discovered during the Cuban missile crisis that his orders of eighteen months ago to the State Department to negotiate those (obsolete) U.S. missiles out of Turkey had never been fulfilled, falling repeatedly into the gumbo of bureaucratic diplomacy.[8]

On the other hand, Kennedy and Lou Harris themselves helped bureaucratize the American presidential campaign process when in the 1960 campaign Kennedy used the information drawn from a Harris survey to manipulate voters in the West Virginia primary. As Harris himself tells the story:

> He [Kennedy] would look back to the West Virginia primary of 1960, where he held a 70% to 30% lead *before* the religious issue was drawn. But *after* the anti-Catholic sentiment had surfaced, he was no better than even up with Hubert Humphrey (41% to 41%) with two weeks to go in the primary. He broke open that historic primary by following advice drawn from his polls that he could shame West Virginia voters for voting like bigots; he won going away 61% to 39%, as compared with our final estimate given to Senator Kennedy that he would win 58% to 42%.[9]

Now politicians always manipulate citizens. What makes the insertion of a scientific pollster between the feelings of the electorate and the actions of a politician interesting is the fact that this involves the separating of citizen and politician by what promises to be an electoral bureaucracy. Could it be that eventually this will lead to an emphasis on how polls are taken rather than on the results of polls — an emphasis on means rather than ends? Already in 1960, Harris reports, there existed in Kennedy's campaign organization an "elaborate research apparatus," headed incidentally by a then relatively unknown Harvard law professor by the name of Archibald Cox, with a "mountain of facts and very little to run a campaign on."[10]

The question being asked here is this: Is it possible to explain Americans' documented estrangement from politics and government in terms of the bureaucratization of politics? It is to this question that the experts examined in the next section speak.

But there is also a further question: If there is to be a bureaucratization of politics, what will be the major difference between old-fashioned politics and bureaucratic politics? The tentative answer suggested here stems out of testimony by and about managers and functionaries as to how it feels in bureaucracy when you command and when you have to obey. The premise is that what most surprises us when we enter bureaucratized politics is the new nature of power itself.

The Bureaucratization of Power

Managers
Thurman Arnold, an insider of Franklin Delano Roosevelt's New Deal, tells two stories about organization men he knew:

> A friend of mine, the head of a moderately large law firm, at great personal loss kept all of his law clerks during the depression. He was also a director of a public utility. As a director he voted to fire employees and cut wages and at the same time actually increased the salary of certain executive officials. While acting for the company he was unconsciously compelled to assume the mythology of the hard-boiled public-utility magnate.[11]

Rather than accepting the mythology of Arnold's interpretation, in what is otherwise a perfect example of the difference in the exercise of power in society and bureaucracy, we might suggest that Arnold's friend exercised power *typically* in each situation. In the social situation of his private law firm, where he very likely had a personal, face-to-face relationship with his subordinates, he held his power carefully and responsibly in hand. In the bureaucratic situation, perhaps because of the distancing effect of bureaucracy and the sense that his relationships were impersonal, he exercised power irresponsibly from the employes' view, but very likely responsibly from the view of the interests of the overall organization. An owner, or senior partner, of a firm can afford to personally absorb financial losses of what is bad management, keeping employes when they are not needed. A manager of a public utility does not wield such personal power. Legally he holds power in trust for others — owners. In any case his position as manager no longer binds him to exercise power in terms of popular legitimacy, which depends on people over whom power is exercised recognizing it as binding. In bureaucracy, people are hired and fired at will, and acts of power do not derive from their consent to an ideological system that would legitimate them but from the psychological dependency of functionaries.*

In other words, it is not only entirely possible, but very probable,

---

*Such dependency in the realm of power relationships brings the relationship closer to one of force than to one of authority. Force rests on psychophysical grounds in human relationships. Authority rests on legitimacy — i.e., a belief in a shared system of ideas that explains or justifies why those in power *should* rule. Force is psychological; authority is ideological.

that power in bureaucracy is something quite different from what it was in society. If so, then the entry of bureaucratic power into the political arena, a part of society, is bound to be perceived as strange by those used to social-political power.

The same analysis holds for the second of Arnold's examples:

> Rosenwald, as head of Sears, Roebuck and Company, paid low wages and was uninterested in better working conditions for his employes. As an individual he was one of our greatest philanthropists. He had a complicated explanation for these two different roles and seemed to believe that he had thought the whole thing out logically. Instances of this kind among our knights errant of business are too commonplace to develop further. Liberals, observing this phenomenon through the spectacles of their theories are unable to understand it.[12]

At this point Arnold adds an explanation totally in accord with our own:

> They therefore assume that businessmen are hypocrites, not realizing that they are observing a fundamental principle of human organization.[13]

This principle is that people are different in bureaucracy than they are in society. But what is even more relevant here is that, being different people, they also develop a different kind of power to make others do their bidding.

Functionaries

How does bureaucratic power feel on the receiving end? How does it differ from political power? A major difference seems to be that instances of conflict, at which subordinates become conscious of power, tend in bureaucracy to revolve around issues of work. In politics conflict revolves around issues of belief.

For several years now I have been asking students in public administration how they like their jobs and, if not, why they keep them. We usually try to focus on a specific job situation in which an employe comes into conflict with a superior. The question then becomes: Why do you obey?

Employes tend to be highly perceptive when it comes to such questions. Some examples:

> I'm a deputy public relations director, and I really know my job. One of the things I do is pull together a newsletter every month. I've got people writing for me, I edit their stuff, I lay out the newsletter. Then the boss takes all my stuff and calls in the art director and does it all over.
>
> He knows I know layout, and I like to be involved on the cover. I think I've got artistic potential, for what it's worth. But he won't let me

have the satisfaction of putting it all together at the end. He's got to be in charge.

Sometimes I think it's his way of telling me I'm lucky to have my job. Lucky to be "allowed" to do as much as I do. I know I could do a better job than they do. And they know it. And they're telling me: we're in charge.[14]

In strict psychological terms, what the boss is here doing is to deny the deputy the chance for full personality development. The boss sees a deputy with highly developed skills on top of which he has a strong sense of knowing what is right. To allow that deputy to satisfy completely his own inner standards — to allow superego development — would be to surrender one specific type of power that bureaucracy allocates to superiors: the power to serve as the subordinate's externalized superego.* By insisting on retaining the final word on a project, the boss both uses the subordinate's strong drive for perfection and denies him the ultimate satisfaction of that drive. The subordinate obeys either because he has become dependent on the boss acting as final judge, perhaps because it relieves him of final responsibility, or because he fears the denial of what small amount of identity he has been allocated by the institution: he can always be demoted into a position where he will be more frustrated. Superego externalization, dependency, and threat to identity become here the psychological bases of bureaucratic power.

Similarly, another deputy director, this one of a public health nursing institution complained of her boss:

She'd give me responsibility alright. A job to do. And when I did it, she'd never say thanks, she'd make sure I wasn't around when she'd hand it to the big boss, and I'd be sent out to do some other job for her. . . . Some nights my boyfriend used to have to come around the office to pick up the pieces.[15]

The example may reflect a second way to exercise bureaucratic power: denial of a sense of ego. Employes, like all human beings, have to be somebody. A superior, in not recognizing their achievements, can deny the subordinate that sense not only of achievement and mastery, but of *being*. † At the same time, the subordinate knows that she or he needs the institution to be afforded any opportunity whatsoever to exercise both skills and limited mastery. This underlying knowledge may not always become conscious, but it is a

*On the externalization of the superego, see chapter 3.
†Mastery is especially a demand of professionals who have to work in bureaucratized institutions. For examples of the conflict involved, see George A. Miller, "Professionals in Bureaucracy: Alienation Among Industrial Scientists and Engineers," in Ada W. Finifter, ed., *Alienation and the Social System* (New York: Wiley, 1972), pp. 164 – 179.

taken-for-granted assumption on which all of us in institutions operate. It is exactly the superior's ability to deny us a sense of ego mastery that serves to remind us that without the institution we might not have the opportunity to exercise even the fragmented mastery that bureaucracy affords.*

The older the functionary, the less likely it is that he or she will be concerned with superego or ego issues and the more likely that pure survival will be exposed as the motivation for obeying. A project manager seventeen years with the U.S. Department of Health, Education and Welfare:

> When I first started, I saw that bureaucracy could be a great tool for opening up opportunities for people who would otherwise never have them, and I felt I was going to be the one to help give them that opportunity. I started out working for [a program supporting community health centers]. Funding wasn't too big in those years, but we had the idea that we were there to actually put health into the neighborhoods.
>
> I guess I was pushing too hard. I'd cut through red tape, tell my superiors how to actually get the job done in such a way they couldn't really get around doing it. I was rocking the boat. My superiors and the people I worked with didn't like me much, but I thought I was a hotshot and somebody would recognize me. When I got promotions I felt I had earned them.
>
> One day my boss called me in and said they needed someone in planning. I was being transferred. I haven't seen a live client in years. I got the message. I'd gone as far as I could. Now I'm concerned with security. I haven't got far to go to retirement.[16]

Behind every exercise of bureaucratic power lies the fact that everything a functionary is inside an institution is owed to that institution, at least in the sense that the institution can always take it away. Civil Service protection is no warranty against transfers, specially created non-jobs, and the daily threats to the identity that the organization giveth and taketh away.

Underlying obedience in bureaucracy is always the fear of being stripped of institutional identity and thus, having previously surrendered one's private personality to the institution, ceasing to be an entity. This is not to deny that other forms of power, aside from the psychological, are exercised in bureaucracy; but it is to assert that the only institutional basis for power, built in as a chief characteristic of this type of administrative structure, is psychological. Ultimately it always rests on fears and drives focused on the issue of institutional identity, especially to the degree that the functionary has no external personality.

*On the fragmentation of the ego as a psychological basis for power, see chapter 3.

In contrast, political power is notorious for its capacity to transcend the psychological and manipulative. In charismatic movements, for example, people at base follow leaders for the psychological reason that their existence is being threatened,* but in their own reports about their experience they follow because the leader is able to crystallize a prophetic message about the ultimate meaning of life (ideology).

With the penetration into politics of this kind of mere psychological power, shorn of all transcendental meaning, the polity would become one of the last holdout backwaters to finally be drained of ultimate meaning and mystery in a process of modernization that Max Weber called "the disenchantment of the world."

Finally, and to complete the circle from the discussion of bureaucratic power to the bureaucratization of politics itself, we can begin to give a new understanding to those who mourned and still mourn the last Romantic president, the passing of a politics and power that moved us through the magic of ideas. As one mourner put it:

> Kennedy was the first president who ever really spoke to me. I really listened to him, and because of him politics became to be meaningful to me. I remember sitting there . . . just listening to that drum beat rolling and rolling.[17]

WHAT THE EXPERTS SAY

Not many experts in the study of politics deal directly with the penetration of bureaucracy into the polity or with the changing nature of power in an increasingly bureaucratized world. Until very recently, the mainstream of American political scientists, for example, had contented itself with studying only official politics. In fact, this mainstream group of the past permitted the study of public administration to simply slip out of the domain of political science altogether, so that today there exist schools and colleges of public administration while the home of political scientists still is the smallest unit of the university — the department. Perhaps the most charitable explanation for this separation of politics from administration as fields of study is that the dominant political scientists felt that administration was, after all, supposed to be free from politics, and that therefore it was not properly part of a discipline focusing on the study of politics.

---

*I try to develop the dynamics of this psychology of charismatic followers in "Freud's Totem Theory as Complement to Max Weber's Theory of Charisma," *Psychological Reports*, 35 (October 1974), 683 – 686, and "Psychology of Charismatic Followers," *Psychological Reports*, 37 (December 1975), 759 – 770.

Recriminations aside, however, just as the arena of politics proper has been shrinking, a handful of political scientists and others concerned with the question "Where is power going?" have grown in influence.*

There is also a second group concerned with the changing nature of power. This group tends to be composed of those whose interest and training lie outside political science proper, probably because few political scientists had an interest in committing professional suicide by redefining their terms.

Bureaucratizing Politics: Mannheim, Bay

Mannheim: Bureaucratizing the Study of Politics
Karl Mannheim, operating from within the field known as the sociology of knowledge — which asks: What is the impact of knowledge on society? And what is the impact of society on knowledge?† — was perhaps the first to raise the question whether politics can be the subject of scientific study. His answer: "No!"[18] As an alternative, he suggests that if a science of politics ever were attempted, it would end up being the study of bureaucracy.

To get to the last point first:

> Every bureaucracy . . . in accord with the peculiar emphasis on its own position, tends to generalize its own experience and to overlook the fact that the realm of administration and of smoothly functioning order represents only a part of the total political reality. Bureaucratic thought does not deny the possibility of a science of politics, but regards it as identical with the science of administration. Thus irrational‡ factors are overlooked, and when these nevertheless force themselves to the fore, they are treated as "routine matters of state."[19]

---

*For surveys of this new generation of political scientists, see the following. For a new political science in the liberal-bourgeois mold, Charles A. McCoy and John Playford, eds., *Apolitical Politics*, which also includes three articles from a left perspective, and George J. Graham, Jr., and George W. Carey, eds., *The Post-Behavioral Era: Perspectives on Political Science* (New York: David McKay, 1972). Useful as a source book for recent work on the left is Michael Parenti's *Democracy for the Few* (New York: St. Martin's, 1974). A third force in the new political science is the phenomenological-existential approach. See Robert A. Isaak and Ralph P. Hummel, *Politics for Human Beings*, and Robert A. Isaak, *Individuals in World Politics* (North Scituate, Mass.: Duxbury Press, 1975).

†Or, as sociologist Joseph Bram has said [personal communication]: The sociology of knowledge asks about any particular statement, "Says who?!"

‡Mannheim here uses the concept "irrational" not in the popular sense of emotional or perhaps "insane," but in the same sense as Max Weber uses the term. The "irrational" is the not yet "rationalized"; it is all those behaviors for which there is as yet no pattern. These are the behaviors which in no sense have as yet become institutionalized, whether by institution we mean a language or custom or an organization like a bureaucracy.

Here Mannheim not only points to a possible source of revolution within bureaucracy, which tends to be blind to individual guerrilla-like activities, but accurately forecast the shape that Hitler's "irrational" revolution would take in Germany — new patterns tearing up the fabric of the old society, while at the same time being clothed in the legality of the old forms.

But the implications of Mannheim's thought for any current science of politics are even more serious. We may "scientize" the study of politics in the sense of looking for patterns of behavior, but to do so will be to overlook what is really political. This is hard for us to understand in the last quarter of the twentieth century, because we already have a political science and it does deal with *patterns* of behavior. Are we to conclude that it is not scientific? On the contrary, Mannheim answers, it may be scientific, but the more scientific it is the less it will deal with actual politics. This is the kind of accusation that makes intuitive sense to the politician, who sneers at the social science advisors he uses and discards when ready. But what kind of sense does it make to those who have a faith in science and sneer at intuition?

Mannheim's warning makes sense because of the way he defines politics:

> Political conduct, however, is concerned with the state and society in so far as they are still in the process of becoming. Political conduct is confronted with a process in which every moment creates a unique situation and seeks to disentangle out of this ever-flowing stream of forces something of enduring character. The question then is: "Is there a science of this becoming, a science of creative activity?"[20]

What Mannheim presents here is a theory of politics as it was before the current state of the bureaucratization of the world. The fact that almost no one in the American science of politics today looks at politics in this way — and, on the contrary, is always on the lookout for "patterns" of politics — can indicate only two things: either Mannheim's concept of politics is wrong, or our concept of politics has been so bureaucratized that we are no longer able to recognize true, creative politics.*

For Mannheim's concept to be "wrong," however, we would have to show that there can be not a single human experience of the kind that Mannheim describes as "politics." Before making a snap judgment, let us consider at greater length what Mannheim means by politics.

---

*The problem here is the same as we have already raised in regard to John R. Searle's concept of language (see chapter 4). There the possibility was discussed that what we speak today in bureaucracy is no longer fully language, but a truncated "language."

Mannheim sharply distinguishes politics from administration. Basing his thinking on that of the Austrian sociologist and statesman Albert Schäffle,[21] he distinguishes between "two aspects of sociopolitical life" discernible at any moment:

> . . . first, a series of social events which have acquired a set pattern and recur regularly; and, second, those events which are still in the process of becoming, in which, in individual cases, decisions have to be made that give rise to new and unique situations.[22]

Still referring to Schäffle, Mannheim summarizes: "The first he called the 'routine affairs of state,' *laufendes Staatsleben;** the second 'politics.'"[23]

> Administration is the domain where we can see exemplified what Schäffle means by "routine affairs of state." Wherever each new case may be taken care of in a prescribed manner, we are faced not with politics but with the settled and recurrent side of social life.[24]

Strictly speaking, then, we might be justified in concluding that true politics exists only in the form of revolution or in a desert land where no society existed before and where the first constitution is being created. Strictly speaking, also, only the first act of *creating* the constitution is pure politics. Every subsequent case in which the same proviso of the constitution is applied to a case circumscribed by that proviso already shifts into administration. Only a subsequent instance in which an old proviso of the constitution is applied to a totally new case — as the courts, for example, changed the concept of "liability," a part of the living Anglo-American constitution, following the advent of railroads and airplanes, not envisioned in the original concept — would again be purely or mainly political.

Actually, Mannheim himself does not draw such sharp distinctions. For example, he suggests that:

> We are in the realm of politics when envoys to foreign countries conclude treaties which were never made before; when parliamentary representatives carry through new measures of taxation; when an election campaign is waged; when certain opposition groups prepare a revolt or organize strikes — or when these are suppressed.[25]

But it is not necessary for Mannheim to follow his initial distinction strictly to the unhappy conclusion it holds for those who today think they are engaged in politics when they are actually

---

*Literally: the ongoing life of the state.

engaged in the routine administration of men and things according to rules long ago settled in a political act. Nor is there probably any use insisting on Mannheim's distinction against those who think they are engaged in a "political science" when what they are studying is not people engaged in the creative act of expressing their needs through politics, but people routinely enacting patterns of "pseudopolitics," whether or not these are related to political expression of human needs.

There is inherent in Mannheim's polarization of politics and administration* a standard of departure that allows us to ask to what extent any given human act is political or administrative. The behavior of diplomats, legislators, campaigners, and even revolutionaries is often so shot through with routine that a penetration of politics by administration can easily be charged — the same way that we are here charging an overall penetration of polity by bureaucracy.

Two conclusions are ultimately unavoidable, if Mannheim's definition of politics is for a moment accepted:

1. Those political scientists who think they have constructed a "science of politics" based on an understanding of past patterns of behavior have in reality created not a science of politics but a science of administration. This has been recognized by politicians themselves who take advantage of this knowledge of patterns — such as those derived from public opinion polls — to manipulate (administer) their constituents into voting for them. In doing so, the politicians, through the "science of politics," change the behavior of citizens from politics to administrative behavior. The politician, through his scientist advisors, becomes the kind of power-holder familiar to us in bureaucracy: the manager.

2. To the extent that political science, as a discipline composed of more than 15,000 living members of a professional organization called the American Political Science Association, is in itself a "knowledge industry," with the authority to give "expert" opinion on what is and what is not politics, scientists themselves are helping reshape the nature of politics as practiced by the citizen. For example, almost every student in college is exposed to at least one course in politics, political science, or American government. To the extent that such courses reinforce, rather than contradict, early socialization about the nature of politics, they create — most conveniently for those making a living out of "political science" — a

---

*Mannheim himself uses the term "polarity," and concedes that "it must be admitted that the boundary between these two classes is in reality rather flexible."

reality out there that just happens to correspond with the expectations of the professionals studying it.*

In any case, Mannheim presents us with an early distinction between a living and creative politics and the dead politics of routine. Ultimately, Mannheim demands a "new kind of knowledge" about politics of a kind that political science has not yet seen:

> It appears then that clear-cut and readily objectifiable knowledge is possible in so far as it is a question of grasping those elements in social reality which, to begin with, we described as settled and routinized components of social life. There does not seem to be any obstacle to the formulation of laws in this domain, since the objects of attention themselves obey a recurrent rhythm of regular sequence.†
>
> When, however, we enter the realm of politics, in which everything is in the process of becoming and where the collective element in us, as knowing subjects, helps to shape the process of becoming, where thought is not contemplation from the point of view of the spectator, but rather the active participation and reshaping of the process itself, a new type of knowledge seems to emerge, namely, that in which decision and standpoint are inseparably bound up together. In these realms, there is no such thing as a purely theoretical outlook on the part of the observer.[26]

Mannheim here attacks the possibility of an objective science of politics. His own position was that such a science would inescapably be bound to the conscious or unconscious political action programs of the scientist.[27] The other alternative is that the scientist becomes detached from the really acute moments of creative political behavior — and ends up unconsciously pursuing a science of administration. It is this latter point that is of special interest to us here.

Christian Bay: Politics as Pseudopolitics When Divorced from Human Goals

One of the first criticisms of current politics as something less than politics — pseudopolitics, to be precise — was launched by the political theorist Christian Bay.‡

---

*I am not suggesting that this is the origin of the bureaucratization of politics. That origin lies in the tendency of people to carry any good idea — like that of institutionalizing political solutions so they will not have to be solved over again and again anew — to the logical, absurd extreme. This tendency has also been observed by Max Weber in his essays in the sociology of religion — Max Weber, *Gesammelte Aufsätze zur Religionssoziologie* (Tübingen: J.C.B. Mohr, 1920–21). But political scientists must carry the burden of having made their small contribution to the legitimation of the apolitical status quo. The individual who aspires to the status of scientist, professional, or intellectual is the last to be absolved from the burden of moral responsibility even in an age where thinking becomes increasingly routinized; such people "know better."

†Compare with Wittgenstein's view of language in chapter 4.

‡First within the revolt of vanguard political scientists against the mainstream

Bay contended, in a landmark article published in 1965, that much of what practitioners and analysts call politics is not politics at all. First he gives a definition of what he means by politics:

> I would define as *political* all activity aimed at improving or protecting conditions for the satisfaction of human needs and demands in a given society according to some universalistic scheme of priorities, implicit or explicit.[28]

While it is possible under this definition to consider administration as political — a fact that results in a widening of the scope of political science — it is at the same time a critique of *all activities* that claim to be political but are not directly related to the fulfillment of human needs. The avowed purpose of Bay's critique was to correct what he saw as a trend among "a growing and now indeed a predominant proportion of leading American political scientists, the behavioralists,"[29] toward achieving science while "strenuously avoiding that dangerous subject, politics."[30]

Bay's central argument is that, contrary to the claim of having achieved science by separating values from the study of politics, "much of the current work on political behavior generally fails to articulate its very real value biases, and that the political impact of this supposedly neutral literature is generally conservative and in a special sense anti-political."[31] Here we are less concerned with the charge of conservatism than with the charge that both political science and its concept of politics have somehow become anti-political.

Bay's argument divides into two subarguments. In the first, he accuses political scientists of having committed exactly that kind of sin we have charged bureaucracy with committing — emphasizing means over ends. The central values of bureaucracy — efficiency, formal rationality, reliability — are all means to ends, as we have pointed out previously.* While these may be proper standards for early bureaucracy, as a tool firmly grasped in the hands of society, the ascendancy of such methods over human needs seems to be the natural result of the rise of bureaucracy over society.

The form taken in political science by this triumph of human tools over people is spelled out by Bay in terms almost exactly parallel to our analysis of bureaucracy. He begins with a definition of politics by Robert Dahl, a man Bay calls "unquestionably" one of the "most influential political scientists of the present generation": "A political system is any persistent pattern of human relationships

---

behavioralists as well as traditionalists. The critique initiated by Bay culminated in what is known in American political science as "the post-behavioral revolution."

*See chapter 2.

that involves, to a significant extent, power, rule, or authority."[32]

What this definition lacks, Bay observes, is "any reference to a public purpose." Just as we have found that means become the supreme standards for behavior for the functionary in bureaucracy, the means of politics have become, Bay finds, the supreme concern of political scientists. That such means are intended to be used for a further, overarching human purpose — the satisfaction of human needs — is ignored:

> Research work on power, rule, or authority can contribute significantly to our political knowledge, even if the data come from contexts not ordinarily thought of as political. But its significance must be gauged in relation to some criteria; until these are articulated and justified, or at any rate chosen, we can only intuit whether our researches on, say, power behavior are tackling significant or trivial issues.[33]

In exactly the same way, the emphasis of bureaucracies on internal efficiency among two links in their long means-means chains is not a guarantee of either accountability to legislators or effectiveness in serving the public. Political scientists have fallen victim, Bay seems to say, to analysis, the devil of science. They have taken apart the political act so much that they have forgotten what the act was intended for. In the same sense, and for the same reason — namely, preoccupation with the analytic in the scientific method — bureaucracies and their staff forget what their public purposes are. They drown in the analytic and forget the transformation with which they are ultimately charged — that is, converting public or private investments into public or private products or services.

Thus Bay calls for a return to developing a political theory that deals with *basic human needs*,[34] an appeal which in itself reflects the likelihood that something has seriously gone wrong with the minds of those who study political science. Specifically, I would like to call what has gone wrong the bureaucratization of thinking about politics.

A second argument that Bay makes is that the dominant experts of his day saw the way American politics was conducted as permanently institutionalized. Bay writes:

> What is anti-political is the assumption, explicit or implicit, that politics, or at any rate American politics, is and must always remain primarily a system of rules for peaceful battles between competing private interests, and not an arena for the struggle toward a more humane and more rationally organized society.[35]

While Bay speaks only tangentially against the bureaucratization of life — the overemphasis on occupational roles, status anxieties, and despair about lack of purpose[36] — his critique against the behavioralist concept of politics can be interpreted as critical of bureaucratization in two ways. First, Bay's comment highlights the fact that Americans see their system of politics as a *finished* business — as a system, an institutionalization. Second, while there is nothing wrong with institutionalization as such, the American system can be said to partake of a typical fault also characteristic of developed bureaucracy — namely, putting the institution's rules above the purposes for which the institution was set up. What Bay is pointing out is that maintaining the "rules for peaceful battles" has become in America more important than seeing to it that someone wins these battles — that is, seeing that the needs of human beings are satisfied through politics.

In summary, we may extend Bay's comments to our own consideration of bureaucracy. When politics has become an end in itself, whether or not it satisfies human needs, it has become an institution very compatible with developed bureaucracy, whose chief trait is also the supremacy of its own life over the lives of the citizens and clients it was set up to serve. We are able, therefore, to discover in the present state of American politics and bureaucracy a kind of "elective affinity," which should make the eventual penetration of politics by bureaucracy all the easier.

Bureaucratizing Power: Berle, Habermas

There is no need to repeat the literature reflecting the transposition of political control from individuals, groups, and the public arena at large to political backrooms,[37] to managers of private bureaucracies in industry and business,[38] to a power elite of politicians and representatives of the military-industrial complex (private and public bureaucracies),[39] and to a new class of bureaucrats as a whole.[40] This literature is readily available.

What needs to be explained are the changes in administrative technique that could bring about the bureaucracy's replacement of polity as the central power instrument in society.

The answers suggested in the following center around the idea that the changing nature of work itself has changed the nature of power. Specifically what can be seen overall is a shift from power based on authority to power based on force. This is not immediately obvious with the first experts to be discussed, A. A. Berle and Gardiner Means, but may become so by the time we reach the thought of Jürgen Habermas.

A. A. Berle and Gardiner Means:
The Changing Meaning of Property

Property has always meant power — at least economic power. But in the modern Western political systems, in which ownership of property has from the beginning been equated with human dignity, property ownership also qualified the owner in the eyes of others to the exercise of power.[41] Property ownership was originally legitimated religiously and later through habit.* Most specifically, the idea of property implied the psychology of autonomous man capable of making over the world in his own image and deserving to preserve the spoils to himself.

Then in the 1930s, A. A. Berle, a law professor at Columbia, and Gardiner C. Means, an economist, discovered something strange was happening to the concept of property just as the modern corporation started taking over from the individualist private enterprisers who had founded modern industry and business.

Ownership of property no longer meant control over the power that went with it. The rich might own property, but managers who often owned little controlled property. Berle and Means summarize their position as follows:

> To Adam Smith and to his followers, private property was a unity involving possession. He assumed that ownership and control were combined. Today, in the modern corporation, this unity has been broken. *Passive property,* — specifically, shares of stocks or bonds, — gives its possessors an interest in an enterprise but gives them practically no control over it, and involves no responsibility. *Active property,* — plant, good will, organization, and so forth which make up the actual enterprise, — is controlled by individuals who, almost invariably, have only minor ownership interests in it.[42]

With this change in the concept of property, important related concepts and behaviors also change. The authors specifically treat the concepts of "wealth," "private enterprise," "individual initiative," "the profit motive," and "competition."[43]

What this implied for the realm of politics — as the activity by which decisions are made that affect how we conduct our daily lives and what we get in them — was that at least the economic basis of power was shifting from the control of owners (the rich) to the control of managers (the skilled). Owners, however, conceived of themselves primarily as members of society, or of economy within society. Managers conceived of themselves first as members of

---

*This is a central argument of Max Weber's *The Protestant Ethic and the Spirit of Capitalism.*

bureaucracy, and only secondarily, if at all, as members of society. In other words, what Berle and Means had found was the basis for the shift of economic power from society to bureaucracy. That basis lay in the superiority of modern management techniques as against old-fashioned attempts of one man to steer an industry single-handedly through personal leadership and lone intellect. Even Henry Ford, founder of the then largest automobile empire, had to yield to the superiority of modern management (bureaucracy) when in the Second World War he was threatened with either giving up his one-man control or having the government take over his empire. In the competition for the control of large enterprises, man is no match for management.

If modern bureaucratic management's superiority in the handling and coordinating of people in vast enterprises — i.e., from the top down — caused the nature of economic power to change, then changes in the nature of power over labor are also implied. It is with changes in the nature of power exercised on the job — that is, with changes in power at the bottom — that Jürgen Habermas concerns himself.*

That the shift from private property to management control in vast bureaucracies implies also a shift of the basis of power from legitimate authority to force is not yet apparent until we examine the nature of power relationships of work. For now, however, the newcomer to the world of bureaucracy should be able to draw from the above an explanation for the impersonality with which power is exercised by his managers. In the modern bureaucracy it is distinctly wrong to say a manager "has" power. In the prebureaucratic stage of administration, he might indeed "have" power in the sense of basing his commands on something he possessed: property. In the modern bureaucratic stage, the manager bases his power not on things he possesses but on qualities: skills. But the only justification for the exercise of management power based on management skills is that these skills exist. Contrary to the power concept based on property, which in turn was legitimated by a whole theology of who

---

*As a final note on Berle and Means's discovery, it may be observed that Means updated the original data on the concentration of economic power in the hands of corporate management in testimony before a U.S. Senate subcommittee in 1964. Means estimated "that the 100 largest manufacturing corporations in 1962 controlled at least 49 percent of the assets of all manufacturing corporations (excluding stocks in other corporations) and 58 percent of the net capital assets — the net land, buildings, and equipment — of all manufacturing corporations." The comparative estimates for 1929 were 40 percent and 44 percent, respectively. (Gardiner C. Means, "Economic Concentration," reprinted in Edward S. Greenberg and Richard P. Young, *American Politics Reconsidered: Power and Inequity in America* [North Scituate, Mass.: Duxbury Press, 1973], p. 77 especially.)

properly could possess property and how it might properly be obtained, the power concept based on skills has no further legitimation than the existence of these skills themselves.

In this sense, modern bureaucracy has developed a forerunner of a new kind of power that is specifically not legitimated in some metaphysics or religion — that is, in some further explanation that tells those over whom it is exercised why such power exercise is right and proper.* Power simply is because it is. Either the manager has the skill to manipulate me, or he doesn't. If there is any rationale of why he *should* possess power, it must be: He is able to manipulate me, therefore it is right that he manipulate me. In other words: He has power, therefore it is right that he should have power. This is a highly circular argument, and one that is easily penetrated by anyone. Systems based on such nonlegitimated exercise of power, lacking a "deeper" meaning or reason for obedience, have historically been short-lived.

Jürgen Habermas:
The Changing Nature of Power on the Job
As a sociologist and philosopher, Jürgen Habermas clearly distinguishes between the nature of power in society and power in bureaucracy, or as he labels the contrasting life worlds, between "institutional frameworks of symbolic interaction" and "systems of purposive-rational action."†

In fact, Habermas distinguishes between the kind of activity that goes on in society and the kind that dominates bureaucracy by calling the first "symbolic interaction" and the second "work." In the world of "symbolic interaction," Habermas seems to argue, we orient all our activities, including our work, toward approval by other human beings. In the world of "work," including bureaucracy, we orient all our activities toward work, making human relations secondary. In the first, work is a means; in the second, work becomes an end.

*This legitimation crisis has created major legal problems, especially in the private sphere, as to who really owns corporations. For a recent example of a solution similar to that of Berle and Means, see David Ellerman, "The 'Ownership of the Firm' Is a Myth," *Administration & Society*, vol. 7 (May 1975), 27 – 42. Rejecting the idea that owners are the firm, Ellerman suggests this definition: "We will call that party — which owns the outputs, is liable for the inputs, and holds the management rights — the firm." (p.27.) This definition holds monumental implications for the legal responsibility of managers of public institutions as well, whose bureaucratization has made the question of public ownership and the reality of public control obsolete.

†Habermas borrows the term "purposive-rational" from Weber, but includes in it, unlike Weber, both instrumental (short-term connecting of means to means) and strategic (long-term connecting of means to ends) action.

How does this transition come about? How does work change power?

In the world of work, Habermas says, violation of a rule, that is, opposition to the exercise of power, has a totally different consequence than such violation has in society; it is punished differently. "*Incompetent* behavior," Habermas states, "which violates valid technical rules or strategies, is condemned per se to failure through lack of success . . . the punishment is built, so to speak, into its rebuff by reality."[44] It is this rule of nature on which the power of managers and technocrats is built. Science has created a world in which human beings first manipulate nature (technology) and, in order to do so, manipulate other human beings (bureaucracy). In contrast to the world of community and society, what matters in the new world is whether such manipulation *works*, not whether it is approved by others. In such a world managers have power as long as they succeed in manipulating functionaries. Their empirical managerial skills, tested again and again, are their power. In the same way, workers exercise "power" over matter if and when, and as long as, matter yields before their hands.

In short, what is right and wrong in a work-oriented world is evident in the success or failure of any given piece of work itself. A "wrong" command is measured in the "failure" of the work to be accomplished. A wrong step in management is punished by failure to get people to respond as intended; it is an error in a natural science of human manipulation. When we order others to obey, then, we are "right" in so ordering if subsequent to our order they obey. We are "wrong," on technical grounds, when they refuse. For power, as has been said before, there is no further justification than that it is — power.

In contrast, what is incompetent behavior in bureaucracy was deviant behavior in society. Not that work done in society did not have its own internal indicators of success or failure, of competence. But there also was a higher standard than competence in a given task. That standard was whether the task itself was considered by society at large as a desirable task, as a means toward an overall end that helped society to survive or achieve whatever other cultural goals it might set for itself. In Habermas's words: "*Deviant* behavior, which violates consensual norms, provokes sanctions that are connected with the rules only externally, 'that is by convention."[45]

In the one world, society, we develop social competence, which resides in our personality. In the world of work, bureaucracy, we develop technical competence skills: "Learned rules of purposive-rational action supply us with *skills*, internalized norms with *per-*

sonality structures. Skills put us in a position to solve problems; motivations allow us to follow norms."[46]

Here we have an explanation not only for the differential perception of the nature of power in bureaucracy and society, but for the sense of *technical* incompetence suffered by those of us who, having gotten along fine with others in society, now must measure up to work standards in bureaucracy. Bureaucracy thoroughly resists the carrying over of social competency into a field where technical expertise is the essential requirement.

The difference between the world of work and the world of social (symbolic) interaction is defined by Habermas as follows:

> By "work" or *purposive-rational action* I understand either instrumental action or rational choice or their conjunction. Instrumental action is governed by *technical rules* based on empirical knowledge. In every case they imply conditional predictions about observable events, physical or social. These predictions can prove correct or incorrect. The conduct of rational choice is governed by *strategies* based on analytic knowledge. They imply deductions from preference rules (value systems) and decision procedures: these propositions are either correctly or incorrectly deduced. Purposive-rational action realizes defined goals under given conditions. But while instrumental action organizes means that are appropriate or inappropriate according to criteria of an effective control of reality, strategic action depends only on the correct evaluation of possible alternative choices, which results from calculation supplemented by values and maxims.[47]

In contrast, the world of society was characterized by communication among people about what they, as a society, wanted to accomplish and what means might properly be used.* This kind of interaction, Habermas calls "communicative action" or "symbolic interaction," because it is defined by shared symbols commonly arrived at in a social context. This view of society — as a world of communications set in a context of mutually perceived problems leading to a shared meaning of symbols — is entirely compatible with John Searle's concept of social language. It is, of course, totally incompatible with machine language of the modern bureaucracy and the computer, which relates not to the norms of people but to

---

*The problem with work in bureaucracy is that, as bureaucracy separates itself out from control by society according to society's overall goals, it becomes difficult for workers to find their work meaningful because there is a high chance that for society's overall goals it is meaningless. In any case, functionaries are often so far removed from the level where such integration between bureaucracy and society can be made, that information about such integration of means (bureaucracy) and ends (society) is simply not available to them. This also affects the degree of legitimacy with which they greet the commands given them. They may obey them because of

getting a piece of work done.* Symbolic interaction, Habermas
writes,

> is governed by binding *consensual norms*, which define reciprocal
> expectations about behavior and which must be understood and
> recognized by at least two acting subjects. Social norms are enforced
> through sanctions. Their meaning is objectified in ordinary language
> communication.[48]

Society dies when science, technology, and bureaucracy demonstrate the superiority of work over social action in achieving the
goal with which modern man is preoccupied — the conquest by man
over matter. But not only society, its ways of applying sanctions, its
ways of power also die.

> The rationality of language games, associated with communicative
> action, is confronted at the threshold of the modern period with the
> rationality of means-ends relations, associated with instrumental and
> strategic action. As soon as this confrontation can arise, the end of
> traditional society is in sight: the traditional form of legitimation breaks
> down.[49]

It is at this point that we experience the transmutation of political
power into technical power. Technical power is superior when it
confronts political power because it can command, in war for example,
instruments of material destruction infinitely superior in effectiveness
to instruments of political power.

A reporter once asked Mahatma Gandhi how he would meet the
power of the atom bomb with his political, in the largest sense,
movement of nonviolence. Gandhi said:

> I will not go underground, I will not go into shelter. I will come out in
> the open and let the pilot see I have not a trace of evil against him. The
> pilot will not see our faces from his great height, I know. But that
> longing in our hearts — that he will not come to harm — would reach
> up to him and his eyes would be opened.[50]

A few years later, Gandhi was killed by a technical tool made possible
by science — a revolver. Purity of heart and moral power, even that
forged into a political movement, cannot resist the ultimate power of

---

the binding psychology of bureaucracy; but they may not necessarily be able to
rationalize them in terms of an ideology, philosophy, or religion — that is, in terms of
systems of knowledge in which are anchored and spelled out people's basic beliefs
about the meaning of the world and their place in it.

*See chapter 4, subsection on differing concepts of language in bureaucracy and
society as established using a Searlean approach.

either technology or bureaucracy, which is force.*

However, as long as people the world over are concerned with the quick and general delivery of the means for purely material survival that science, technology, and bureaucracy promise, we are tempted by the irresistible appeal of power based on control over material work, and over people to do the work. This power, organized into vast institutions, is, because it controls both humans and matter as material tools, superior to political power related to organizing people through symbolic interaction toward cultural goals. Here we find not only a description of the transmutation of power, from political into technical and administrative, but an explanation for the death of public politics. When power can be properly exercised only by experts, because these demonstrate their ability to exert control over people and machines, then the claim of the old participants in politics, citizens and politicians, to have a part in controlling such power is rejected. In fact, both the citizen and the politician are disqualified from the new apolitics. They are replaced by functionaries and by experts, including experts over people — managers — and experts over matter — professionals. Habermas comments on this:

> Old-style politics was forced, merely through its traditional form of legitimation, to define itself in relation to practical goals: the "good life" was interpreted in a context defined by interaction relations.[51]

The new substitute system is one of a "politics"† by experts and administrators. These now make decisions not only for their proper sphere, technology and bureaucracy, but for all spheres of life.‡ Their ascendancy over politicians is assured as long as people bow to the superiority of expertise:

> The solution of technical problems is not dependent on public dis-

---

*To argue that the immense material power of either modern industrial, business, public administrative, or military organizations can be wielded only if people are properly motivated by attachment to ideas and a sense of what is just and proper is to speak from the standpoint of an obsolete social reality. The reality of power and obedience in bureaucracy is that people do what they do because they are psychologically pressured to do it. Psychology replaces ideology as the ultimate motivation. Motivation replaces legitimation. It is therefore of doubtful value to predict, as Habermas has done more recently, a "legitimation crisis." See Jürgen Habermas, *Legitimation Crisis* (Boston: Beacon Press, 1975). Late bureaucracy's transformation of the basis of power has very handily circumvented just such a legitimation crisis by lowering the consciousness of people to the psychological-physiological level.

†Put into quotation marks here for the same reason that "language" had to be put into quotations in chapter 4: no one from the old system of politics would recognize technical and administrative decision-making today as politics in the old public sense.

‡This expert control over decisions affecting the public is what I have previously labeled "apolitics."

cussion. Rather, public discussions could render problematic the frame-work within which the tasks of government action present themselves as technical ones.[52]

For this reason the new secret decision-making of bureaucratic politics is also forced to enter into, and attempt to wipe out, the realm of the old-style public politics. Following this bureaucratic takeover, it may be correct, as Habermas says, that "the new politics of state interventionism requires a depolitization of the mass of the popula-tion."[53] Further, in exactly the same way that Christian Bay pointed out above, "to the extent that practical questions are eliminated, the public realm also loses its political function."[54] When politics be-comes removed from paying attention to designing means to reach ultimate social goals, and instead concerns itself only with the short-term maintenance of the internal standards of efficiency, reli-ability, and control that the advent of bureaucratic decision-making means, then it can no longer be called politics.

In this way, Habermas presents, through an exposition of the changed meaning of power, an explanation for the replacement of polity by bureaucracy. Fundamentally, this explanation says that bureaucracy contains a different kind of power than does society. This kind of power is incompatible with traditional politics as a way of reaching social goals but is, at least initially, superior to it in promising or reaching material goals. By the time that superiority could appear to be doubtful, the personal investment of bureaucrats, and their inability to evade the psychological power grip exercised over them, makes a rethinking of the preference for bureaucratic over political systems impossible. Therefore bureaucratic power triumphs over political power. Bureaucracy replaces polity.

BUREAUCRACY, POWER, AND POLITY

The practical result of the depolitizing of politics is that sense of frustration and meaninglessness citizens experience when confronted with the pseudoreality of public politics:

> A national politics which has both parties posturing without joining for debate on issues; manufacturing mass images and construing "democ-racy" as a plebiscitary decision between sets of administrative appeals. There is no discussion of the dilemmas of the society but rather different packages presented as to how to deliver to specific groups.[55]

This is exactly how Christian Bay, as a political scientist, defines pseudopolitics.[56] And citizens of society and polity, expecting to see some connection made through politics between their human needs and public policy, do not need to be experts to sense something is radically wrong when they enter the skeleton that is left of the body politic.

As a further result, citizens can explain to themselves the strangeness of the bureaucratized political world by the absence of politics from it:

> The very existence of a *political* process is today questionable and it is perhaps more accurately viewed as a planning mechanism for the economy and a service delivery system for the needs of organizable groups. The inflexibility of the federal budget priorities and the limited power that the Congress has over these allocations reveal the regulative nonpolitical character of the American state. Add to this structural inflexibility the further rigidity resulting from decision-making procedures, such as cost-effectiveness or the Planning, Programming, Budgeting System* that technically constrain the action of either political party when it comes to power. But perhaps the most serious political distortion is the growth of the nonpublic decision-making procedures of government.[57]

Similarly, understanding the changed nature of power, the functionary in an official bureaucracy can now rest assured that power applied by his managers to him is, as long as it is in harmony with the bureaucracy's overall technical needs, not political at all. In a real sense, therefore, it is true when your supervisor tells you: "Nothing personal in this, Joe, but you're fired. You just didn't fit in." Should a personal political judgment, of individual self-interest, nevertheless creep into a manager's judgment, we can expect that manager to be eventually punished by his or her own acts; acts of management will, over the long run, not work and he or she, too, will be replaced — unless the bureaucracy as a whole and all its members want to face the prospect of going under.

In summary, as strangers in the land of bureaucracy we can expect to see two strange sights both related to politics and power. Bureaucracy will itself become more political in the sense that decisions on behalf of the public will increasingly be made by experts and managers of public and private enterprises. One reason that such politics in bureaucracy will not look political is not only that it is not public, but that the kind of power exercised is no longer ideological but merely psychological, constituting physical and psychological force. Secondly, what is left of the social-political arena will become

---

*The defeat of PPBS in the federal government, after its official institution by President Lyndon B. Johnson, is generally interpreted as the outcome of a battle between politicians, who saw PPBS as an instrument depriving them of political (or, more exactly, pseudopolitical) power, and long-term planners who claimed such power for themselves on the grounds that only experts could make long-term political decisions for the United States. It is my personal opinion that, if the trends discussed here are real, PPBS may have lost a battle but not the war.

bureaucratized, which means that bureaucratic power will replace political power: politicians will look more and more like managers or will be run by managers. Ideology and ideals will still play roles in political campaigns — but only apparently, as tools to be manipulated by campaign managers. People will no longer vote, they will be voted. The sense of alienation will increase because, though we will feel pressured psychologically to take part in politics — just as the functionary in bureaucracy is pressured psychologically to take part in that system — we will not have a sense that the political system into which we are impressed is in any sense legitimate. In truth, we will be likely to feel on many occasions that it, like bureaucracy, is illegitimate and for the same reasons.

In bureaucracy, we can no longer see who the people are who set it up, we no longer even know our fellow workers, and we do not know the people whom it serves. As the political system becomes bureaucratized, we are likely to increasingly ask questions like the following: Why should those who designed and maintain the system — the Founding Fathers and politicians — have a *right* to do so? What purpose does participating in politics serve? Is there a higher purpose, some kind of meaning to political routines like voting? And finally, in both bureaucracy and bureaucratized polity, we will ask: Why should we as workers and citizens serve or support the clients allocated to us? That is, what is the overarching rationale that justifies that these specific clients or citizen groups deserve our public service and our tax dollars. This future is already here.

SUMMARY

Administration of the bureaucratic kind is not an effective replacement for traditional politics. The ultimate reason for this transcends the objection that nonpublic decision-making and the psychological manipulation of human beings by human beings exclude processes essential to the healthy polity.

Bureaucracy cannot ultimately become a polity, an instrument for finding and maintaining the good life, because of the very nature of its inhabitants. These inhabitants are not in touch with the needs of others because they do not socially treat others as human beings, but rather as cases. Psychologically, none of them is a human being entire of himself and is therefore incapable of either the range of human feeling that makes man man or of the full range of cognitive thinking operations for problem solving. The very success of the best bureaucracy with its integration of interdependent functionaries means ultimately that there may be integration and interdependence, but not a single human being. Culturally, the functionaries of systems are

acquainted with only the internal values of their machinelike enterprise, but have no experience in struggling to define and determine
ultimate values. Their very language, reflecting a mode of thought
and a mode of operation, makes impossible the causal thinking
requisite for attempting to answer the ultimate questions of human
existence.*

As long as such characteristics leave their mark on modern
systems of administration, they are incapable of superseding the
polity in effectiveness, no matter how hard they struggle to overcome
the bad name of bureaucracy by calling themselves open systems and
the like. In combination with science, bureaucracy can calculate the
cost of pursuing certain society-wide goals against others. In combination with technology, bureaucracy can administer most efficiently the pursuit of one set of goals against others. But there is
nothing in the social relations, culture, psychology, language, and
thought of the bureaucrat that gives him the capacity to replace the
political philosopher or the political process. Unfortunately, there is,
of course, all the power in the world available to him and no reason to
think that the bureaucrat will restrain himself from the use of power
any more than any of the rulers who preceded him.

Against all this pessimism, which logically derives from the
description of the innate tendencies of the rationalization of the
world, of which bureaucracy is the administrator, only one hope
remains for a revolution toward freedom and survival. That hope lies
in the remembrance, by some of us, that other experiences and other
ways of life, aside from the bureaucratic one, are possible.

Left to us as power instruments are all those kinds of power
which bureaucracy has not yet absorbed into its systems of control.
Bureaucracy's power is mainly, but also merely, psychological. Orig-
inating in a great idea — that humanity might conquer its difficulties
by applying science to administration — bureaucracy's continuing
power is basically idea-less. Because successful administration rests
on the reliability of functionaries, they must be kept away from great
ideas. Efficiency, duty, and the experience of being a cog in the wheel
do not replace the questioning of the ultimate meaning of life; the
absurdity of life terminated by death; the experiences of love, hate,
justice, and oppression; or the final hope and terror of salvation and

---

*For these reasons it would be a mistake to consider modern institutions "private
political systems," as Alain Touraine has done. Rather, following a school of thought
from Aristotle to Christian Bay, such institutions must be considered "*pseudo*-political
systems." What characterizes them is the built-in inability to conceive of an adaptive,
life-assertive ultimate "good" for its members while nevertheless making ultimate
decisions governing their lives. Cf., Alain Touraine, *The Post-Industrial Society —
Tomorrow's Social History: Classes, Conflicts and Culture in the Programmed Society*, trans.
Leonard F.X. Mayhew (New York: Random House, 1971), p. 145 ff.

damnation. In Jürgen Habermas's words, "The industrially most advanced societies seem to approximate the model of behavioral control steered by external stimuli rather than guided by norms."[58] Bureaucracy has not yet developed a successful ideology, and it is possible that inherently it never can.*

The study of the new form of power applied by bureaucracy will then be essential to opposing its more blatant claims to hegemony over mankind. Against mere psychological dependency can be brought to bear the promise of freedom through ideas. It still has to be shown whether a system of organization basing itself on the inability of its people to think causally or attach themselves affectively to ideas once thought through to their consequences is ultimately superior in a war waged by the truly political, those who understand and are moved by reason, responsibility, and legitimacy. The fact that for most of its functionaries, bureaucracy, as the incarnation of the widest and fullest use of reason at the point of its design, has become the grave of reason is an indication of its self-destructive impulses.

NOTES

1. Max Weber, "Parliament and Government in a Reconstructed Germany," Appendix II to *Economy and Society* (New York: Bedminster Press, 1968), p. 1393.

2. Ibid., p. 1403. Weber's italics.

3. Separate studies recently undertaken and based on Gallup and Harris polls, along with research undertaken by the main academic research organization, the Survey Research Institute at the University of Michigan, are Robert S. Gilmour and Robert B. Lamb, *Political Alienation in Contemporary America* (New York: St. Martin's, 1975), Ada W. Finifter, ed., *Alienation and the Social System* (New York: John Wiley, 1972), William Watts and Lloyd A. Free, eds., *State of the Nation* (New York: Universe Books, A Potomac Associates Book, 1973), and Louis Harris, *The Anguish of Change* (New York: W.W. Norton, 1973).

4. Harris, *Anguish of Change*, p. 12. Confidence in business, religious, scientific, medical, military, and other leaders dropped similarly.

5. Gilmour and Lamb, *Political Alienation*, p. 17.

6. Harris, *Anguish of Change*, p. 15.

7. James David Barber, *The Presidential Character: Predicting Performance in the White House* (Englewood Cliffs, N.J.: Prentice-Hall, 1972), p. 328.

*While Habermas nevertheless speaks of "the ideological power of the technocratic consciousness," we must ask ourselves whether we can still seriously apply terms like ideology to the idea-less society he himself describes. While the effect of a forced adherence to norms of technicality through a psychology of dependence may indeed be "ideological" in the sense of preserving the status quo, what characterizes the "logos" of the new "ideology" (to take the word apart to its roots) is its specific freedom from the presence of ideas. But given the absence of ideas we return to the material "logos" in which we may discourse about raw nature and even have a theory of man in his base material form, but we no longer speak of how man discourses with himself through ideas.

8. Ibid., p. 336.

9. Harris, *Anguish of Change*, p. 18.

10. Ibid., p. 20.

11. Thurman Arnold, *The Folklore of Capitalism* (New Haven: Yale University Press, Yale Paperbound, 1959), p. 353.

12. Ibid., pp. 353 – 354.

13. Ibid. Italics mine for emphasis.

14. Class discussion in Organization Theory, New York University, Graduate School of Public Administration, spring term 1976.

15. Ibid.

16. Ibid.

17. Gilmour and Lamb, *Political Alienation*, pp. 51 – 52.

18. Karl Mannheim, *Ideology and Utopia* (New York: Harcourt, Brace & World, 1956), chapter III, "The Prospects of Scientific Politics: The Relationship between Social Theory and Political Practice," pp. 109 – 191.

19. Ibid., p. 119.

20. Ibid., p. 112.

21. See Albert Schäffle, "Ueber den wissenschaftlichen Begriff der Politik," *Zeitschrift für die gesamte Staatswissenschaft*, vol. 53 (1897).

22. Mannheim, *Ideology and Utopia*, pp. 112 – 113.

23. Ibid., p. 113.

24. Ibid., p. 113.

25. Ibid.

26. Ibid., p. 170.

27. Ibid., p. 117: "It is our task definitely to establish the thesis that in politics statements of a problem and the logical techniques involved vary with the political position of the observer." On positions taken in the recent battle in American political science over this issue, see also Isaak and Hummel, "Post-Behavioralism and the New Political Science," *Politics for Human Beings*, pp. 249 – 250, and the works cited at the beginning of this section.

28. Christian Bay, "Politics and Pseudopolitics: A Critical Evaluation of Some Behavioral Literature," *The American Political Science Review*, LIX (March 1965), 39 – 51. Reprinted in Charles A. McCoy and John Playford, eds., *Apolitical Politics: A Critique of Behavioralism* (New York: Crowell, 1967), pp. 12 – 37; this citation, p. 15.

29. For expositions of behavioralism in political science, see Heinz Eulau, Samuel J. Eldersveld, Morris Janowitz, eds., *Political Behavior: A Reader in Theory and Research* (Glencoe, Ill.: Free Press, 1956), Austin Ranney, ed., *Essays on the Behavioral Study of Politics* (Urbana, Ill.: University of Illinois Press, 1962), and Sidney Ulmer, ed., *Introductory Readings in Political Behavior* (Chicago: Rand McNally, 1961). The members of the behavioralist movement originally contrasted themselves against institutionalists and constitutionalists, whom they accused of spending too much time studying politics by looking at the way institutions and constitutions were supposed to work. Instead, the behavioralists said they were looking at the actual political behavior of living people — what *is* rather than what *ought* to be. This distinction between "is" and "ought" precipitated itself in the behavioralists' claim that in order to find out what "is," political scientists had to separate themselves from any attachment to values — become "value-free." This possibility is put in serious question by the works of epistemologists, including Max Weber's theory of knowledge. For a recent contention that "science, like the economy, has its own political philosophy," see Ernest Gellner, *Legitimation of Belief* (London: Cambridge University Press, 1974), pp. 168 – 184.

30. Bay, "Politics and Pseudopolitics," in McCoy and Playford, *Apolitical Politics*, p. 12. Bay is here referring to an earlier and much-cited comment by Alfred Cobban that political science is "a device, invented by university teachers, for avoiding that dangerous subject politics, without achieving science." (Cobban, "The Decline of Political Theory," *Political Science Quarterly*, 48 [1953], 335.)

31. Ibid., p. 14.

32. Ibid., p. 14. Bay here graciously overlooks the fact that Dahl's definition is not a definition of politics at all but a definition of a political system. This discrepancy is all

the more striking since the title of the chapter in which the definition appears asks the question: "What Is Politics?" Dahl never answers this question.

The slip-up can, however, be understood in terms of Karl Mannheim's accusations that social scientists often mislabel as politics already existing *routines* of problem solving. Systems are such routines institutionalized. Dahl is probably thinking of what Mannheim would call administration when he defines politics not in terms of individuals creatively expressing their needs and finding solutions in the public arena, but in terms of needs and solutions already created long ago by people long since dead and incorporated into a "system." Dahl's stand reflects the advance of the bureaucratization of politics even in the concepts of scientists.

33. Ibid.

34. Ibid., especially p. 30.

35. Ibid., pp. 22 – 23.

36. Ibid., p. 36.

37. See Peter Bachrach and Morton S. Baratz, *Power and Poverty: Theory and Practice* (New York: Oxford University Press, 1970) on public politics as the preoccupation of people with nondecisions.

38. For a summary of related literature, see Michael Parenti, *Democracy for the Few* (New York: St. Martin's, 1974), pp. 14 – 16 and 25 – 29.

39. See C. Wright Mills, *The Power Elite* (New York: Oxford University Press, 1956) and, interestingly, Dwight D. Eisenhower, "The Ticklish Problem of Political Fund-Raising — and Spending," *Reader's Digest*, January 1968.

40. See Milovan Djilas, *The New Class* (New York: Praeger, 1957).

41. For a thorough presentation of this argument, see H. Mark Roelofs, *Ideology and Myth in American Politics* (Boston: Little, Brown, 1976).

42. Adolf A. Berle and Gardiner C. Means, *The Modern Corporation and Private Property*, rev. ed. (New York: Harcourt, Brace & World, 1968), p. 304.

43. Ibid., pp. 305 – 308.

44. Jürgen Habermas, "Technology and Science as 'Ideology'," in Habermas, *Toward a Rational Society: Student Protest, Science and Politics* (Boston: Beacon Press, 1971), pp. 81 – 122. Citation from p. 92.

45. Ibid.

46. Ibid.

47. Ibid., pp. 91 – 92.

48. Ibid., p. 92. Contrast this view of social action with that of Talcott Parsons in his systems view of society. See chapter 1, subsection on Parsons.

49. Ibid., p. 96.

50. Erik H. Erikson, *Gandhi's Truth: On the Origins of Militant Nonviolence* (New York: W.W. Norton, 1969), p. 430.

51. Habermas, *Toward a Rational Society*, p. 103. The argument that only citizens, because they are amateurs, are qualified to set societal goals and that experts and specialists are specifically disqualified from such activity is also made, and in vain, by Alfred Schutz in a classical article attempting to justify a return to the old-style politics: "The Well-Informed Citizen: An Essay on the Distribution of Knowledge," in Schutz, *Collected Papers* The Hague: Martinus Nijhoff, 1964), pp. 120 – 134.

52. Ibid., p. 103.

53. Ibid., p. 103.

54. Ibid., p. 104.

55. Claus Offe, "Political Authority and Class Structure," *The International Journal of Sociology*, Spring 1972, cited in Trent Schroyer, *The Critique of Domination: The Origins and Development of Critical Theory* (Boston: Beacon Press, 1975), p. 240.

56. "Pseudopolitical in this paper refers to activity that resembles political activity but is exclusively concerned with either the alleviation of personal neuroses or with promoting private or private-interest group advantage, deterred by no articulate or disinterested conception of what would be just or fair to other groups." (Bay, "Politics and Pseudopolitics,"in *Apoliticrl Politics*, p. 15.)

57. Schroyer, *The Critique of Domination*, pp. 240 – 241.

58. Habermas, *Toward a Rational Society*, p. 107.

6
Bureaucracy
The Terminal
World

The case for bureaucracy as a different world has now been made. There is considerable evidence that the newcomer entering bureaucracy from society enters what, in the social evolution of mankind, is an entirely new world. Not only is that world new as a place of work, but it threatens to absorb all of social and private life into its patterns. Finally, when that new world's all-encompassing claims to regulating human life are compared to the adaptive survival functions previously left to the polity, the essential incapacity of bureaucracy to deal with ultimate human questions is exposed, and the bureaucratized society is revealed as potentially humankind's terminal society.

For these reasons, we are faced with three tasks: (1) recognizing bureaucracy wherever it appears so we can orient our actions toward it, (2) learning how to handle bureaucracy so that we can survive in it and still retain human potential, and (3) overcoming bureaucracy.

RECOGNIZING BUREAUCRACY

The major lesson I learned from the present investigation is to trust people when they complain about strange experiences in their work world. The bureaucratic experience is the point of departure for any analysis of this new social world, if that analysis is to be meaningful to all those who live in it, not just for those who run it. This experience can be encountered not only at work, but in unexpected recesses of social life apparently immune to the invasion of rationalization. How, then, can we recognize that invasion?

Bureaucratic Transformations

I intend to answer this question first by giving in quick summary the series of society-to-bureaucracy transformations considered earlier. In a sense this listing is a replacement for the six characteristics of bureaucracy Max Weber observed at the turn of the century. In bureaucracy:

Socially

cases replace *people*
functions replace *actions* and *social relations*

Culturally

means replace *ends* as ultimate norms
operational *codes* replace social *norms*
effectiveness replaces *ethics*

Psychologically

role replaces *person*
office or *work identity* replaces *personality*
motive replaces *ideas*
motivation replaces *legitimation*
conditioning replaces *socialization*
team replaces *ego*
teamwork replaces *mastery*
hierarchy replaces *superego*
system replaces *integrated personality*
stimulus-response controls replace
    social norms as controls
id satisfaction replaces *ego satisfaction*

Linguistically

command replaces *dialogue*
analogous reasoning replaces *causal reasoning*

Politically

pseudopolitics replaces *politics* (the needs
  of *systems* are put before the needs of *people*)
managers and *experts* replace *politicians*
functionaries replace *citizens*
administration replaces *politics*
psychological power replaces *ideological power*
corporations, public or private, replace, or become superior to,
  nations or the *state*
management replaces *leadership*

Bureaucratic Behavior

The separation of the actors' attachment to action — including the
acceptance of means values as against ends values, the detachment of
affect from action, and the detachment of the speaker from what is
spoken — makes possible the arbitrary and unhindered disposition
of both offices and operations according to the needs and intentions
of the designers of the system at large. The sociological, cultural,
psychological, and linguistic disconnection of what bureaucrats do
from their own wills first *frees* the bureaucracy at large to construct
command posts and channels of operations for exercising unhindered
its own will. This does not yet guarantee that the bureaucracy's will is
carried out, but it removes any obstacles and is the precondition to
functionaries' willingness and need to carry out commands. This
willingness deprives functionaries of personal power to act, of
knowledge of ends values, of existence as a private personality apart
from bureaucratic identity, and of the ability to trust other speakers.*
As long as these characteristics of human existence are officially
stripped from them, they become and remain psychologically dependent on the substitutes that bureaucracy provides. These are
rewards for converting personal actions into officially sanctioned
functions, for not allowing personal values to interfere with means
values, for allowing any speech at all to be put in their mouths as long
as it is functional.

In short, functionaries surrender their social, cultural, and language capacities that normally channel their human energy in order
to make that energy freely available to the system. In return they are
given not only material rewards but the means of existential recognition as well. Deprived first of human personality, they are given
institutional identity. Henceforth any act against the institution, as
judged by the institution itself, is an act by functionaries against the
only point of existence they have — their institutional identity. The

---

*Rather they must have faith in the functionality of the totality of spoken words, even
if specific words addressed to them in a given instance are lies.

psychology of absolute dependence replaces the psychology of mastery.

It must finally be understood that for functionaries the bureaucracy is not simply the replacement for society, culture, individual psychology, and meaningful language activities. For functionaries, bureaucracy is their own life world. And, since for all practical purposes it makes all decisions affecting how they conduct their lives, it is their polity.

That all the ancient and continuing human meanings have been removed from these five concepts cannot be a concern to the functionary. Whatever the limitations on humanity, adaptation to bureaucracy's demands is the only way for successful functionaries to be alive. While it must be admitted that bureaucratic life deprives them of exercising capacities of social, ends-oriented, self-reliant, and self-conscious beings, bureaucracy has the functionary not by his human nature, but by his animal nature. As a friend once put it so aptly: "Ripping the affective synapses that link people together condemns us to inhabit cells collected into a penitentiary by the sterile ties of the economic and demographic interdependence we need to keep us alive as animals."[1]

This keeping alive as animals might seem enough to a starving man and might even be considered as the beginning of a new civilization that would let bloom the truncated human beings first living in it — were it not for the demonstrated inability of bureaucracy to become a polity, a group of interdependent human beings capable of making decisions for its own survival. But bureaucracy is specifically designed to make decisions about means, not ends. And there is no evidence, despite the fact that late bureaucracy does exercise the power to dictate ends, that bureaucracy at any stage of its development has developed the capacity to make decisions about life-affirmative adaptive ends. With its tendency to universalize behavior, bureaucracy in fact reduces variability of behavior and orientation, an evolutionary imperative favoring the survival of any species. Judging the overall system from what it does to individuals, bureaucracy further has a tendency to wind down life, not to give and continue life. All that is living is replaced by mechanism. But the end of mechanism is entropy, not the negentropy of biological life.

Bureaucracy becomes an instrument of power without compare because it is able to remove all human obstacles to power. In doing so it also removes the only human purpose for the exercise of power — the affirmation of human life. From its very beginning, bureaucracy claims it has to destroy man to save him.*

---

*The logic of bureaucratization as the concrete institution of Western rationalization as a historical process finally ends in absurdity well expressed by a U.S. Army officer in Vietnam: We had to destroy the town to save it.

CONTROLLING BUREAUCRACY

What can we do about bureaucracy? Once we understand the nature of bureaucracy, and especially the bases for its dehumanizing tendencies, this would seem to be an unavoidable question for all of us. For we all work in or with bureaucracy — as citizens, legislators, managers, functionaries, professionals, and clients.

Of course, if we really understand the bases of bureaucracy in the past, present, and future development of Western civilization, we may see it as the carrying institution of an irresistible rationalization process that will ride roughshod over any opposition. In that case, we may as well cave in.

Ultimately we will all make our own choices. Mine rests on a belief — that continuing the life of humankind is the ultimate value — and a judgment — that bureaucracy, despite its apparent contributions to material continuity, threatens to become a terminal disease whose symptoms, such as killing off humanity and leaving only the animal, are already well established.

A Reactionary Response

This leaves us with only a single practical possibility for resistance. As a tactic it is no more than a path of reaction, not one of transcendence. But I do not believe we have the power for much more.

The public and its legislators, accustomed to the immense variety of complex services that bureaucracy does render, are no longer capable of rejecting the human cost that bureaucracy imposes as the price of rationalistic means of control. The best we can do is to admit we are caught up in the process of rationalization and have recourse to whatever humanizing elements still possess the public's social and political imagination to moderate the extremes of bureaucratization.

In other words, if bureaucracy is progressive, we must, as long as we all still have an investment in tradition, balance that progress by becoming reactionary. Where bureaucracy promises more speed, we must extol the virtues of slowness and deliberation. Where bureaucracy promises efficiency, we can do with some production lags and even occasional breakdowns that give us time to breathe and rethink whether we really need to do what is being done. Where bureaucracy vows to clean politics out of administration, let us counterpose citizens groups, commissions, participatory councils and legislatures, politically appointed watchdogs and ombudsmen — for while these will bring "corruption," they are also the only way of introducing some guarantee that political goals, in the best sense, will not be totally displaced by engineering goals. In this respect, liberal democracy can be praised for one of its central faults: its fragmented myriad governments, each gauging a finger into the bureaucratic pie from above as well as from sideways and below.* As the political sphere itself becomes bureaucratized, † this attempt at countervailing power will become ineffective and already has become so. ‡

Controlling the bureaucratization process at the design level is more difficult in private enterprise. In the sphere of influence of most large production industries — ranging from automobiles to food and what used to be called luxuries — bureaucratization has hedge-hopped from the central control apparatus of the industry itself right over the heads of the sales force into the reservoir of customers. By redefining the consumers' needs to coincide with what the industry has to sell, advertising now makes it unnecessary to allow sales-people the degree of independence they used to assert. In an earlier age, they were the bridges between rationalized industry and the relatively less-rationalized social realm in which consumers lived. But that was in an age in which there was still a boundary between economy and society; traders would not dream of bringing Wall Street home in their briefcases nor sales managers of exposing their families to the pressures of a sales pitch. Today the market, via television, is in the home, and the salesperson need only fill out the sales form provided by the central accounting office. The good salesperson is no longer the one with the biggest foot in the door and the greatest empathy for people living in society; it is the person with the greatest ability for translating a computerized marketing and promotion report into the strategy and tactics of the organized follow-up.

What this indicates is that as the techniques of control over previously independent consumers in open markets improve and increase, earlier reasons for leaving large portions of an enterprise relatively free of top-down control disappear. The sales force is usually the last hold-out.

Other hold-outs, especially in large conglomerates, are the

*For example, in federal agencies: the president through appointive power from above, congressional committees through the purse power from the side, and the multitude of state and local baronies from below. See for a defense of this practice Vincent Ostrom, *The Intellectual Crisis in American Public Administration* (University of Alabama Press, 1973).

†See chapter 5.

‡As in the case of government agencies purportedly created in the public interest to control the tendency of private bureaucracy to control public life. It should by now be obvious that control instruments to control control instruments merely spread the disease they are supposed to cure. This has been a complaint of American political conservatives for a long time, and as usual there is an element of validity in a complaint that finds so much of a popular echo.

managers of line companies who, because they produce the goods, must still have some concern with initiative and inventiveness as well as with concrete output. These increasingly run afoul of the staff operatives surrounding or constituting the central leadership of what is in effect a holding company at the top. Staff, of course, succeed when they can demonstrate control. And control eventually comes to have nothing to do with ultimate purpose or product. It is its own justification. Thus bankers who know nothing about making computers, nor about the computer market, may exercise control over a computer firm and hire and fire computer designers and engineers. The conflict between the world of finance and the world of production is not a new one. What seems to be new is the growing, and probably irreversible, ascendancy of staff (control) over line (production) in the most modern enterprises.

A telling, but probably ineffective, attack on the dominance of staff over line appeared in a book by a former line manager of the International Telephone & Telegraph Corporation. The top line manager described the conglomerate as "a management organization that operated like a central bank for both funds and talent." He added, "Conglomerates assembled large, knowledgeable staffs to audit and control the acquisitions in many diverse business activities."[2] What typically distinguished the staff controllers from the production doers was their concern for internal control values rather than ultimate goals or purposes:

> The ITT staffs were peppered with graduates of the management consulting profession, people who could appreciate the manipulation of power as almost an academic exercise.* They seemed to have no psychic need for profit and loss responsibility and were the stuff great audit groups are made from.[3]

Traditional entrepreneurs, of course, view profit and loss as the "stuff" of concrete work and production. Their orientations, as with many line people today, are toward substance, while the staff orientations focus on procedure:

> The system of a staff man overseeing each major line function [series of enterprises in the same product line] did not encourage an entrepreneurial business climate. But the staffs did provide direction, and could marshall a number of diverse technical skills very quickly to solve a problem.[4]

Because of such power it is doubtful that conglomerates or the

---

*The parallel to military staff people who play war games with nuclear weapons counting the slaughtered in convenient abstractions like "megadeaths" is unavoidable. Staff people everywhere are the most detached from human contact and human values, as well as from human language.

internationals in general will find any need to curb bureaucratization. Any organization that can control its environment can bury its errors. This applies as much to an organization's ability to persuade through saturating the information channels of the marketplace as to its ability to overthrow the government of Chile or subvert the government of the United States. Even at an earlier stage of development, General Motors and other auto manufacturers proved the dominance of internal methods and centers of control, even when the result was a million cars that had to be recalled every month or so to correct technical disasters.

The recall of automobiles illustrates a further problem with bureaucracy — its penetration into the field of law. Of course it is the law, and the principle of liability, that forces recalls, but that defective cars are allowed to leave the premises of a producer at all, and in the millions, reflects on the ability of the bureaucratized automobile manufacturers to force aside the law in practice, making only an occasional symbolic bow in its direction. Even when ever-increasing *"control"* still yields an ever-worsening *product*, the answer is more "control." The march of bureaucratization appears irresistible.*

With the supercession of owners by managers, and their emphasis on internal, not ultimate, production values, it is difficult to see how the decline of modern industry and business into muscle-bound control mechanisms can be stopped. A. A. Berle and Gardiner Means

---

*The point to be made is that, contrary to defenders of bureaucratization who distinguish between "good" and "bad" bureaucracies, this response is in no sense a deviation from "good" bureaucracy. It is the logical development of a tendency built in to all bureaucracy that can be explained in terms of the prerogative assigned to an institution to itself define the categories under which it will act. When the outside world changes and no longer fits these categories, the only possible bureaucratic instinct is to tighten application of the categories. Politicians who try to redirect the focus of an agency in such cases are treated in exactly the same way as clients; in fact, they have become clients at that point at which they surrendered the administration of original substantive purpose to subcategorization by managers into actions "administratable" on procedural grounds.

Thus it is erroneous to classify as "pathological" such bureaucratic realities as the fact that the State Department, for example, for the last twenty years has been "applying the principles of the late 1940s in an increasingly rigid way to international conditions that were constantly changing." (From a report of a task force on creativity set up in 1970 as cited by George E. Berkley, *The Craft of Public Administration* [Boston: Allyn and Bacon, 1975], p. 120.)

The cure for bureaucracy's tendency to assert the dominance of procedural over substantive concerns is for legislators not to leave the *structuring* of an agency, which is the translation of *substance* into *procedure*, entirely to experts in procedure — administrators.

Once this translation had been undertaken, the State Department's very structures became frozen decisions based on a division of labor designed to achieve a by-gone substance. The fact that this division of labor still reflected the substance of the original reality which gave rise to it, even after twenty years, is to be counted a *success* of bureaucracy, not a failure.

suggest some possible, and necessary, legal changes to bring the controllers back under the control of the public, but with the decline of the public arena itself, it is difficult to see how, without awakening some self-interest in the minds of managers themselves, much can be done. Berle and Means wrote:

> Neither the claims of ownership or those of control can stand against the paramount interests of the community. The present claims of both contending parties now in the field have been weakened . . . It remains only for the claims of the community to be put forward with clarity and force.[5]

That was back in 1932. In the meanwhile so little has been done to win public control over either the private or the "public" bureaucracies that we are left with the initial reactionary* proposal of Berle and Means:

> Rigid enforcement of property rights as a temporary protection against plundering by control would not stand in the way of the modification of these rights in the interest of other groups.† When a convincing system of community obligations is worked out and is generally accepted, in that moment the passive property of today must yield before the larger interests of society.[6]

I intend to say some hopeful words about the latter part of this proposal at the end of this chapter.

What Can Managers Do?

What is left for top administrators and managers to do is to create and encourage humane alternatives to bureaucratized management wherever possible — in the full recognition of the probability that all such techniques, even those most clearly opposed to mindless control, will eventually be converted by the control apparatus into its own uses. Among these alternatives are the politization of an organization, the encouragement of countervailing bureaucracies, the establishment of open systems and feedback loops, and the formation of T-groups.

Politization of the Organization
Avoidance of Michel's iron law of oligarchy has been cited by S. M. Lipset, M. Trow, and J. S. Coleman as achieved in the International

---

*In this chapter I have begun using the term for the first time in a kindly sense of the person about to be guillotined whose struggle to cling to life also must have seemed "reactionary" to the progressives sharpening the blade.

†Unfortunately I sense it is too late for that. What has been plundered has been our very humanity itself. No court can restore it.

Typographical Union through the creation of two political parties and the denial of salaries to officials.* This is an example of internal politization.

An example of external politization is the development of political contacts between street-level-functionaries and clients. This was done successfully by the New York City welfare bureaucracy when it was threatened with staff cutbacks from above. By mobilizing existing and potential welfare recipients to apply for all the benefits for which they are eligible, the welfare bureaucrats both saved their jobs and increased client accessibility to the bureaucracy. There is here a potential lesson for reformers — threaten a cutback unless functionaries can produce evidence of client demand or client satisfaction.

Countervailing Bureaucracies
Establishment of countervailing bureaucracies is initially a political process, but it can also become a management tool.

In the political process, care must taken not to confuse countervailing agencies with satellite agencies. The so-called independent agencies of the federal government set up to "regulate" private bureaucracies of industry, business, and finance are not countervailing and never were. Their initial and continuing purpose, reflected in private enterprise's usual demand for their original establishment, is to provide the permanence, stability, and predictability of materials, labor, and consumers in the various marketplaces.

Secondly, an organization that at the beginning of its life cycle is countervailing — early labor unions, for example — follows the natural tendency of rationalization and ends up being integrated into the universal system of rationalistic values, rules, and structures, which all modern organizations favor. A labor union is caught in a double-bind. Unless it bureaucratizes itself, it cannot muster the power necessary to oppose private enterprise. If it does bureaucratize, its officials will soon begin to share private management's values and begin to see the reasonability of sharing control over their members rather than competing for it. Classical examples are provided by the older American labor unions like the AFL-CIO and the UAW. Similar examples are provided by the West German experience with sharing management power by putting labor officials into directorships of corporations; such officials soon become managers with the same motivations as the rest — profit, growth, stability, and productivity.

For managers themselves vast opportunities exist in fields in which the need for both substantive professionals and administrative

*See S. M. Lipset, M. Trow, and J. S. Coleman, *Union Democracy* (Glencoe, Ill.: The Free Press, 1956).

experts has been institutionalized. Although such a mingling is often perceived as a management "problem" — for example, by hospital administrators having to deal with doctors — it is in reality an opportunity for the humane administrator.

Although usually totally unrealistic from a management point of view, those socialized into the professions, such as doctors and nurses, can bring to bear two humanizing influences on an organization primarily concerned with such efforts as keeping costs down, encouraging a turnover in beds, and fitting patients with an infinite number of types and extent of diseases into a finite number of manageable categories.

First, medical professionals are socialized into a professional ideology that, at least superficially, asserts the primacy of human life. Despite horrible examples of desertion from that standard, it is surprising to what extent doctors and nurses usually try to adhere to that standard in power struggles with administrators. The reason, aside from the overlapping of professional and social values, lies in the fact that the defense of professional values is not so much a defense of such values in themselves as a defense of professional freedom and power.

Secondly, in such arguments professional personnel bring to bear an important and often effective source of power — their professional organization.

Hospital administrators conscious of the dehumanizing tendencies of all bureaucracies, given their mechanistic internal values, can become successful humanizers if they can play off the professionals and their values and organization against their own bureaucracy. Chances are they will lose money that way, and their heads will fall; but the interim also has its rewards.

A counterexample is presented by the careers of professional city managers who, certain of a continuing and growing market for the benefits of their rationalized services, are willing to allow themselves to be fired every several years as a trade-off for imposing their professional values on a polity in the meanwhile. The lesson for administrators of all kinds who retain a social conscience is that it still is possible to fight a rearguard action on behalf of society in situations in which there is a large enough market for one's special skills.

Open Systems and Feedback Loops
As the example of the New York City welfare workers showed, it is sometimes possible to open up a system, even from the managerial and functionary level.

The question must always be asked, however: What is the impact on the bureaucratic tendency toward control? An open system, as long as its own survival is measured ultimately by its ability to control, tends to absorb that part of its environment toward which it has been opened — and then close again. Welfare recipients thus cease being clients. They learn the categories of the bureaucracy that has been opened to them and reap the benefits. But they themselves are thus more thoroughly integrated into the control system, even to the extent that they begin to perform an important survival function for the agency by constituting a stable, growing, and controllable market of demand.

The same tendency is inherent in internal and external feedback loops. Suggestion boxes, complaint sessions, and the like are notorious among lower-ranking functionaries as not-so-subtle methods of control. Through their use the worst excesses and sometimes the worst offenders or complainers can be weeded out. The result is a resumption of an illusion of harmony.

Equally blatant is the development of external feedback loops for administrative systems. Environmental impact studies, effectiveness calculations, cost-benefit analyses, social accounting — all fall into the same ultimate fate. While initially proclaimed as sources of input from the social or political arena and thus constituting a constraint on control, they eventually are exploited as opportunities to bureaucratize areas not previously rationalized. Thus environmentalists must wade through mountains of red tape and learn the rationalized categories and language to comply with the requirements for creating environmental impact statements. Qualitative social and cultural standards of effectiveness and cost must be converted into quantitative measures, the tool of bureaucratic control. The term "social accounting" contains in its own internal contradiction its ultimate fate: essential values of society are not susceptible to accounting methods and accounting is not ultimately compatible with the maintenance of prebureaucratic cultural values. Social accounting is in itself an attempt to convert the patterns of society and the norms of society's culture into patterns and norms an accountant can understand.

Again, the lesson for the manager is that such tools can be humanizing at their inception, but contain within them the seeds of self-destruction. The answer once again for controlling bureaucracy is a temporary holding action: adopt the new methods, then discard them in a few years. Never allow the cycle of growth toward over-rationalization to fully develop.

T-Groups to TM

A popular counterpoise to the nature of bureaucracy itself has been the use of group training programs (T-groups) where bureaucracy deviates most radically from society. The T-group encounter sessions combat an inability to engage in social relationships, a rigid adherence to bureaucratic values, the use of bureaucratic language as a shield to hide behind, and even the loss of an authentic and integrated personality. As one commentator reports:

> These sessions seek to expand interpersonal consciousness, develop authenticity in interpersonal relations and spontaneous behavior, eliminate behavior that stems from hierarchical positions and substitute collaborative behavior, and develop ability to solve conflicts through problem-solving rather than through bargaining, coercion, or power-manipulation.[7]

But when we analyze the values here juxtaposed, we find that we have collaboration versus conflict and bargaining, problem solving versus coercion and power manipulation. Without engaging in a thorough critique, we can suggest that what is being juxtaposed here is the further enhancement of already established bureaucratic values and the further denigration of social ones, specifically traditional political values. This reading depends, of course, on the understanding that when the terms "coercion" and "power manipulation" are used in the T-group context, they refer to traditional political forms of power, not to the bureaucratic type of power which, in effect, assures the T-groups' "desirable" values — collaboration and problem solving.*

The one outright attack on bureaucracy contained in T-group ideology is the attempt to "eliminate behavior that stems from hierarchical positions," but the seriousness of this demand is put in question: if anyone really wanted to abolish hierarchical behavior, they would abolish hierarchy. I suspect that what is meant here is the abolition of sovereign behavior rooted in a hierarchical position converted into a private — and therefore social and political, though not strictly bureaucratic — power base.

The remaining plea for spontaneity must be viewed within the same institutional strictures, which are not loosened by the introduction of T-group training. In part they may reflect an honest recognition of the dearth of creativeness which rationalization enforces, but there appears to be no halt called to such rationalization. If anything the T-group, by opening up the individual to immense social pressure exerted on behalf of the "good of the organization," is an attempt to penetrate even the most private thoughts and attitudes of the individual and take these apart for later reintegration under bureaucratic auspices.

Unintentionally perhaps, Charles Perrow opens up a vast array of apparent antibureaucratic social phenomena to the same suspicion

---

*For the difference, see chapter 5.

that analysis of the difference between bureaucracy and society in T-groups leads us. He concludes:

> We should bless T-groups because they do for managers what pot, flower power, psychedelic experiences, encounter groups, and hard-rock music do for the far-out younger generation. The search for authenticity and spontaneity should be never-ending, and if it must occur in the guise of better productivity in organizations, let it.[8]

Here the relationship between apparent humanizing activities and bureaucratic interests stands revealed, though Perrow stands it on its head.

Private corporations have sponsored and endorsed such "mind-blowing" activities as transcendental meditation (TM) for exactly the same reason that the robber baron capitalists of old used to endorse and finance established religions.[9] The functionary who takes advantage of "yoga and lunch" returns to his or her job refreshed in body and spirit, productivity goes up, and the need to confront bureaucracy is handily reduced by the noon to 1 P.M. escape into the worlds of "out-of-body travel" or "astral projection," the loosening of vocationally tightened muscles, and the momentary retreat into a "strange" world of love, spirit, and soul, purchased with the money provided by holding down a job. Here the rationalizers of the job world manage to convert what used to be everyday social experiences into carefully conducted safaris into what is now advertised as exotic and esoteric — and *back* again. Rather than constituting a constraint, such counterpoises are eventually exposed as the ultimate in bureaucratization — the rational organization of the irrational.

What Can Functionaries Do?

The immediate routes of escape for the functionary, therefore, seem to be blocked in exactly the same way that Max Weber foresaw at the beginning of the century.

It has been the attempt of each of the central chapters of this book — on social relations, values, the psyche, language, and politics — to demonstrate how and why we are locked into bureaucracy, the institutional reflection of the rationalization of the world.

In a speech at the University of Munich in 1918, Weber still saw the possibility to take a political stand:

> . . . it is immensely moving when a *mature* man — no matter whether old or young in years — is aware of a responsibility for the consequences of his conduct and really feels such responsibility with heart and soul. He then acts by following an ethic of responsibility and somewhere he reaches the point where he says: 'Here I stand; I can do

no other.' That is something genuinely human and moving. And everyone of us who is not spiritually dead must realize the possibility of finding himself at some time in that position.[10]

Today, we are spiritually deadened, and the structure of the world is so designed that no such handy intersections of space and time are provided at which we can take such a heroic stand as did Martin Luther, the individual Weber quotes.

Bureaucratic training prevents us from feeling and living close to our fellow man; we are no longer adept in social relations. The dominant values tell us nothing of human ends for which it might be possible to take an ethical stand. There can never be an ethics of efficiency, only a technique. Language itself, one-directional and acausal, prevents our becoming conscious of who is ultimately responsible for the orders we receive and the structurally inherent functions we perform. Nor does it provide a clue to the final consequences of our actions. It is quite possible that no matter which action we choose, we are engaged only in a choice among evils.[11]

Weber, of course, meant for his audience to take political responsibility. His description is that of the ethical political man. But the realm of politics itself has since shrunk and been rationalized. It would seem difficult for any functionaries of an organization to escape into politics and to use public power against the apolitics of the organization. Such escapes tend to not only cost them their livelihood, but to the extent that their personalities have been converted into institutional identity, they deprive them of psychic existence.

Nor is it any longer possible to follow the advice of this most human of scientists in his essay "Science as a Vocation" that "we shall set to work and meet the 'demands of the day,' in human relations as well as in our vocation."[12] The demands of our day are almost totally bureaucratic, and the arena of human relations has shrunk to next to nothing.

If we cannot act our way out of the iron cage, we must begin to think our way out. I would like to address a few final words to that prospect in the next and last section.

TRANSCENDING BUREAUCRACY

Critics of this book might argue that it offers nothing new that is empirical. They would be wrong. Every analysis undertaken here — sociological, cultural, psychological, linguistic, and political — begins with the experiences of people. The assumption has been that the experience of people is what is empirical.

The Bureaucratization of Science

In a time of the bureaucratization of everything, science itself has not escaped. If we wish to free ourselves from bureaucracy, it is essential that we begin by examining the way through which we get knowledge about reality. In the modern era, the approved way is the scientific method. But which scientific method?

Empirical Versus Experiential Science
Here we must distinguish between two kinds of science — science that has itself become bureaucratized and science that remains empirical because it is based on experience, not on dogma. We can call the first kind of science "pseudoscience," because by destroying or fragmenting what is empirical before examining it, it fails to be empirical. Truly scientific methods, in contrast, are empirical because they begin with the actual behavior and experiences of people *before* science forces them into its own preconceived notions and categories.

One thing I have not done in this book is to begin with the theory of Max Weber and force it on the people whose experiences I have presented. Rather I accepted their stories as valid in themselves and then searched for new or old concepts that might explain them. Thus complaints were initially accepted as valid *because* they were complaints rather than being rejected because the respondent was misled in interpreting his or her feelings. When we see people in agony, as we do in bureaucracy, we must accept that agony as real simply because it is real to them. I believe a truly empirical science must always begin with what is given, then construct explanations afterward.

In an era in which every "scientist" claims the right to impose his or her own theory on an unsuspecting reality,* what is most trustworthy is not the immense variety of theories, each in the pay of a would-be master, but the shared empirical reality with which anyone living life must deal.† But the most trustworthy access to that reality — in our case, to people living in bureaucracy — is through

*In survey research, for example, few respondents suspect, though this is changing especially among minority groups, that the results will be used to control them.

†The relativity of various theories, none of which makes a claim to final truth, is a natural outgrowth of what has been called the era of value-relativism in science. Theories simply coexist in multiplicity side by side; none makes a claim to epistemological truth, though each makes a claim to providing better opportunities for control than the rest. On value-relativism, see Arnold Brecht, *Political Theory: The Foundations of Twentieth-Century Political Thought* (Princeton, N.J.: Princeton University Press, 1967).

what people feel and afterward say and do. Certainly, we must be highly suspicious of "scientists" who limit what they pick up of that reality to those fragments that fit their preconceived categories, especially when their approaches are shot through with the qualities we have exposed as bureaucratic and therefore control oriented.

Pseudoscience in Organizations

Thus systems analysts and functionalists look at functions and roles apart from the people who perform them, reflecting the social condition of bureaucracy which separates actors from their actions and from their social relationships. Experimental psychology studies cognitive behavior as if it existed in real life separate from affective behavior, thereby becoming the perfect handmaiden to today's dominant form of organization, which forces functionaries to coolly calculate their work without regard to personal feelings about the people at whom their work is directed. Similarly, communications theory and lately the new linguistic "science" of semiotics study language signs apart from their context — what is spoken apart from the speaker. This reinforces the dehumanizing reality of bureaucratic language.

All the dominant "sciences" are dominant exactly because they play a support role for today's dominant organizations, an effectiveness enhanced by their ability to disguise the hidden costs of their control activities by ignoring complaints from the controlled as unreal or dysfunctional — and something to be stamped out.

A science that insists that its preconceived notions truly reflect how people really are can pride itself in coming close to reality only by changing it. It is no more a science than it would be science if I defined all chickens as characterized by broken necks — and then went about breaking them. The analogy is not intended to be humorous; it is exact. It follows that the dominant pseudosciences of today "work" only if they are associated with the immense control mechanisms of modern organization. They have limited validity only in association with bureaucracy – either inside institutions or in society through the popular acceptance of bureaucratic values.

Since bureaucracy forces functionaries to do what they are ordered to do, there is nothing surprising when pseudoscience, using the very categories of bureaucratic design itself, actually finds behavior fragments "out there" that fit the preconceived categories. Such "sciences" simply ignore those experiences that are the most important to people themselves, what Habermas called the central questions of people's collective existence and of individual life history: justice and freedom; violence and oppression; happiness and gratification; poverty, illness, and death; victory and defeat; love and hate; and salvation and damnation.[13]

The limitations of such pseudoscience are reflected in its most difficult problem: tying the fragments of its findings together and making sense out of them. The problem arises very simply from the refusal of pseudoscience to accept the unity of experience as it is presented by living people themselves. Because pseudoscience first fragments such experience by fitting it into arbitrary categories not causally linked together, it later faces the problem of linking such fragments together. Since such fragments can no more be linked together in normal social life than a Greek vase can be reconstructed out of several disconnected fragments without a model to go by, the pseudoscience ultimately has recourse to the control power of the organizations for which it works, and it *forces* the pieces together. Much of the agony of workers in bureaucracy is the result of such idiocy.

A second limitation affects the ability of pseudoscientists them- selves to address their questioning to the fundamental structural causes of operational management problems. The dominant scientific method in the social sciences and management sciences today works through the use of correlations. But correlating disparate events, without causal explanation (and causal explanation is at the least left in abeyance in modern social and management science), is reasoning by analogy. The technicians of these dominant sciences therefore engage in exactly the same type of reasoning as does the bureaucrat: analogous thinking replaces causal thinking.*

Not only does the bureaucratized pseudoscience ignore the central issues of human experience, because such issues are a threat to the lopsided style of life dictated by organizations, but its popular propagandists arrogantly argue that such central experiences them- selves are invalid. The implication being that, if we insist on having such experiences and raising difficulties for rationalistic organization, we are not only somehow deviant, but menaces who no doubt require "institutionalization" — a most appropriate word.[14] Thus a recent advocate of "structuralism":

> Structuralism is a method, not a program or an ideology, and its usefulness has begun to change the face of research and discussion in a wide variety of disciplines. At the same time, it frees [!] us from asking questions that have no answers — Where is life's inherent meaning? What can I do about alienation? — without risking the usual alter- natives of nihilism or solopsism.[15]

*See chapter 4.

Such popularizations are not to be sneezed at. They have a wide impact on popular thought. And they often manage to expose the essences of the "science" involved, the central assumptions "scientists" hide in esoteric language. Beginning with the claim that structuralism is not an ideology, the statement deserves careful examination. First we can ask what ideology is. Ideology can be considered a system of justification through ideas in defense of someone's self-interest. We may ask: In whose interest is it to say that structuralism is *not* an ideology? Especially when the writer then asserts that to continue to ask questions about the experience of meaning and alienation — something *we* have an interest in — is absurd.

Obviously, if structuralism lays these questions to rest, it works in the interest of bureaucracies, public and private, which we have just finished establishing as the chief perpetrators of human alienation, including the separation of meaning from man.

As to whether the only alternatives to structuralism are nihilism or solipsism, this question is also important. It reflects on the wider question of whether these are the only ways to transcend bureaucracy. Of this later.

The point to be made here is that it would be surprising — indeed, a first in the history of the world — if the dominant "sciences" of today were not also *de facto* ideologies defending the dominant institutions of power — bureaucracies.[16]

If this accusation is correct, then the first step to transcending bureaucracy is to free ourselves from using its bought pseudo-sciences, which prevent us from seeing the world as it is while helping bureaucracy make the world what it "must" be.

The Humane Sciences

How shall we select the sciences that can help man conquer bureaucracy? First, they must have at their center a concern for people. A science that is concerned with making the world safe for actions without the actor, for bits of energy pretending to be acts of speech, for an organizational psyche outside the human head is not a science that can make the world safe for people. Functions, machine norms, stimuli and responses, holes in computer cards, and power without purpose are not suitable focuses for a science of human beings. These fragments are always something less than human. The problem for humans, as the analysis of bureaucratization has shown, is to reconstitute themselves out of their fragments.

It must be accepted as the foundation principle of a humane

science that such a science is not possible if its unit of analysis is something less than humans.

Which Sciences Are Humane?

Compared to functionalism, human engineering in industrial psychology and sociology, behaviorism, contextless linguistic analysis, and political science ignoring needs, there are some sciences which are relatively less dangerous to humans and at the same time powerful enough to uncover scientistic and bureaucratic dehumanization. These include Weberian sociology, phenomenology, and Freudian and existential psychology.

Weberian sociology takes as its unit of analysis two actors in the field of their mutual orientation to each other. Its application to bureaucracy's destruction of social relationships (as seen in chapter 1) shows that a dated sociology can still pry the lid off our current reality.*

Phenomenology, by arguing that the source of all meaning springs from within each man himself, asserts the future potential of man as the creator of his own world rather than as victim. The guiding light in phenomenological sociology has been Alfred Schutz. The most moving summary of the fundamental unit of phenomenological analysis, however, may be drawn from the historian and political philosopher Eric Voegelin, who asserted the ultimate indivisibility of human experience in a different context in this way:

> Human society is not merely a fact, or an event, in the external world to be studied by an observer like a natural phenomenon. . . . It is a whole little world, a cosmion illuminated with meaning from within by the human beings who continuously create and bear it as the mode and condition of their self-realization.[17]

Those who want to assure themselves of a method of analysis that ensures the continuing emphasis on man as engaged in the process of social creation, rather than on man as frozen into the structures of decisions made in a by-gone era, may find phenomenology rewarding.

Freudian psychology and *existential psychology* in emphasizing the problem of man's inner unity have made possible the analysis of the role of bureaucratic structures not only in tearing apart man's psyche, but in ripping out of it his capacity for exercising conscience and for mastery over his work and his world. I believe that the psychologies of child development, especially those, such as Jean Piaget's, that are

---

*Max Weber at one point wrote that he hoped his sociology would be out of date within fifty years. He would have been disappointed in our ability to do better.

genetically based, will give us further power to show to what extent bureaucracy forces us to think, act, and talk at childish levels.*

The psychologies of the management sciences, of course, fragment both the psychology and the behavior of man in bureaucracy. There is a dual movement toward an all-encompassing psychology of man in bureaucracy. The first part of this is B. F. Skinner's behaviorism, which does provide a theoretically unified explanation of man's behavior in a rationalized world, perhaps the first such unified psychology since Freud. Skinner then proceeds to make his science useless as a way of transcending the dehumanized psychic dynamics he so well describes by arguing that man has always been manipulated as he is today and that this might as well be done rationally. Further, he "solves" the problem of individual atomization by asserting that there have never been individuals. A science that solves my problem, which I experience, by saying the problem doesn't exist fails to meet the test of any proper science — dealing with the empirical.

The "organization psychology" of Edgar Schein, by taking man's psyche out of himself and formally endowing the organization with a psyche, serves the useful purpose of doing openly what the bought industrial psychologies have always assumed. With great finality it demonstrates the bankruptcy of a trend in psychology, saying that administrative structures have psyches while men do not. A true psychology of bureaucracy still remains to be constructed, if we expect to gain from it more than the ability to manipulate others and achieve the ability to overcome bureaucracy itself.

What Can Humane Science Do?

It would be wrong, however, to expect from the more humane sciences a return to society or individualism as we have experienced these in the past. Historical experience teaches us that new ways of looking at ourselves and the world triumph only in periods of transition, when combined with the self-interest of those whose power is on the rise. For example, Weber found that the creation of entrepreneurial and industrial society, with its all-motivating work ethic, did not arise from the development of the Protestant ethic alone, but from the confluence of that way of looking at the world with the material power for conquering nature that science, in-

---

*I believe further research in this area will demonstrate a parallel between the analogous reasoning implied by bureaucratic language and the reasoning by organic analogy utilized in autistic thinking as discussed by Piaget. See Jean Piaget, *The Language and Thought of the Child* (Cleveland and New York: World, Meridian Books, 1955), especially p. 63.

dustry, and modern commerce had begun to make available to Western man.

Assuming that current trends toward the humane sciences — with their emphasis on "self-actualization"* — are more than a passing fad, where could we find powerful groups of people who would find it in their material interest to support and join forces with such sciences?

I believe this question deserves fuller exploration than is possible here, but a short summary of a probable scenario of postbureaucratic development in the future is appropriate at this point because of its likely impact on the immediate future of administration.

Control and Growth

Modern bureaucracy in public service arose out of the need of private groups — industrial entrepreneurs, financiers, and merchants — to have the state regulate the world so that the huge investments and reinvestments characterizing modern capital enterprise could be justified. Out of this came rationalized state administration of the legal system (emphasizing the enforcement of contract), the regulation of labor, the state supervision of commerce and finance, and finally state stabilization of markets. Today we criticize bureaucracy for its inflexibility, stability, and immutability in the face of change. But in the past these qualities perfectly reflected the purpose for which it was set up — to provide controls over a society that had, from the viewpoint of capital enterprisers, too much change in it.[18]

A recent survey by the National Academy of Public Administration of almost a hundred "experienced and well-informed leaders in public affairs" predicts the future conversion of bureaucracy into change-oriented and temporary organizations.[19] We must ask ourselves in whose interest such conversion might be. In fact, much has been made both by academicians and in the popular media of the radical social and cultural changes that emerged out of the 1960s and still affect us today: varieties of new life styles, the decline of the family, the rise in hedonism ranging from the sexual to smoke-dreams of the mind, the politization of previously ignored groups like the poor and longforgotten ethnics. Surely, it is being suggested, public service institutions must cease being rigid and treat-

*The term is Abraham Maslow's. See his *Motivation and Personality*, 2nd ed. (New York: Harper and Row, 1970). For applications to modern organizations, see Chrys Argyris, *Integrating the Individual and the Organization* (New York: John Wiley, 1964), and Frederick Herzberg, Bernard Mausner, and Barbara Synderman, *The Motivation to Work* (New York: John Wiley, 1959).

ing all people in a homogenous way. They must, it is argued, become more flexible and adaptive and they must tune in to the increasing variety of needs represented by increasing numbers of small groups and even individuals.

This argument for abandoning rigid and monocratic bureaucracy in favor of flexible institutions with a decentralized focus sounds even more plausible when the changing needs of private economic institutions are considered. Times of rapid social and cultural change are also times of great opportunity for the entrepreneur. Each of the changes first noticed in the 1960s has been exploited by entrepreneurs, who have responded to "new needs" with new products and services.

In fact, it was private enterprise that first produced the insight that if the range of human needs could be widened and demand manipulated, the result would be an entire new foundation for the survival and growth of the American economic system. Everyone would benefit. Profits would rise along with gross national product, and so would wages and the delivery of consumer goods and services.

Surely such variety, diversity, and growth are not compatible with the presence of stultifying control mechanisms in society of the type exemplified especially by public bureaucracy. Here lay the promise of transcendence of all of bureaucracy's shortcomings. Surely bureaucracy itself would have to change.

But let us go softly into that promissory future.

What have we learned about the impact of bureaucracy on the human being? The fact is that it is exactly that rigid mammoth of which we now seem to wish to rid ourself that has produced the kind of consumer that business now would have us go and multiply.

Socially, bureaucracy has cracked the unit of social relationships: two individuals relating to one another in reciprocity and relative equality. The bureaucratic relationship has trained us to look always upward toward superiors. Culturally, what we look to them for is the answer to the question what is good or bad for us; bureaucracy has made it impossible to maintain personal norms. Psychologically, the process of bureaucratization has destroyed the integrity of the individual, made him into a being of dependency, and opened up his reservoir of human needs (the id) to direct manipulation from the outside. Linguistically, we have been trained to be mute and not talk back while becoming wide open to the imperatives flowing down the chain of command and out of the loudspeakers and screens of the modern media. Politically, we have learned to accept that we are powerless and lack the imagination to dream what human power can be.

In the end, it is bureaucracy itself that has produced the kind of dehumanized human fragment — socially crippled, culturally norm-less, psychologically dependent, linguistically mute, and politically powerless — that has become the economy's favorite object of manipulation.

If we fail to see the human fragmentation behind the surface hustle and bustle of the bureaucratized world, we will also commit the error of looking to such fragments as the source of renewed attempts at humanizing the institutions that created them.

The fact is that modern business and industry are in a relation-ship of symbiosis with bureaucracy, public or private. The latter institutions turn human beings into the raw material for eternal growth — not of humanity but of an abstract system in which ultimately even the top managers must be not human beings but machines.

If there are hidden opportunities for transcendence, they are not easily exposed. Modernity as a way of life has infinite capacities for closure against any escape from itself.

If fate in modern times is, as Max Weber said, the consequence of man's action contrary to his intention, we have been well and truly had.

NOTES

1. Kalman H. Silvert, *Man's Power: A Biased Guide to Political Thought and Action* (New York: Viking, 1970), p. 158.

2. Thomas S. Burns, *Tales of ITT — An Insider's Report* (Boston: Houghton Mifflin, 1974), p. 60.

3. Ibid., p. 65.

4. Ibid.

5. A.A. Berle and Gardiner Means, *The Modern Corporation and Private Property*, rev. ed. (New York: Harcourt, Brace & World, Harvest Book, 1967), p. 312.

6. Ibid.

7. Charles Perrow, *Complex Organizations: A Critical Essay* (Glenview, Ill.: Scott, Foresman, 1972), pp. 115 – 116.

8. Ibid., p. 118. For a perfect example of the destruction of the individual by a T-group, along with the violation of his privacy and human dignity, see the account of Robert Tannenbaum, I.R. Wechsler, and F. Massarik, *Leadership and Organization: A Behavioral Science Approach* (New York: McGraw-Hill, 1961), p. 123. A long excerpt is reprinted in Perrow, *Complex Organizations*, pp. 116 – 117.

9. For the parallel between the effect of old religions and new cults in the context of American culture, see Lawrence Chenoweth, *The American Dream of Success:*

The Search for Self in the Twentieth Century (North Scituate, Mass.: Duxbury Press, 1974), especially pp. 14 – 19.

10. Weber, "Politics as a Vocation," in H.H. Gerth and C. Wright Mills, eds., *From Max Weber: Essays in Sociology* (New York: Oxford University Press, Galaxy Book, 1958), p. 127.

11. The likelihood of this probability is demonstrated in the work of Tadeusz Borowski. For an introduction, see Andrej Wirth, "A Discovery of Tragedy," *The Polish Review*, 12 (Summer 1967), 43 – 52.

12. Weber, "Science as a Vocation," in Gerth and Mills, *From Max Weber*, p. 156.

13. Jürgen Habermas, *Toward a Rational Society* (Boston: Beacon Press, 1971), p. 96. For the confrontation between such values, still recognized in society, and the bureaucratic culture, see chapter 2.

14. See Thomas Sasz, *Ideology and Insanity — Essays on the Psychic Dehumanization of Man* (Garden City, N.Y.: Doubleday, Anchor, 1970).

15. Perry Meisel, "Everything You Always Wanted to Know About Structuralism but Were Afraid to Ask," *The Village Voice*, August 23, 1976, p. 93. For an introduction to structuralism, see Jacques Ehrmann, ed., *Structuralism* (Garden City, N.Y.: Doubleday, Anchor, 1970).

16. In sociology an entire specialty, the sociology of knowledge, affirms this accusation. For a handy summary essay on the various approaches to the sociology of knowledge, see Peter Berger and Thomas Luckmann, *The Social Construction of Reality: A Treatise in the Sociology of Knowledge* (Garden City, N.Y.: Doubleday, Anchor, 1967), especially "Introduction: The Problem of the Sociology of Knowledge," pp. 1 – 18. The classical writers in the sociology of knowledge include Karl Mannheim, Werner Stark, Robert Merton, and Berger and Luckmann. Recent work on how different professions and work groups produce different forms of knowledge, including self-knowledge, has been done in Georges Gurvitch, *The Social Frameworks of Knowledge* (New York: Harper & Row, Harper Torchbook, 1972) and Joseph Bensman and Robert Lilienfeld, *Craft and Consciousness: Occupational Technique and the Development of World Images* (New York: John Wiley, 1973). Gurvitch includes a study on how people come to know one another in factory and administrative groups, while Bensman and Lilienfeld have a chapter on bureaucratic and planning attitudes deriving from the work situation.

17. Eric Voegelin, *The New Science of Politics: An Introduction* (Chicago: University of Chicago Press, 1952), p. 27.

18. For the argument that bureaucracy best fitted the "routine tasks of the nineteenth and early twentieth centuries," see also Warren G. Bennis and Philip E. Slater, *The Temporary Society* (New York: Harper and Row, 1968), p. 56.

19. See Richard L. Chapman and Frederic N. Cleaveland, *Meeting the Needs of Tomorrow's Public Service: Guidelines for Professional Education in Public Administration* (Washington, D.C.: National Academy of Public Administration, 1973).

Selected Readings

A major purpose of this book has been to rediscover ways of studying the bureaucratic experience that would be critical and creative. With this in mind, the following references for each of the five central chapters are divided, where possible, into two parts: books, and on occasion articles, that lend themselves to a critical perspective on bureaucracy, and those that lend themselves to acceptance or defense of bureaucracy.

BUREAUCRACY AS THE NEW SOCIETY

Critical

Berger, Peter, and Thomas Luckmann. *The Social Construction of Reality.* Garden City, N.Y.: Doubleday Anchor, 1967.

Berger, Peter, Brigitte Berger, and Hansfried Kellner. *The Homeless Mind: Modernization and Consciousness.* New York: Vintage, 1974.

Blumer, Herbert. *Symbolic Interactionism: Perspective and Method.* Englewood Cliffs, N.J.: Prentice-Hall, 1969.

Mead, George Herbert. *Mind, Self and Society.* Chicago: University of Chicago Press, 1934.

Mehan, Hugh, and Houston Wood. *The Reality of Ethnomethodology.* New York: Wiley, 1975.

Schutz, Alfred. *Collected Papers.* 3 vols. The Hague: Martinus Nijhoff, 1967.

––––––. *The Phenomenology of the Social World.* Translated by George Walsh and Frederick Lehnert. Evanston, Ill.: Northwestern University Press, 1967.

Weber, Max. "Basic Sociological Terms," and "Bureaucracy" in *Economy and Society: An Outline of Interpretive Sociology.* Edited by Guenther Roth and Claus Wittich. Translated by Ephraim Fischoff et al. New York: Bedminster Press, 1968.

Transitional

Gerth, Hans H. and C. Wright Mills. *Character and Social Structure.* New York: Harcourt, Brace, 1953.

Goffman, Erving. *Asylums*. Garden City, N.Y.: Doubleday Anchor, 1961.
————. *The Presentation of Self in Everyday Life*. Garden City, N.Y.: Doubleday Anchor, 1959.
Merton, Robert K. "Bureaucratic Structure and Personality," and "Continuities in the Theory of Reference Groups and Social Structure" in *Social Theory and Social Structure*. New York: Free Press, 1968.

Pro-bureaucratic

Merton, Robert K. "Manifest and Latent Functions" in *Social Theory and Social Structure*. New York: Free Press, 1968.
Parsons, Talcott. *The Social System*. New York: The Free Press of Glencoe, 1964.
Radcliffe-Brown, A. R. *A Natural Science of Society*. Glencoe, Ill.: Free Press, 1957.

BUREAUCRACY AS THE NEW CULTURE

Critical

Birenbaum, Norman. "Culture" in *The Crisis in Industrial Society*. New York: Oxford University Press, 1969.
Habermas, Jürgen. "Technology and Science as 'Ideology'" in *Toward a Rational Society*. Translated by Jeremy Shapiro. Boston: Beacon, 1971.
Weber, Max. "Bureaucracy" in *Economy and Society: An Outline of Interpretive Sociology*. Edited by Guenther Roth and Claus Wittich. Translated by Ephraim Fischoff et al. New York: Bedminster Press, 1968.

Transitional

George, Alexander L. "The 'Operational Code': A Neglected Approach to the Study of Political Leaders and Decision-Making," *International Studies Quarterly*, June 1969.
Harris, Louis. *The Anguish of Change*. New York: Norton, 1973.
Leites, Nathan. *The Operational Code of the Politburo*. New York: McGraw-Hill, 1951.
Watts, William, and Lloyd A. Free. *State of the Nation*. New York: Universe Books, 1973.

Pro-bureaucratic

Parsons, Talcott, and Edward A. Shils. "Values, Motives, and Systems of Action" in *Toward a General Theory of Action*. Edited by Talcott Parsons and Edward A. Shils. New York: Harper & Row, 1962.

THE PSYCHOLOGY OF BUREAUCRACY

Critical

Marcuse, Herbert. *Eros and Civilization: A Philosophical Inquiry into Freud*. New York: Vintage, undated; original edition Boston: Beacon, 1955.
Mitscherlich, Alexander. *Society Without the Father*. Translated by Eric Mosbacher. New York: Schocken, 1970.

[Additional readings in Freudian and existentialist psychology are listed in the chapter.]

Transitional

Skinner, B. F. *Beyond Freedom and Dignity*. New York: Vintage, 1972.

Pro-bureaucratic

Schein, Edgar H. *Organizational Psychology*. Englewood Cliffs, N.J.: Prentice-Hall, 1965.

[Most industrial and organizational psychology falls into the pro-bureaucratic category.]

THE LANGUAGE OF BUREAUCRACY

Critical

Bernstein, B. "Social Class, Language, and Socialization" in *Language and and Social Context — Selected Readings*. Edited by Pier Paolo Giglioli. Baltimore: Penguin, 1972.

Dilman, Ilham. "Wittgenstein on the Soul" in Royal Institute of Philosophy, *Understanding Wittgenstein*. New York: St. Martin's, 1974.

Searle, John R. *Speech Acts: An Essay in the Philosophy of Language*. London: Cambridge University Press, 1969.

Transitional

Gellner, Ernest. *Legitimation of Belief*. London: Cambridge University Press, 1974.

Pro-bureaucratic

Chomsky, Noam. *Aspects of the Theory of Syntax*. Cambridge, Mass.: M.I.T. Press, 1965.

———— "Some Empirical Assumptions in Modern Philosophy of Language" in *Philosophy, Science and Method*. Edited by Signey Morgenbesser, Patrick Suppes, and Morton White. New York: St. Martin's, 1969.

De Saussure, Ferdinand. *Course in General Linguistics*. Translated by Wade Baskin. New York: McGraw-Hill, 1959.

Eco, Umberto. *A Theory of Semiotics*. Bloomington, Ind.: Indiana University Press, 1976.

BUREAUCRACY AS POLITY

Critical

Bachrach, Peter, and Morton S. Baratz. *Power and Poverty: Theory and Practice*. New York: Oxford University Press, 1970.

Bay, Christian. "Politics and Pseudopolitics: A Critical Evaluation of Some Behavioral Literature." *The American Political Science Review*, 59, 1 (March 1965), 39 – 51.

Berle, A. A. and Gardiner C. Means. *The Modern Corporation and Private Property*. Revised edition. New York: Harcourt, Brace, 1968.

Edelman, Murray. *The Symbolic Uses of Politics*. Urbana, Ill.: University of Illinois Press, 1967.

Habermas, Jürgen. *Legitimation Crisis*. Boston: Beacon, 1975.

Isaak, Robert A. and Ralph P. Hummel. *Politics for Human Beings*. North Scituate, Mass.: Duxbury Press, 1975.

Smith, Michael P. "The Ritual Politics of Suburban Schools" in *Politics in America: Studies in Policy Analysis*. Edited by Michael P. Smith and Associates. New York: Random House, 1974.

Pro-bureaucratic

Almond, Gabriel A. and G. Bingham Powell. *Comparative Politics: A Developmental Approach*. Boston: Little, Brown, 1966.

Easton, David. *The Political System*. New York: Alfred A. Knopf, 1964.

———— *A Framework for Political Analysis*. Englewood Cliffs, N.J.: Prentice-Hall, 1965.

Index